30 Days to Experiencing Spiritual Breakthroughs

30 DAYS TO

EXPERIENCING

SPIRITUAL

BREAKTHROUGHS

DR. BRUCE H. WILKINSON

Multnomah® Publishers *Sisters, Oregon*

30 DAYS TO EXPERIENCING SPIRITUAL BREAKTHROUGHS
published by Multnomah Publishers, Inc.

©1999 by Bruce Wilkinson

ISBN 1-57673-982-1

Cover design by The Office of Bill Chiaravalle
Cover illustration by Mike Wepplo

Scripture quotations are from:

The Holy Bible, New King James Version (NKJV) © 1982, 1984 by Thomas Nelson, Inc.

New American Standard Bible® (NASB) © 1960, 1977, 1995
by the Lockman Foundation. Used by permission.

The Holy Bible, King James Version (KJV)

The American Standard Version (ASV) © 1901

The Holy Bible, New International Version (NIV) © 1973, 1984 by International Bible
Society, used by permission of Zondervan Publishing House

The Revised English Bible (REB) © 1989 by Oxford University Press
and Cambridge University Press

The Living Bible (TLB) © 1971. Used by permission of Tyndale House Publishers, Inc.
All rights reserved.

The New Testament in Modern English, Revised Edition (Phillips)
© 1958, 1960, 1972 by J. B. Phillips

Multnomah is a trademark of Multnomah Publishers, Inc.,
and is registered in the U.S. Patent and Trademark Office.
The colophon is a trademark of Multnomah Publishers, Inc.
Printed in the United States of America

For information:
MULTNOMAH PUBLISHERS, INC.•POST OFFICE BOX 1720•SISTERS, OREGON 97759

DEDICATION

This book is dedicated to a person with whom I have worked for over twenty years in the ministry of Walk Thru the Bible and have been privileged to watch her experience numerous spiritual breakthroughs throughout the years. She not only continues to pursue excellence in her life but has never stopped growing spiritually ever since I first met her in 1978. I hereby dedicate this book to:

Jill Milligan

Over these twenty years, WTB promoted her more than anyone else in the ministry's entire history. Her visionary leadership is widely renowned and only exceeded by her ever deepening commitment to the Lord Jesus Christ. The board of directors and executive team of Walk Thru the Bible hold her in highest esteem. She not only leads the women's ministries at her local church but also continues to disciple women, leading each of them to experience spiritual breakthroughs.

Just recently I shared with her that my wife, Darlene, and I thought she was one of the greatest examples of the "Proverbs 31 Woman" we'd ever met. Indeed, "Her children rise up and call her blessed; her husband also, and he praises her: 'Many daughters have done well, but you excel them all'" (Proverbs 31:28–29, NKJV).

Today, she is the vice president for LifeChange Videos and oversees a vast and ever growing ministry outreach of Bible teaching via video across our nation. It was at her continuing encouragement that this entire series titled The Three Chairs: Experiencing Spiritual Breakthroughs! was produced. It is a privilege to honor her—a woman who I believe is great in the eyes of both heaven and earth—in this small way.

Table of Contents

SECTION FOUR:
Experiencing Spiritual Breakthroughs in Your Walk with God

CONCLUSION

Introduction
The Road Ahead

In my thirty years of ministry, I have asked audiences around the world how they would describe their spiritual progress at the moment. "Think of yourself as a pilgrim on a journey," I've said. "Where would you put youself on the road? How would you best describe the degree of your forward motion in your walk with God?"

Do you know what I've discovered? Only a few Christians see themselves as making significant progress spiritually. The majority use words like "seems like I'm going in circles," "a little off track right now," or just plain stuck.

But here's the good news—more than 80 percent of the Christians I've talked to have a deep desire to grow, to change, and to make spiritual breakthroughs to God's very best for their lives!

Since you're reading this book, I suspect you're one of them. You're contemplating striking out in a new direction spiritually. Maybe you've been sensing for some time that you need to get past some old obstacles in your life that have kept you from experiencing a deeper and more satisfying spiritual walk with God.

Every single page of this book has been crafted to make your spiritual quest a success. Each of the thirty readings will, I believe, present you with a key that will open a different lock in your life. Each lock, once open, will set you free in a new area. Chains will fall away. Gates, long barred, will swing open. New possibilities will become immediately apparent.

How do I know? Because every teaching is Bible-based. And because the seasoned mentors you'll meet in these pages have gone ahead of you on the journey. Their advice is tested by personal experience and measured against the powerful, changeless truths of God's Word. Insightful teachers like Charles Swindoll, Elisabeth Elliot, James Dobson, Joni Eareckson Tada, Howard Hendricks, Gary Smalley and others—each will introduce you to truth that transforms.

30 Days to Experiencing Spiritual Breakthroughs is actually part of a much larger series of life-changing resources. These include the book *Experiencing Spiritual Breakthroughs* and a number of video and audio resources for personal and group use that you'll find listed at the back of this volume. I hope you'll take advantage of them to aggressively pursue your own spiritual growth. If you've ever attended a Walk Thru the Bible seminar, watched a LifeChange video such as the Biblical Portrait of Marriage or Personal Holiness in Times of Temptation, or read the Daily Walk, YouthWalk, or Family Walk, then you already know the heart of our ministry. Everything that Walk Thru develops focuses on one thing— to guide you into real and lasting life change for God's glory.

As you'll soon discover, the principle of the Three Chairs is woven as the common thread throughout nearly every page of this book. I've been communicating and writing about the Three Chairs for more than twenty-five years nationally, and more recently, around the world. In every case, whether in sports stadiums, at Christian colleges, before national conventions of businessmen and educators, or to arenas in South Africa or Australia, the response to the message has been consistently the same: Lives have changed.

Each of the Chairs represent a different level of commitment toward God:

- **The First Chair stands for commitment.** The person has chosen to wholly love and serve God.

- **The Second Chair stands for compromise.** The person has chosen to try to get for themselves the best that both God and the world have to offer.
- **The Third Chair stands for conflict.** The person has chosen not to respond to God in any meaningful way, remaining at odds with eternal spiritual realities.

If you are a Christian, then you have sat in every one of these Chairs at one time of your life or another. The Chair in which you habitually sit controls all of your life—your values, your goals, your relationship with God, your character, your marriage, your children, how you spend your time and money.

I've noticed that when people begin to grasp the implications of these principles, lights flash on all across their lives. Nearly everyone recognizes where they sit and why. Many reach for a spiritual breakthrough on the spot.

Never has leaving spiritual mediocrity behind been more urgently needed. Secular pollsters have all reported the same statistic: the lifestyles, values, and choices of Christians and non-Christians are basically indistinguishable! Instead of demonstrating the incredible power of Christ to change lives, the church today embarrassingly demonstrates just the opposite. I am convinced that the Lord is calling believers back to a life of commitment and godliness.

So, my friend, mark out the next thirty days, and open your heart. The Master of life change—the Holy Spirit Himself—waits to guide you step by step toward the freedom, growth, and fulfillment that your Lord has had in mind for you since time began. You've begun an exciting journey, one you can undertake with both anticipation and confidence. "For it is God who works in you both to will and to do for His good pleasure" (Philippians 2:13).

ACKNOWLEDGMENTS

The purpose of this page is to make known the facts behind this book—to share the credit where the credit truly is due.

The first honor must be given to the man who worked alongside to develop this powerful tool for spiritual growth, Mr. Steve Kroening. Steve is an editor par excellence and is able to uncover the very best of the very best of anything that is written on the subject. His heart for the Lord is ever growing, and this project reflects his commitment for us to experience the joy of spiritual breakthroughs. Thanks, Steve; it's been a pleasure!

The second honor must be given to the incredible authors whose writings unveiled the secrets behind experiencing spiritual breakthroughs. Most of these men and women are personal friends or acquaintances, and I know that their lives match their words. When words and ways are one, we call it personal integrity. Thank you, fellow servants of the King, for sharing your heart on these thirty breakthroughs!

The third honor must be given to the entire LifeWay Resources team specifically under the leadership of Dr. Gene Mims and his leadership team. His encouragement and visionary Kingdom leadership stimulated this concept beyond what we could have ever dreamed or imagined. Our partnership at Walk Thru the Bible with LifeWay Resources in this entire process has been nothing but the greatest pleasure. John Kramp, John Ross, Rich Murrell, Mike Miller, Lee Sizemore, Jimmy Hester, and many others were a tremendous example of servant excellence!

The fourth honor must be given to the wonderful team at Multnomah Publishers under the innovative leadership of

Don Jacobson. It is a distinct honor to publish this book with Multnomah because of their strong commitment to produce material of excellence and eternal value. Special thanks must be given to Eric Weber, who guided this complex process and its rather demanding deadlines with the greatest of ease.

I've saved the best for last. The highest honor must be given to our great Lord. His commitment to lead us through spiritual breakthrough after spiritual breakthrough could be the only foundation for such a book. How I thank and praise Him for His unswerving loyalty and faithful commitment to move all of His sons and daughters through one spiritual breakthrough after another—all en route to the final breakthrough—the ultimate transformation into the very image of the Lord Jesus Christ.

Set Your Heart to Experience Spiritual Breakthroughs

Bruce H. Wilkinson

I was stuck!
I mean really stuck!
Back then I called it my "midlife crisis."

I was nearing forty and nothing was working right. The ministry wasn't satisfying. I wanted everything I didn't have. Even the proverbial red sports car and all that goes with it looked awfully good to this middle-aged married man. So did quitting the ministry. I didn't know what I wanted to do instead—maybe work at a bagel shop or something. Anything else…but *something* else.

Eventually, it all came to a head. I knew I had to do something, but no matter what I tried, it didn't work. So I turned to one of my mentors who had been used by the Lord numerous times during the previous twenty or so years, Dr. Howard G. Hendricks, a distinguished professor from Dallas Theological Seminary. I called him and told him I was stuck and that I needed help.

After only two sentences, he told me he was there for me

and that I should catch a plane the next day to go see him. He canceled some meetings and set the whole afternoon aside for me. Such friendship is a rare treasure.

When I finally sat in his office the next afternoon, I was uncomfortable and distressed. Not because of "Prof," as we affectionately call him, but because of the internal turmoil that was raging in me. He asked me a few questions and listened quietly. He didn't say much. I can remember sweating, just trying to explain for him as best as I could my turmoil and confusion. For as long as I live, I will never forget what he said next.

"Bruce, I can help you. Will you do what I say?"

"Well," I asked, "what do you want me to do?"

He sat quietly for a moment and then said soberly, "Will you do what I say regardless of what I ask?"

I couldn't believe it! He wanted my commitment before telling me what it was going to be! He was keeping me purposely in the dark!

I just sat there. Sweat dripped down my forehead. I couldn't speak. I just looked at the floor.

After a while, he said, "Bruce, do you believe I love you?"

"Yes, Prof, I know you love me."

"Then trust me."

There it was, out in the open. "Trust me." That was the problem.

For the longest time, I sat there considering his words. I knew he loved me. I knew he could be trusted. But could I trust him this far? Could I agree to do whatever he asked, even before he told me what it was? He was asking me to trust him without an answer to the question *why*.

After what seemed like an eternity, I finally found the words: "Yes, Prof, I know you love me—and I know that I can trust you. I will do anything you ask me to do."

He smiled with affection and gave me two different things to do. Everything in me screamed in opposition. What he was suggesting was the very opposite of what I wanted to do! I told him that I would set aside all of the emotion and arguments in my heart and that I would do exactly what he asked me to. Then I flew home.

I did exactly what he said.

And within three or four weeks, I was set free.

What a breakthrough!

ARE YOU STUCK?

In your spiritual life have you ever been stuck? It's really not too different from getting your car stuck in the mud or snow. You try to go forward, but nothing happens. You try to go in reverse, and still nothing happens. You might even try turning the wheels in different directions. But all the while, you're just digging yourself deeper and deeper.

You may be in this type of situation even as you're reading this. Perhaps you feel like the Israelites did when they were wandering around in the desert: continually going in circles, never really getting anywhere, eating the same spiritual diet day after day, and all you see on the horizon is more sand.

How did the Israelites handle their seemingly desperate situation? For years, they grumbled. They even decided it would be better to go back to Egypt and live in slavery than deal with the responsibilities of their newfound freedom. But that just caused their situation to get worse. They were really stuck! And they remained there for forty years.

Perhaps you don't even realize you're stuck. You may have become so comfortable with your life that you really see no reason to change it. Then you don't even know what you're missing. You've become so content with living in the desert that you may never experience the "Promised Land."

What is it that causes us to get stuck in the first place? Well, for the Israelites, it was unbelief. They were so frightened of the giants living in the Promised Land that they didn't believe God would give them the land as he promised. Once they acted on that unbelief, they were stuck. (The most tragic aspect of the Israelites' unbelief is that they never got unstuck. This generation wandered around in the desert until they died.)

I have a feeling the same could be true for you and me— we simply don't believe God!

THE THREE CHAIRS

The whole story of the Israelites and the Exodus can be broken up into three different periods of time: (1) the years of slavery, (2) the years of wandering, and (3) the years of abundance.

Obviously, the years of slavery refer to the four hundred years the Israelites spent in captivity in Egypt, the years of wandering pertain to the forty years they spent in the desert, and the years of abundance concern the years of plenty in the Promised Land under Joshua's leadership.

Each of these time periods represents a new generation. The generations of Israelites that lived in Egypt were slaves. They lived their lives in complete submission to the Egyptians. They were well taken care of, had plenty of good food and shelter, and lived fairly comfortable lives, but they were still slaves.

The second generation that left Egypt experienced the incredible exuberation of being delivered from slavery. They saw firsthand the miracles of God and experienced the power of His guiding hand. But they didn't know how to handle the responsibilities of freedom. They continually forgot about God's miracles and power, and tried to do things their own way. As we've already seen, the results were not pleasant.

The third generation, though, did things the right way. They remembered the things God did to get their forefathers out of Egypt, and they remembered His promises about the Promised Land. As a result, their belief was greatly rewarded with a land flowing with milk and honey. They saw God destroy their enemies, and they lived a life of abundance and blessing.

To make all of this more visual and practical, I have used three different chairs to represent each of these generations. Picture three chairs in your mind: the First Chair is the one on your right side, the Second Chair is in the middle, and the Third Chair sits on the left.

The First Chair in our metaphor is the godly chair, and those who sit in it remain close to Him. Joshua and the generation of Israelites who went into the Promised Land sat in this chair. They had a deep devotion to God. They trusted Him and knew their lives were firmly in His hand. They had an intimate relationship with the Lord and lived their lives to serve Him.

Joshua once said to this generation: "Now therefore, fear the LORD, serve Him in sincerity and in truth, and put away the gods which your fathers served on the other side of the River and in Egypt. Serve the LORD!... But as for me and my house, we will serve the LORD" (Joshua 24:14–15, NKJV). What a testament to their devotion!

Notice how Joshua referred to the other two generations of Israelites? The first group he mentioned was their fathers, who served other gods on the other side of the river. What is the difference between these Israelites and the Israelites in Egypt? The former group had experienced the power of God's salvation in their lives. They had been delivered from the tyranny of other lords. But as Joshua explains, they refused to put away the gods they had served in Egypt. They had come under the blood of the Passover but were not serving the Lord with their whole heart. To put it in modern terms, they were sitting comfortably in the Second Chair.

The Israelites in Egypt, on the other hand, had never experienced God's salvation. They were slaves to a master other than God and worshiped pagan gods. They were firmly seated in the Third Chair.

Are you beginning to understand the progression? God's desire for the life of an unbeliever is that he move from the Third Chair (where there is no relationship with Christ) into the Second Chair (where there is salvation, but a lot of baggage), and then quickly into the First Chair (where the baggage is thrown out).

Unfortunately, many people who move from the Third Chair into the Second get stuck there for far too long, just as the Israelites did in the desert. Or worse, they move on into the First Chair but then slide back into the Second Chair. Both situations are unfortunate. In fact, both are dealt with in Scripture.

If you keep reading the Israelites' story, you'll see that Joshua's descendants and the generation that outlived him (the fourth generation) don't do a very good job of holding on to the First Chair. This generation still believed in the Lord, but there was one significant difference: their faith wasn't original. They hadn't dealt personally with the Lord. Instead, they relied on the faith of their parents and the stories of what

God had done in their parents' generation. That alone had been enough to develop faith in God. They believed all the facts *about* God, but they didn't experience Him personally.

The next generation (the fifth) took an even bigger step backward. Judges 2:10 says this "generation arose after them who did not know the LORD nor the work which He had done for Israel" (NKJV).

EXPERIENCING SPIRITUAL BREAKTHROUGHS

So the movement can go both ways. Obviously, God wants us moving to the First Chair.

But some of us may be stuck. I was. I needed the help of a good friend to get out of the Second Chair and back into the First Chair. It took a little time, but I finally experienced the spiritual breakthrough I'd been searching for.

That's what this book is about: experiencing spiritual breakthroughs in your life, in your marriage, in your family, and in your walk with God.

I've arranged for some of the strongest leaders in the Christian community to guide you to the First Chair in several areas of your life. That's right! Every area of your life must be moved into the First Chair, and for thirty days these leaders will help you experience the breakthroughs you'll need to get there.

If you follow the steps they've outlined, I promise you'll encounter the abundant life God so desires for you to experience.

Trust me!

Experiencing Spiritual Breakthroughs in Your Life

"Character is always lost when a high ideal is sacrificed on the altar of conformity and popularity."

CHARLES R. SWINDOLL

Put an End to the Downward Spiral

CHARLES R. SWINDOLL

To begin, let's take a look at how easy it can be to move from the First Chair to the Second Chair. Many times, it's not one event in particular that causes us to change our seating arrangement. Rather, it's usually a slow erosion that eats at us over a long period of time. But Chuck Swindoll isn't content to let that erosion continue. While it may not be one single event that leads to our downfall, there can be a powerful spiritual breakthrough that moves us back to where we belong.

Some of my most pleasurable memories take me back to a little bay in Mexico. My maternal granddad owned a small cottage on that bay and was generous to share it with his extended brood. Throughout my adolescent years our family spent summer vacations down there: boating, swimming by the hour, jumping off piers, seining for shrimp, early-morning fishing, late-night floundering, but mainly laughing and relaxing.

While those years passed in family togetherness and fun, an ugly erosion was taking place. The waters of the bay were eating away at the bank of land between the cottage and the sea. Year after year, thanks to the rising and falling tide, a few hurricanes, and the normal lapping of waves at the shoreline, chunks of earth were being consumed by the bay. In all our busy activities and lazy hours of relaxation, no one ever talked about it or bothered to notice. In my childish innocence I never even thought about it. But I shall never forget the day all that changed. I did a little experiment late one summer day that made an indelible impression on my mind.

The previous year, our class in junior high school had studied erosion. The teacher did a good job of convincing us that even though we cannot see much happening or hear many warnings, erosion can occur right under our eyes. Just because it's silent and slow doesn't mean it isn't devastating. So, all alone the last day of our vacation that summer, I drove a big stake deep into the soil and then stepped off the distance between the stake and the sea—about fifteen feet, as I recall.

The next year we returned. Before sundown the first day we arrived, I returned to the stake and stepped off the distance; a little under twelve feet remained. The bay had gobbled up another three-plus feet—not in big gulps, understand, but an inch here and another inch or so there during the year that had passed. A downward spiral was underway. I've often wondered if I ever return to that place of happy family memories, would the cottage still be standing, or would it have surrendered to the insatiable appetite of the sea?

A friend of mine who attended an elite college in the Midwest many years ago told me a similar story. There was this massive tree—sort of a treasured landmark where students had met for decades. No one could even imagine that campus without the giant oak that spread its limbs for all to enjoy. It seemed to be a perpetual part of the landscape... until. One day, with an enormous nerve-jolting *C-R-A-C-K,* the mighty giant gave up the ghost. Once down, all who grieved its passing could see what no one had bothered to notice. A downward spiral had continued for years. Month by month, season after season, an internal erosion was taking place. Just because it was silent and slow didn't mean it wasn't dying.

So It Is with Character

My interest is not simply with a cottage or a college...not nearly so much as with character. Ever so slightly, invisible moral and ethical germs can invade, bringing the beginning stages of a terminal disease. No one can tell by looking, for it happens imperceptibly. It's slower than a clock and far more silent. There are no chimes, not even a persistent ticking. An oversight here, a compromise there, a deliberate looking the other way, a softening, a yawn, a nod, a nap, a habit...a destiny. And before we know it, a chunk of character falls into the sea, a protective piece of bark drops onto the grass. What was once "no big thing" becomes, in fact, bigger than life itself. What started with inquisitive innocence terminates at destructive addiction.

The same downward spiral can impact a family. It's what I often refer to as the domino effect. What is tolerated by Mom and Dad flows down to son and daughter. As Jeremiah once wept, "The fathers have eaten sour grapes, and the children's teeth are set on edge" (Jeremiah 31:29). The tragedy is that it doesn't stop there. Those kids grow up, shaping a nation's future. Reminds me of a line out of John Steinbeck's letter to Adlai Stevenson:

There is a creeping all-pervading gas of immorality which starts in the nursery and does not stop until it reaches the highest offices, both corporate and governmental.

Sociologist and historian Carle Zimmerman, in his 1947 book *Family and Civilization*, recorded his keen observations as he compared the disintegration of various cultures with the parallel decline of family life in those cultures. Eight specific patterns of domestic behavior typified the downward spiral of each culture Zimmerman studied.

1. Marriage loses its sacredness...is frequently broken by divorce.
2. Traditional meaning of the marriage ceremony is lost.
3. Feminist movements abound.
4. Increased public disrespect for parents and authority in general.
5. Acceleration of juvenile delinquency, promiscuity, and rebellion.
6. Refusal of people with traditional marriages to accept family responsibility.
7. Growing desire for and acceptance of adultery.
8. Increased interest in and spread of sexual perversions and sex-related crimes.

That last one generally marks the final stage of societal disintegration. The "creeping all-pervading gas" may be invisible, but according to Zimmerman, it can be lethal.

Before closing today's reading with a shrug, spend sixty seconds scrutinizing your life. If you're married, step off a mental measurement of your marriage...your family. Think hard. Don't lie to yourself. Ask and answer a few tough questions. Compare the way you were with the way you are. Look within the walls of your moral standard, your once-strong commitment to ethical excellence. Any termites in the timber? Don't be deceived by past years of innocence and fun. An ugly erosion may be taking place that you haven't bothered to notice. Just because the changes are silent and slow doesn't mean things aren't deteriorating.

Taken from *The Quest for Character* ©1982 by Charles R. Swindoll, Inc. Published by Zondervan Publishing House. Used by permission. Available at your local Christian bookstore.

So what is the breakthrough that will stop the downward spiral? It could be simply acknowledging that you're going the wrong direction. When Alcoholics Anonymous begins working with an alcoholic, the biggest and hardest obstacle to overcome is to get the person to admit he or she is an alcoholic. But once that breakthrough occurs, the restoration can begin. So it is with other spiritual breakthroughs. Take a moment and, in prayer, confess to the Lord if you've been going the wrong way and desire to go the right direction. Repent of your unbelief that caused you to stray in the first place and ask the Lord to restore your intimate relationship with Him.

Then to stay in the First Chair and deepen your walk with Christ, I urge you to read Chuck Swindoll's book The Quest for Character. *It will show you the importance of character and how you can develop the traits of a First Chair Christian.*

EVALUATION QUESTIONS

1. Take some time and evaluate where you are in stopping the downward spiral. Where would you rate yourself on the following scale?

1	5	10
Not even close to experiencing this breakthrough.	I've begun the journey, but I've got a ways to go.	I've experienced a breakthrough, and I'm living the abundant life.

2. What would you consider to be the biggest hindrance to your stopping the downward spiral right now?

3. What one action should you take to experience this breakthrough right now? I challenge you to do it.

*"No man is ever more than four steps from God:
conviction, repentance, consecration, and faith."*
ROY L. SMITH

*"Many of our fears are tissue-paper thin, and
a single courageous step would carry us clear through them."*
BRENDAN FRANCIS

*"The greatest of all disorders is to think
we are whole and need no help."*
THOMAS WILSON (1663–1735)

*"It is not the man who has too little, but
the man who craves more, who is poor."*
LUCIUS ANNAEUS SENECA (C. 4 B.C.–A.D. 65)

"Contentment consists not in great wealth but in few wants."
EPICTETUS (C. 55–135)

Break Down the Obstacles to Intimacy with Christ

JOSEPH STOWELL

Sitting in the Second Chair can be very comfortable. The effort that it takes is minimal—for the most part, you can just sit back and relax. But it takes work to reach the First Chair; that's why many folks never leave the Second Chair. If you've decided to leave the Second Chair and move to the First Chair, I have to warn you that there are many obstacles that can keep you from reaching your goal. However, overcoming these obstacles will produce an intimate relationship with Christ. And gaining intimacy with Christ is the greatest spiritual breakthrough you can possibly experience. Join Joseph Stowell as he leads the way.

I have to assume that most college campuses are a lot like Moody, where one of the most exciting places on campus is the campus post office. As long as you have a clear conscience, the daily mail is a lot of fun. Students go looking for a letter from that special guy or girl at home. A check from Mom or Dad. A box of cookies. That grade on the last major test.

I wonder what would happen if we were to pull a letter out of our stack of mail that had "Christ: The Universe" as the return address. While we would no doubt be concerned about what might be inside, knowing that He is well aware of all our shortcomings, we would be riveted to its text. We need to be riveted to the text of the letter Christ wrote to the church of Laodicea (Revelation 3:14–22). It is intensely personal and highly relevant to our search for intimacy. It could have been written to us. Near the end of the letter there is a compelling invitation:

> Behold, I stand at the door and knock. If anyone hears My voice and opens the door, I will come in to him and will dine with him, and he with Me. To him who overcomes I will grant to sit down with Me on My throne, as I also overcame and sat down with My Father on His throne. He who has an ear, let him hear what the Spirit says to the churches. (vv. 20–22)

Although many times we have taken this passage as being about salvation, the context dictates that it's really about a relationship with Christ for those who have already come to know Him.

Christ is standing at the door of our hearts, knocking. The metaphor is powerful. It means that Christ is intentionally, aggressively, passionately pursuing us. There are no qualifiers here. He isn't speaking just to the few really select, highly spiritual, worthy people at Laodicea. He is addressing all of the Laodiceans: the weak and the strong, the rich and the poor, those with disabilities, and those who are marginalized. Christ portrays Himself as intentionally pursuing intimacy with us.

If Christ makes Himself so accessible, why is it that we don't open the door? There are at least three reasons for our reticent response.

THE FIRST REASON: FEAR

Though God does pursue us and though Christ is there knocking, some of us may be afraid to open the door. Many of us have longed for intimacy in human relationships—with our father, mother, or someone else—only to find that our hopes for intimacy were not only dashed and broken but that as we made ourselves vulnerable, we were wounded in the process. We are afraid. We just don't know if we can ever trust again.

Thomas Keating, in his book *Intimacy with God*, speaks to this problem:

> The Christian's spiritual path is based on a deepening trust in God. It is trust that first allows us to take that initial leap in the dark, to encounter God at deeper levels of ourselves. And it is trust that guides the intimate refashioning of our being, the transformation of our pain, woundedness, and unconscious motivation into the person that God intended us to be.
>
> Because trust is so important, our spiritual journey may be blocked if we carry negative attitudes toward God from early childhood. If we are afraid of God or see God as an angry father-figure, a suspicious policeman, or a harsh judge, it will be hard to develop enthusiasm, or even an interest, in the journey.[1]

I have a prayer for those of us who keep God far away, who hear the knocking but fear to risk opening the door. It is the prayer of Mark 9:24: "Lord, I believe; help thou mine unbelief." (KJV). We need to pray, "Lord, I want to trust You" and then move toward trusting Him and being venturesome enough to reach out and open the door to God. We need to grasp the truth that God will not disappoint us. He will not abuse us. He will not use us. No one who has ever trusted God and moved toward intimacy has ever ultimately been disappointed—ever.

THE SECOND REASON: SELF-SUFFICIENCY

But for some of us, the fact that Christ is still on the outside may have something to do with the problem of the Christians at Laodicea. Revelation 3:14–19 tells the story of a lot of our lives:

To the angel of the church in Laodicea write:

The Amen, the faithful and true Witness, the Beginning of the creation of God, says this: "I know your deeds, that you are neither cold nor hot; I wish that you were cold or hot. So because you are lukewarm, and neither hot nor cold, I will spit you out of My mouth. Because you say, 'I am rich, and have become wealthy, and have need of nothing,' and you do not know that you are wretched and miserable and poor and blind and naked, I advise you to buy from Me gold refined by fire so that you may become rich, and white garments so that you may clothe yourself, and that the shame of your nakedness will not be revealed, and eye salve to anoint your eyes so that you may see. Those whom I love, I reprove and discipline; therefore be zealous, and repent.

Christ says, in effect, to the Laodiceans, "You are luke-warm. I wish you were like iced tea on a hot day or like hot tea on a cold day. I just wish you had an edge to you, but because you are neither hot nor cold, you are distasteful to me."

Why would God say that about His people? He said it because of their sense of self-sufficiency. They were rich and had no material needs, so they thought they didn't need God. They relied on what they consumed from the material world in order to satisfy, sustain, and secure themselves.

I find it interesting that all these "self" terms we throw around the church make us wilt with instant guilt. Just say the word *self-centered* and we wince. *Self-indulgent. Self-serving.* But when we think of self-sufficiency our eyes glaze over with pious apathy. We don't think it's as bad as the other "self" words. But it's a big issue to God. Christ said of the Laodiceans that though they had all the "stuff"—comforts, companions, commodities—they were "wretched and miserable and poor and blind and naked" (v. 17). They needed Christ.

But Christ didn't give up on the Laodiceans, just like He doesn't give up on us. In 1 Timothy 6, Paul tells believers to stop fleeing after earthly riches and to "pursue righteousness, godliness, faith, love, perseverance and gentleness" (v. 11, NKJV). God wants to make us rich in the right ways. He wants to fill our lives with truly valuable treasures. He wants to give us "gold refined by fire" (Revelation 3:18, NKJV). He wants us to have His peace, comfort, presence, and power. He wants to make us rich in a relationship that has access to all His resources: He wants to clothe our nakedness with white robes, the gowns of His children, and to anoint our eyes with the salve of His presence so that we can see (v. 18). And, as He told the Laodiceans, He wants us to repent of our self-sufficiency (v. 19). It's all because He loves us.

THE THIRD REASON: DISCONTENTMENT

Laurence Shames, in his penetrating analysis of Americans' preoccupation with consumption, The Hunger for More, writes:

> More. If there's a single word that summarizes American hopes and obsessions, that's it. More success. More luxuries and gizmos. We live for more—for our next raise, our next house; and the things we already have, however wonderful they are, tend to pale in comparison with the things we might still get.[2]

A friend who is an heiress to a massive estate told me that she wished she could have the days back again when getting a mug for Christmas would please and satisfy her. She remarked that there was a certain wonder and pleasure to find joy and satisfaction in small things.

What she had forgotten was that even those of us who can find pleasure in a new mug soon find that it too becomes commonplace. There is that ever-present craving for all that is more, bigger, or better.

I love heavy, large porcelain mugs. It's probably a male thing. My all-time favorite is my Chicago Bulls mug. That is, it was, until I visited the Hot Shot Cafe in Asheville, North Carolina. You have to experience the Hot Shot Cafe to appreciate what a privilege it is. It's where the local of the locals hangs out. Old jukebox and all. No pretense. Just good ol' home cookin' and an authentic rude waitress. On the shelf behind the cash register were Hot Shot Cafe mugs. I knew I needed one. It was a compulsion I couldn't resist. So I left some of my hard-earned cash behind and took it home where it would take its place among the other mugs I have bought through the years to satisfy my longings.

If it were only the mugs in our lives—or the teddy bears, or CDs, or antiques, or cars—it wouldn't really be all that big a deal. But it's the dynamic that drives my need for just one more mug that drives the bigger issues of life as well.

Shames goes on to say,

> During the past decade, many people came to believe there didn't have to be a purpose. The mechanism didn't require it. Consumption kept the workers working, which kept the paychecks coming, which kept the people spending, which kept inventors inventing and investors investing, which meant there was more to consume. The system, properly understood, was independent of values and needed no philosophy to prop it up. It was a perfect circle, complete in itself—and empty in the middle.[3]

The biblical word for satisfaction is the word *contentment*. We are called to be content with what we have since we have God—and He is fully sufficient. That doesn't mean we don't ever want something or that we don't enjoy a purchase here and there. It means that we are not controlled by the passion to consume. Having Him, we have it all. Anything extra is a bonus. Paul testified that he had learned both how to have plenty and how to have little and in both cases to be content (Philippians 4:11–13). In 1 Timothy 6 he writes:

> But godliness actually is a means of great gain when accompanied by contentment. For we have brought nothing into the world, so we cannot take anything out of it either. If we have food and covering, with

these we shall be content. But those who want to get rich fall into temptation and a snare and many foolish and harmful desires which plunge men into ruin and destruction. For the love of money is a root of all sorts of evil, and some by longing for it have wandered away from the faith and pierced themselves with many griefs. (vv. 6–10, NASB)

The King James Version puts it this way: "Godliness with contentment is great gain." We often reverse the formula to say "godliness plus gain is contentment" when in reality godliness plus contentment equals gain. The writer to the Hebrews reminds us to "make sure that your character is free from the love of money, being content with what you have; for He Himself has said, 'I will never desert you, nor forsake you,'" so that we confidently say, "The Lord is my helper, I will not be afraid. What will man do to me?'" (Hebrews 13:5–6, NASB).

Contentment is not just reflected in our relationship to things. We can be discontented with our spouse, our job, our place in life, our education, or a long list of other things. Sometimes discontentment can motivate us to righteousness or a zealous commitment to God. This is a healthy kind of discontentment. The kind of discontentment, however, that signals a vulnerability to aloneness is a discontentment that seeks personal satisfaction and security in "just one more thing, one more experience, one more friendship."

There is no way that we will want to turn our backs to the far country and our faces toward home until we are ready to realize that Christ is our all-sufficient source and as such enables us to live in the calm peace of a contented life.

When we hear Him knocking, it is the trusting, God-sufficient, contented heart that hurries to answer. Opening the door generates the pleasure of experiencing His promise, "I will come in to him and will dine with him, and he with Me" (Revelation 3:20, NASB).

Can you hear Christ knocking at the door of your heart? If you're sitting in the Second Chair, he's there, waiting for you to open the door. He desires to come in and dine with you. But you're being held back by fear, self-sufficiency, and discontentment. You've just read how these obstacles can be overcome. Are you ready to experience a breakthrough in your intimacy with Christ? Then all you have to do, as Joseph Stowell explains in his book Far from Home, *is get up and answer the door. "The very second we do," says Stowell, "we find that God is there, ready to come in. It's a union that our souls will never forget." Won't you open the door to your heart today? If you, like the prodigal son, have found your-self way off course, far from where you thought you'd be, read Dr. Stowell's book. It will meet you where you are and help you get back to where you're supposed to be.*

EVALUATION QUESTIONS

1. Take some time and evaluate where you are in experiencing this breakthrough. Where would you rate yourself on the following scale?

1	5	10
Not even close to experiencing this breakthrough.	I've begun the journey, but I've got a ways to go.	I've experienced a breakthrough, and I'm living the abundant life.

2. What would you consider to be the biggest hindrance to your experiencing this breakthrough right now?

3. What one action should you take to experience this breakthrough right now? I challenge you to do it.

1. Thomas Keating, *Intimacy with God* (New York: Crossroad, 1994), 22.

2. Laurence Shames, *The Hunger for More* (New York: Time Books, 1989), preface, x.

3. Ibid., 80.

"Do not consider painful what is good for you."
EURIPIDES (C. 484–406 B.C.)

"No pain, no palm; no thorns, no throne; no gall,
no glory; no cross, no crown."
WILLIAM PENN (1644–1718)

"If you don't invest much, defeat doesn't hurt and
winning is not exciting."
DICK VERMEIL

"Repentance is an attitude rather than a single act."
RICHARD OWEN ROBERTS

"Penitence does not grow by our looking gloomily on
our own badness, but by looking up to God's loveliness,
God's love for us."
WILLIAM CONGREVE (1670–1729)

"You never will be the person you can be if pressure, tension, and
discipline are taken out of your life."
JAMES G. BILKEY

Discipline Yourself to Win the Prize

ERWIN LUTZER

There's a moment in every athlete's quest where the realization hits that he's either won the prize or not. It's a glorious moment for the winner, but it's not so glorious for the loser. In athletics there's only one prize—winning. And the only way to reach it is to train with rigorous persistence. The same is true of Christianity. The Second Chair Christian, of course, isn't interested in training—he's interested in the pleasures of life. The First Chair Christian, on the other hand, isn't concerned about the pain that comes with training. No, he's interested in the prize. Sometimes spiritual breakthroughs aren't experienced without training and rigorous persistence. But ask any athlete who has won the prize if he has any regrets. I think you know what his answer will be. Follow carefully the wise words of Erwin Lutzer, and experience a breakthrough that will make you a winning believer.

*T*here is a story about a frustrated basketball coach, Cotton Fitzsimmons, who hit on an idea to motivate his team. Before the game he gave them a speech that centered around the word pretend. "Gentlemen, when you go out there tonight, instead of remembering that we are in last place, pretend we are in first place; instead of being in a losing streak, pretend we are in a winning streak; instead of this being a regular game, pretend this is a playoff game!"

With that, the team went onto the basketball court and was soundly beaten by the Boston Celtics. Coach Fitzsimmons was upset about the loss. But one of the players slapped him on the back and said, "Cheer up, Coach! *Pretend* we won!"

Many of us appear to be winning in the race of life, but perhaps it is all "pretend." Standing before Christ, we will soon see the difference between an actual victory and wishful thinking. We will see what it took to win and what it took to lose. We'll discover that we're playing for keeps.

Paul loved to use athletic contests as an analogy for living the Christian life. The famous Greek marathon and the Isthmian Games in Corinth were ready illustrations of how to run the race that really counts. We are running the race, Paul taught, and we are running to win.

> Do you not know that those who run in a race all run, but only one receives the prize? Run in such a way that you may win. Everyone who competes in the games exercises selfcontrol in all things. They then do it to receive a perishable wreath, but we an imperishable. Therefore I run in such a way, as not without aim; I box in such a way, as not beating the air; but I discipline my body and make it my slave, so

that, after I have preached to others, I myself will not be disqualified. (1 Corinthians 9:24–27, NASB)

Let's not miss Paul's point: *Whatever makes a winning athlete will make a winning Christian.* If we were as committed in our walk with God as we are to golf or bowling, we will do well in the Christian life. We can take what we learn in our tennis lessons and apply it to Christian living. Think of the energy, time, and money spent on sports. If we transferred such resources to the race that really counts, we would all be winners.

Society does not develop saints. There is nothing in our culture that will encourage us to have the stamina and encouragement to become winners for Christ. Indeed, we shall have to buck the world at every turn of the road; we shall have to rely on God and His people to help us develop the disciplines that lead to godliness.

RULES OF THE RACE

Let's introduce the analogy:

First, in Greece you had to be a citizen in order to compete in the games. Of course, all citizens were not in the races, but if you were eligible, you had to give proof of citizenship. Just so, you have to be a citizen of heaven in order to qualify for the race that Paul speaks about.

However, there is this difference: All citizens of heaven are enrolled in this race. This is not optional; there are no other events offered during this time frame. You do not run this race to get to heaven; you run this race in order to receive the prize. This race began on the day you accepted Christ as your Savior.

Second, this is one race in which everyone has the potential of winning, for we are not competing with others but with ourselves. We will be judged individually by God. To be determined is the question of what we did with what God gave us. Thus we all have our own personal finish line, our own personal coach, and our own personal final judgment.

Some people don't compete in sports because they fear failure. The humiliation of coming in last is just too much for those who are sensitive to public opinion. But fearful or not, this is one race we run every day. We are best served by setting aside our fears and running as best we can. Yes, this is one race you and I can win.

What are those rules that make great athletes and thus make "great" Christians? Each of us can translate them into daily living.

THE FIRST RULE: DISCIPLINE

When Paul speaks of those who compete in the games, he uses the Greek word *agonizomai* from which we get our word *agonize*. "Everyone who agonizes in the games...." You and I are simply unable to grasp the hours of agony that go into athletic conditioning.

In August, drive past a football field and watch the young athletes sweating under the hot sun. Clad in heavy clothes, padding, and a helmet, their faces grimace with distress and even pain. If they did this because their lives were threatened, we might understand. What is difficult for some of us to grasp is that they do this voluntarily—all for a trophy that will be kept in a glass case and soon be forgotten in this life and most assuredly not remembered in the next. They voluntarily play, and they will torture themselves in order to win.

Athletes must give up the bad and the good, and strive for only the best. They must say no to parties and late nights.

They cannot have the luxury of any personal enjoyment that conflicts with their ability to concentrate and to practice. Every distraction must be eschewed. I'm told that Mike Singletary of the Chicago Bears would work out with his team, then go home and do more exercises. Then, late at night when the house was quiet, he would watch videos of opposing teams to see how he might win against them.

Translate that into the disciplines of living the Christian life. Imagine the spurt of growth we would enjoy if we were to memorize Scripture, pray, and study the opposition with the same intensity with which athletes attack their game. Just think of what would happen if we were to hone our spiritual sensitivities, our spiritual appetites, and our spiritual muscles. We could take on the world....

There are many ways to fail in the Christian life. But all of them begin with lack of discipline, a conscious decision to take the easy route. Paul says, "I discipline my body and bring it under control." The lie is that the body cannot be disciplined, for indeed it can, especially with the help of the Holy Spirit, who gives us self-control.

I'm not asking you to add to your busy and cluttered life but rather to substitute the spiritual disciplines in favor of the priorities you have adopted. If you had to have dialysis every day because of kidney malfunction, you would find the time to do it. We must approach our walk with God with the same single-minded determination. Paul says, "This one thing I do!" not "These forty things I dabble in."

If you struggle with discipline, begin with this:

• Spend twenty minutes in prayer and meditation every morning before nine o'clock.
• Read a chapter of a good Christian book each day.

• Join a group of believers (a Bible-study class, prayer group, etc.) for fellowship and accountability.
• Learn to share your faith, and take the opportunities that God brings across your path.

Discipline itself does not produce godliness. We are not made spiritual by being "under the law," depending on our own strength to win God's approval. Rather, the purpose of these disciplines is that we might learn to draw our strength from Christ.

THE SECOND RULE: DETERMINATION

We've already referred to the passage in the book of Hebrews that tells us how to run the race. There we are given the rule book on how to run successfully. "Therefore, since we have so great a cloud of witnesses surrounding us, let us also lay aside every encumbrance and the sin which so easily entangles us, and let us run with endurance the race that is set before us" (Hebrews 12:1, NASB).

You've heard Bible teachers say that this "cloud of witnesses" is a reference to those who have gone to heaven and are now watching us here on earth. But, in context, it is clear that the witnesses are the heroes of Hebrews 11, and *we are motivated, not because they see us, but because we see them!*

Specifically, we look back to men like Abraham, Joseph, and Moses and conclude that if they could run the race successfully, so can we. We learn from them that endurance is always possible if we remember where we are headed. We are to glance at these heroes and gaze on Jesus.

What are the rules of the race?

First, we must *keep our weight down*. We are to "lay aside every weight." Some people have to join a spiritual Weight Watchers group. There are some things that might not be sins but are weights—habits and actions that take time and energy from that which is better.

Second, we are to *keep our feet free*. We must be free from the sin that does so easily "entangle" us. Sin tangles our feet, makes us stumble, and eventually will cause us to lose the race. Just think of the many people who began with a small weight or sin and ended up wounded on the sideline of the racetrack.

Those of us who are still in the race have an obligation to help those who have stumbled so that they too can cross the finish line.

In the 1992 Olympics, Derek Redmond of Great Britain popped his hamstring in the 400-meter semifinal heat. He limped and hobbled around half the Olympic stadium track. The sight of his son's distress was too much for Jim Redmond, who had been sitting near the top row of the stadium packed with sixty-five thousand people. He rushed down flights of stairs and blew past security people who challenged his lack of credentials to be on the track.

"I wasn't interested in what they were saying," he said of the security guards. He caught up to his son on the top of the final curve, some 120 meters from the finish. He put one arm around Derek's waist, another around his left wrist. Then they did a three-legged hobble toward the finish line.

Derek had no chance of winning a medal, but his determination earned him the respect of the crowd. His father said, "He worked eight years for this. I wasn't going to let him not finish." Whether or not his father knew it, he was acting biblically.

"Therefore, strengthen the hands that are weak and the knees that are feeble, and make straight paths for your feet, so that the limb which is lame may not be put out of joint, but rather be healed" (Hebrews 12:12–13, NASB). Some people have to be helped across the finish line. Some have stumbled over their own feet; others have been tripped by family members and so-called friends. We must help those who have fallen into the snares of the devil; we must lift up the fallen, bind up their wounds, and help them on their journey toward home.

Determination will do it.

THE THIRD RULE: FOCUS ON THE FINISH LINE

Every runner knows the danger of distractions and potholes. We not only have to know how to win, but we must also know why many people have lost the race.

Please remember that chapter divisions in the Bible are not inspired! Paul does not conclude his thoughts about winning the race at the end of 1 Corinthians 9, but continues his thought into the next chapter: "For I do not want you to be unaware, brethren" (10:1, NASB). That little word "for" is a bridge that continues Paul's warning.

In chapter 9 Paul says, "I discipline my body and make it my slave, so that, after I have preached to others, I myself will not be disqualified" (v. 27). He feared that even he might lose the race!

When he begins chapter 10, he uses the Israelites in the desert as an illustration of those who lost the race. These were people redeemed out of Egypt; they had crossed the Red Sea and had experienced the daily provision of God, and yet they fell short of the prize.

First, Paul speaks of the blessings they enjoyed. They were given all they needed to run successfully.

> For I do not want you to be unaware, brethren, that
> our fathers were all under the cloud, and all passed
> through the sea; and all were baptized into Moses in

the cloud and in the sea; and all ate the same spiritual food; and all drank the same spiritual drink, for they were drinking from a spiritual rock which followed them; and the rock was Christ. (vv. 1–4, NASB)

Next, Paul describes their failure in the face of innumerable blessings. "Nevertheless, with most of them God was not well pleased" (v. 5). Then follows a list of their sins: idolatry, immorality, and ingratitude. Many of these people were saved in the Old Testament sense of that word: They will be in heaven. Nevertheless, they were displeasing to God and will not win the prize.

The contrast is between their many undeserved blessings and their failures. They began the race with all the resources for the journey, yet they stumbled badly, far from the finish line. Not only did they not make it into Canaan, they never even lived successfully in the desert, where God supplied all of their needs.

The same sins beset us today. Our only hope of winning is to repent; indeed, our lives should be lived with an attitude of repentance. Ask the Holy Spirit to show you the sins that might keep you from finishing well. If Paul feared that he might be disqualified, you and I are most assuredly vulnerable.

We look back and say, "Abraham won. David won. Joseph won. So did a host of people who did not see deliverance but trusted God anyway." We can do the same! But let us always remember what it cost them.

Nothing fades as quickly as flowers. In the hot sunlight they last but a few hours. It was for such a wreath that the athletes competed in ancient Greece. Paul called it a "corruptible crown."

In contrast, there is an incorruptible crown given to those who serve Christ. It is guaranteed to last forever. We must covet the prize of the high calling of God in Christ Jesus. Paul was not embarrassed to say that he desired to win the crown; he did not think it unspiritual to seek the approval of Christ and the honor associated with it.

On a businessman's desk was this sign:

In twenty years what will you wish you had done today?
Do it now!

Do you want to win the race? Whatever it takes, just "do it now!"

Taken from *Your Eternal Reward* by Erwin W. Lutzer, ©1998 by Erwin W. Lutzer. Used by permission of Moody Press. Available at your local Christian bookstore.

Procrastination will kill just about any chance you have of experiencing a spiritual breakthrough. "Do it now!" is Erwin Lutzer's exhortation to you to get up off your Second Chair today and begin moving to the First Chair. In his book, Your Eternal Reward, *Lutzer reminds you to keep your eyes focused on the prize. If you need to get up from where you're sitting right now and physically move to another seat to symbolize your intentions, do it now! Whatever it takes to help you make the decision to begin training, do it now! You won't regret it. Today is the day you must say, "Today I will remember the goal; I will focus on Christ no matter what storm might come my way!" And Erwin Lutzer's book is a great resource to encourage you to keep your focus on your eternal reward. I strongly encourage you to read it.*

EVALUATION QUESTIONS

1. Take some time and evaluate where you are in experiencing this breakthrough. Where would you rate yourself on the following scale?

1	5	10
Not even close to experiencing this breakthrough.	I've begun the journey, but I've got a ways to go.	I've experienced a breakthrough, and I'm living the abundant life.

2. What would you consider to be the biggest hindrance to your experiencing this breakthrough right now?

3. What one action should you take to experience this breakthrough right now? I challenge you to do it.

"A man wrapped up in himself makes a very small bundle."
BENJAMIN FRANKLIN (1706–1790)

"Dear Heavenly Father:
I'm working on a puzzle, pure and simple.
It is I.

Dear Searching Child:
Here's the answer to your puzzle, pure and simple.
It is I."
ETHELYN A. SHATTUCK

"Beware of no man more than yourself;
we carry our worst enemies with us."
CHARLES HADDON SPURGEON (1834–1892)

"If I am half-full of myself, there is no way I can be full of God."
RICHARD OWEN ROBERTS

"It is not my business to think about myself. My business is to
think about God. It is for God to think about me."
SIMONE WEIL (1909–1943)

"Self…is not to be annihilated,
but to be rightly centered in God."
OSWALD CHAMBERS (1874–1917)

"Self is the opaque veil that hides the face of God from us."
A. W. TOZER (1897–1963)

Take Courage and Examine Yourself Differently

HANNAH WHITALL SMITH

Examine yourselves, whether ye be in the faith.
2 CORINTHIANS 13:5, KJV

When Paul and his friends were on their way to Damascus, they could have been focused on just about anything: their job, the sand, the camels, maybe even their destination. But they certainly weren't focused on what God wanted them to be focused on. As a result, God caused Paul to have a major spiritual breakthrough. God refocused Paul's vision by blinding him to the physical word and opening his eyes to the spiritual. Is it possible that in your attempts to move to the First Chair you've had your eyes on the wrong prize? If so, the spiritual breakthrough you're about to experience will be monumental. It might not be as dramatic as Paul's, but the end result could help you arrive at the same destination.

*P*robably no subject connected with the religious life has been the cause of more discomfort and suffering to tender consciences than has this subject of self-examination, and none has led more frequently to the language of "much less." And yet it has been so constantly impressed upon us that it is our duty to examine ourselves, that the eyes of most of us are continually turned inward and our gaze is fixed on our own interior states and feelings to such an extent that self, and not Christ, has come at last to fill the whole horizon.

By "self" I mean here all that centers around this great big "me" of ours. Its vocabulary rings out the changes on "I," "me," "my." It is a vocabulary with which we are all very familiar. The questions we ask ourselves in our times of self-examination are proof of this. Am I earnest enough? Have I repented enough? Have I the right sort of feelings? Do I realize religious truth as I ought? Are my prayers fervent enough? Is my interest in religious things as great as it ought to be? Do I love God with enough fervor? Is the Bible as much of a delight to me as it is to others? All these and a hundred more questions about ourselves and our experiences fill up all our thoughts, and sometimes our little self-examination books as well, and day and night we ring out the changes on the personal pronouns "I," "me," "my" to the utter exclusion of any thought concerning Christ or any word concerning "He," "His," "Him."

WHAT DOES THE BIBLE SAY

The misery of this many of us know only too well. But the idea that the Bible is full of commands to self-examination is so prevalent that it seems one of the most truly pious things we can do, and miserable as it makes us, we still feel it is our duty to go on with it in spite of an ever-increasing sense of hopelessness and despair.

In view of this idea, many will be surprised to find that there are only two texts in the whole Bible that speak of self-examination and that neither of these can at all be made to countenance the morbid self-analysis that results from what we call self-examination.

One of these passages I have quoted at the head of this chapter: "Examine yourselves, whether ye be in the faith" (2 Corinthians 13:5, KJV). It does not say examine whether you are sufficiently earnest, or whether you have the right feelings, or whether your motives are pure, but simply and only whether you are "in the faith." In short, do you believe in Christ or do you not? A simple question that required only a simple, straightforward answer, yes or no. This is what it meant for the Corinthians then, and it is what it means for us now.

The other passage reads: "Wherefore whosoever shall eat this bread, and drink this cup of the Lord, unworthily, shall be guilty of the body and blood of the Lord. But let a man examine himself, and so let him eat of that bread, and drink of that cup" (1 Corinthians 11:27–28, KJV). Paul was here writing of the abuses of greediness and drunkenness that had crept in at the celebration of the Lord's Supper, and in this exhortation to examine themselves, he was simply urging them to see to it that they did none of these things but partook of this religious feast in a decent and orderly manner.

In neither of these passages is there any hint of that morbid searching out of one's emotions and experiences that is called self-examination in the present day. And it is amazing that out of two such simple passages should have evolved a teaching fraught with so much misery to earnest, conscientious souls.

The truth is there is no Scripture authority whatever for this disease of modern times, and those who are afflicted with it are the victims of mistaken ideas of God's ways with His children.

WHO ARE YOU LOOKING AT

It is a fact that we see what we look at and cannot see what we look away from, and we cannot look unto Jesus while we are looking at ourselves. The power for victory and the power for endurance are to come from looking unto Jesus and considering Him, not from looking unto or considering ourselves, or our circumstances, or our sins, or our temptations. Looking at ourselves causes weakness and defeat. The reason for this is that when we look at ourselves, we see nothing but ourselves, and our own weakness, and poverty, and sin; we do not and cannot see the remedy and the supply for these, and as a matter of course we are defeated. The remedy and the supply are there all the time, but they are not to be found in the place where we are looking, for they are not in the self but in Christ, and we cannot look at ourselves and look at Christ at the same time. Again I repeat that it is in the inexorable nature of things that what we look at that we shall see and that, if we want to see the Lord, we must look at the Lord and not at the self. It is a simple question of choice for us, whether it shall be I or Christ; whether we shall turn our backs on Christ and look at ourselves, or whether we shall turn our backs on ourselves and look at Christ.

I was very much helped many years ago by the following sentence in a book by Adelaide Proctor: "For one look at self, take ten looks at Christ." It was entirely contrary to all I had previously thought right, but it carried conviction to my soul and delivered me from a habit of morbid self-examination and introspection that had made my life miserable for years. It was an unspeakable deliverance. And my experience since leads me to believe that an even better motto would be, "Take no look at self at all, but look only and always at Christ."

PUT OFF THE SELF-LIFE

The Bible law in regard to the self-life is not that the self-life must be watched and made better but that it must be "put off." The apostle when urging the Ephesian Christians to walk worthy of the vocation wherewith they had been called, tells them that they must "put off" the old man, which is corrupt according to the deceitful lusts. The "old man" is, of course, the self-life, and this self-life (which we know only too well is indeed corrupt according to deceitful lusts) is not to be improved but to be put off. It is to be crucified. Paul says that our old man is crucified, put to death, with Christ, and he declares of the Colossians that they could no longer lie, seeing that they had "put off the old man with his deeds." Some people's idea of crucifying the old man is to set him up on a pinnacle and then walk around him and stick nagging pins into him to make him miserable, but keeping him alive all the time. But if I understand language, crucifixion means death, not making miserable, and to crucify the old man means to kill him outright and to put him off as a snake puts off its dead and useless skin.

It is of no use, then, for *us* to examine self and to tinker with it in the hope of improving it, for the thing the Lord wants us to do with it is to get rid of it. Fenelon, in his *Spiritual Letters*, says that the only way to treat self is to refuse to have anything to do with it. He says we must turn our backs on this great big "I" of ours and to say to it, "I do not know you and am not interested in you, and I refuse to pay any attention to you whatever." But self is always determined to secure attention and would rather be thought badly of than not to be thought of at all. And self-examination, with all its miseries, often gives a sort of morbid satisfaction to the self-life in us and *even* deludes self into thinking it a very humble and pious sort of self after all.

The only safe and scriptural way is to have nothing to do with self at all, either with good self or with bad self, but simply to ignore self altogether and to fly our eyes, and our thoughts, and our expectations on the Lord and on Him alone. We must substitute for the personal pronouns "I," "me," "my" the pronouns "He," "Him," "His" and must ask ourselves, not "Am I good?" but "Is He good?"

The psalmist says: "Mine eyes are ever toward the Lord, for he shall pluck my feet out of the net." As long as our eyes are toward our own feet and toward the net in which they are entangled, we only get into worse tangles. But when we keep our eyes toward the Lord, He plucks our feet out of the net. This is a point in practical experience that I have tested hundreds of times, and I know it is a fact. No matter what sort of a snarl I may have been in, whether inward or outward, I have always found that while I kept my eyes on the snarl and tried to unravel it, it grew worse and worse, but when I turned my eyes away from the snarl and kept them fixed on the Lord, He always sooner or later unraveled it and delivered me.

Have you ever watched a farmer plowing a field? If you have, you will have noticed that in order to make straight furrows, he is obliged to fix his eyes on a tree, or a post in the fence, or some object at the farther end of the field, and to guide his plow unwaveringly toward that object. If he begins to look back at the furrow behind him in order to see whether he has made a straight furrow, his plow begins to jerk from side to side, and the furrow he is making becomes a zigzag. If we would make straight paths for our feet, we must do what the apostle says he did. We must forget the things that are behind, and reaching forth to those which are before, we must press toward the mark for the prize of the high calling of God in Christ Jesus.

To forget the things that are behind is an essential part of the pressing forward toward the prize of our high calling, and I am convinced this prize can never be reached unless we will consent to this forgetting. When we do consent to it, we come near to putting an end to all our self-examination, for if we may not look back over our past misdoings, we shall find but little food for self-reflective acts.

We complain of spiritual hunger and torment ourselves to know why our hunger is not satisfied. The psalm says: "The eyes of all wait upon thee, and thou givest them their meat in due season." Having our eyes upon ourselves and on our own hunger will never bring a supply of spiritual meat. When a man's larder is empty and he is starving, his eyes are not occupied with looking at the emptiness of his larder but are turned toward the source from which he hopes or expects to get a supply of food. To examine self is to be like a man who should spend his time in examining his empty larder instead of going to the market for a supply to fill it. No wonder such Christians seem to be starving to death in the midst of all the fullness there is for them in Christ. They never see that fullness, for they never look at it, and again I repeat that the thing we look at is the thing we see.

We grow like what we look at, and if we spend our lives looking at our hateful selves, we shall become more and more hateful. Do we not find as a fact that self-examination, instead of making us better, always seems to make us worse?

Beholding self, we are more and more changed into the image of self. While on the contrary if we spend our time beholding the glory of the Lord—that is, letting our minds dwell upon His goodness and His love, and trying to drink in His spirit—the inevitable result will be that we shall be, slowly perhaps, but surely, changed into the image of the Lord upon whom we are gazing.

The only way to treat all forms of self-reflective acts, of whatever kind, is simply to give them up. They always do harm and never good. They are bound to result in one of two things: either they fill us full of self-praise and self-satisfaction, or they plunge us into the depths of discouragement and despair. Whichever it may be, the soul is in this way inevitably shut out from any sight of God and of His salvation.

One of the most effectual ways of conquering the habit is to make a rule that, whenever we are tempted to examine ourselves, we will always at once begin to examine the Lord instead and will let thoughts of His love and His all-sufficiency sweep out all thoughts of our own unworthiness or our own helplessness.

What we must do, therefore, is to shut the door definitely and resolutely at once and forever upon self and all of self's experiences, whether they be good or bad, and to say with the psalmist, "I have set the Lord [not self] always before me; because he is at my right hand, I shall not be moved. Therefore my heart is glad, and my glory rejoiceth; my flesh also shall rest in hope."

Taken from *The God of All Comfort* by Hannah Whitall Smith. Published by Moody Press. Available at your local Christian bookstore.

What a breakthrough! What a change in direction! Now you can see why Paul made such a difference in this world—he had his eyes firmly focused on his Savior. The encounter Paul had with Jesus on the road to Damascus moved him from the Third Chair to the First Chair in a flash. We have no record of Paul ever backsliding into the Second Chair. Why? Because he kept his eyes firmly focused on Christ. Now you can follow in his footsteps. Who knows, this breakthrough you've just experienced may change the world. I guarantee it will change your world.

EVALUATION QUESTIONS

1. Take some time and evaluate where you are in experiencing this breakthrough. Where would you rate yourself on the following scale?

1	5	10
Not even close to experiencing this breakthrough.	I've begun the journey, but I've got a ways to go.	I've experienced a breakthrough, and I'm living the abundant life.

2. What would you consider to be the biggest hindrance to your experiencing this breakthrough right now?

3. What one action should you take to experience this breakthrough right now? I challenge you to do it.

*"God sends no one away empty except
those who are full of themselves."*
D. L. MOODY (1837–1899)

*"Most of the trouble in the world is caused by people
wanting to be important."*
T. S. ELIOT (1888–1965)

*"Pride is spiritual cancer;
it eats the very possibility of love or contentment,
or even common sense."*
C. S. LEWIS (1898–1963)

*"Pride is the ground in which all the other sins grow,
and the parent from which all the other sins come."*
WILLIAM BARCLAY (1907–1978)

*"Self-complacency and spiritual pride
are always the beginning of degeneration.
When I begin to be satisfied with where I am spiritually,
I begin to degenerate."*
OSWALD CHAMBERS (1874–1917)

Replace Your Pride with Genuine Humility

J. OSWALD SANDERS

One sin that is sure to keep you out of the First Chair is pride. It will prevent you from experiencing many of the spiritual break- throughs that we talk about in this book. What that means is that you must experience a spiritual breakthrough in regard to your pride. Otherwise, you're destined to live your life in the Second Chair, wandering through the desert and never experiencing the abundant life. Heeding the words of Oswald Sanders will help you experience this breakthrough and gain victory over your pride.

The Bible does not tell how sin entered the uni- verse, but we are told how it entered our world and that it originated before it made its pres- ence felt here. It is characteristic of Scripture revelation that while it does not tell us everything we would like to know, it tells us all we need to know to enable us to meet the exigencies of life and to live victoriously over sin and circumstances. To do this, it is not necessary that we know the primal origin of sin, but it is essential that we know the nature and character of the fundamental sin that has blighted the world ever since it was entertained by our first parents.

In Genesis, the original temptation to sin was presented by the Devil, who himself had fallen from his lofty position. Two Old Testament passages throw light on the nature of his sin (Ezekiel 28:11–19; Isaiah 14:12–15), passages that primarily refer to the king of Tyre and the king of Babylon. But the meaning of these Scriptures obviously cannot be exhausted by mere men. The Ezekiel passage runs:

> Thou sealest up the sum, full of wisdom, and perfect in beauty. Thou hast been in Eden the garden of God; every precious stone was thy covering.... Thou art the anointed cherub that covereth.... Thou wast perfect in thy ways from the day that thou wast created, till iniquity was found in thee.... And thou hast sinned: therefore I will cast thee as profane out of the mountain of God.... *Thine heart was lifted up* [was proud] because of thy beauty... I will cast thee to the ground. (Ezekiel 28:12–17, KJV, italics mine)

How reminiscent of the words of our Lord, "I beheld Satan as lightning fall from heaven" (Luke 10:18, KJV). Or again the Isaiah passage:

> How art thou fallen from heaven, O Lucifer.... For thou hast said in thine heart, I will ascend into heaven, I will exalt my throne above the stars of God: I will sit also upon the mount of the congregation.... I will ascend above the heights...*I will be like the most High.*

Yet thou shalt be brought down to hell. (Isaiah 14:12–15, KJV, italics mine)

The historical characters to whom these passages had primary reference could not exhaust the full significance of these extraordinary statements, which without doubt have a deeper meaning. This method of revelation of truth is employed elsewhere in Scripture, for instance, in the messianic psalms, where the psalmist, though apparently referring to himself, made statements that in their fullness could refer only to the Messiah (Psalms 2, 22, and 110). This is confirmed elsewhere in Scripture. So we have grounds for inferring that these passages have a secondary application to Satan, who occupied the lofty office of guardian and protector of the throne of God. He was the daystar, holding a position of unsurpassed glory near the Sun of Righteousness.

What caused his downfall? The fundamental sin of pride, the sin of seeking to establish a throne of his own. Instead of guarding the throne of God, which he was set to protect, he struck at it and attempted to dethrone the Almighty. Pride led to self-exaltation, which expressed itself in self-will. The essence of his sin was that he wanted to be independent of God. Pride is the self-sufficiency of a selfish spirit that desires only unrestrained independence. "I will exalt *my throne* above the stars of God.... I will be like the Most High." This is the fundamental sin that tries to enthrone self at the expense of God.

Though Satan was cast down, in his fall he wrested the scepter of sovereignty of the world from man, and now he rules as god of this world. In Eden he sowed the seeds of the same tragic sin. "In the day ye eat thereof...ye shall be as gods," he promised in Genesis 3:5, KJV. Compare this with his "I will make myself like the Most High." Satan fell through pride. Adam and Eve fell through pride and implicated the whole human race in their ruin. You and I fall through pride, the fundamental sin that lies at the root of every other sin, the desire to be master of our own lives and to be independent of God. Since this is so, it is little wonder that pride leads the list in every catalog of sins compiled by the church.

GOD HATES PRIDE

No sin is more hateful and abhorrent to God. Sins of the flesh are revolting and bring their own social consequences, but against none of those does God speak with such vehemence as He does of pride.

"Him that hath...a proud heart will I not suffer [endure]" (Psalm 101:5).

"The proud he knoweth afar off" (Psalm 138:6).

"These six things doth the Lord hate; yea, seven are an abomination unto him: a proud look" (Proverbs 6:16–17).

"Pride...do I hate" (Proverbs 8:13).

"Every one that is proud in heart is an abomination to the Lord" (Proverbs 16:5).

"A proud heart...is sin" (Proverbs 21:4).

"The pride of man shall be brought low" (Isaiah 2:17, ASV).

"God resisteth the proud" (James 4:6).

No further words are necessary to express the hatred, the revulsion, the antipathy of God to pride and arrogance, to conceit and haughtiness. It is an abomination to Him. Can we condone what God hates? Can we entertain what is an abomination to Him? God opposes the proud and holds them at a distance. There is no meeting point between a proud heart and God, but a broken and contrite spirit He will not despise.

THE ESSENCE OF PRIDE

The word "proud" in James 4:6 signifies literally "one who considers himself above other people." It is an offense to both God and man. The Greeks hated it. Theophylact called pride "the citadel and summit of all evils."

Pride is a deification of self. It thinks more highly of itself than it ought to think. It arrogates to itself the honor that belongs to God only. It caused Rabbi Simeon Ben Jochai to say with becoming humility, "If there are only two righteous men in the world, I and my son are the two. If only one, I am he." It was the sin of Nebuchadnezzar that brought him down to the level of the beasts. The valet of the last German kaiser said, "I cannot deny that my master was vain. He had to be the central figure in everything. If he went to a christening, he wanted to be the baby. If he went to a wedding, he wanted to be the bride. If we went to a funeral, he wanted to be the corpse."

Pride is characterized by independence of God. It was at the heart of Adam's sin. Instead of being dependent on God, he desired to be as God and brought ruin on the whole race. Pride desires to be beholden to neither God nor man. It is perfectly self-sufficient, in striking contrast to the Son of God, who said, "I can of mine own self do nothing" (John 5:30). He gloried in His dependence on His Father. Pride glories in being self-made.

It involves a certain contempt for others. "God, I thank thee, that I am not as other men are…or even as this publican" (Luke 18:11). It relegates every other mortal to a minor role in life. It uses other people as a backdrop to display its own brilliance. The proud man considers others beneath him, the hoi polloi, the common herd. Instead of pouring contempt on all his pride, he pours his contempt on others whom he esteems less worthy than himself.

Pride is essentially competitive in its nature. C. S. Lewis points out that no one is proud because he is rich, or clever, or good looking. He is proud because he is richer, or more clever, or better looking than someone else. It involves a comparison that always goes in favor of the one who made it.

Pride defiles everything it touches. There are germs that transform nourishing food into virulent poison. Pride transforms virtues into vices and blessings into curses. Beauty plus pride results in vanity. Zeal plus pride makes for tyranny and cruelty. Human wisdom compounded with pride brings infidelity. In speech, pride manifests itself in criticism, for criticism is always made from the vantage point of conscious superiority. Pride will find cause for criticism in everyone and everything. It lauds itself and belittles its neighbor.

Scripture is replete with illustrations of the folly and tragedy that follow in the train of pride. It was pride of his kingdom and power that moved King David to number Israel (1 Chronicles 21:1), a sin that resulted in divine judgment. Gripped by pride, Hezekiah showed his covetous enemies "all the house of his precious things, the silver, and the gold...and all that was found in his treasures" (2 Kings 20:13)—and lost them all. Nebuchadnezzar's pride fed on his own achievements: "Is not this great Babylon, that I have built for the house of the kingdom by the might of my power, and for the honour of my majesty?" (Daniel 4:30). But his haughty spirit went before a gigantic fall. "While the word was in the king's mouth, there fell a voice from heaven, saying...'The kingdom is departed from thee. And they shall drive thee from men, and thy dwelling shall be with the beasts of the field: they shall make thee to eat grass as oxen'" (Daniel 4:31). When his sanity was restored, the center of his worship was shifted from himself to God. "Now I Nebuchadnezzar praise and extol and honour the King of heaven" (Daniel 4:37). Pride is a species of moral and spiritual insanity.

THE CURE OF PRIDE

Pride must be radically dealt with. William Law wrote, "Pride must die in you or nothing of heaven can live in you.... Look not at pride only as an unbecoming temper, nor at humility only as a decent virtue.... One is all hell and the other all heaven."

Steps on the road to cure are:

Perception. Humility, the antithesis of pride, has been defined by Bernard as the virtue by which man becomes conscious of his own unworthiness. We will never conquer a sin of which we are unconscious or over which we do not grieve. We must hate what God hates. Self-knowledge is not easy to come by, as we are all so prepossessed in our own favor. We see the splinter in our brother's eye with great clarity but, with strange inconsistency, fail to detect the plank in our own. We need to genuinely ask God to expose us to ourselves. When we see ourselves as we truly are, we will sink in self-abasement. Is it not true that we would not be very comfortable if others knew all our secret thoughts, saw all the pictures that hang on the walls of our imagination, perceived all our hidden motives, observed all our covered deeds, heard all our whispered words? Are we humbled that God knows us for the persons we truly are? If we realize the facts about ourselves as they really are, all grounds for pride will be demolished. Do I know a lot? What I know is infinitesimal compared with what remains to be known. Am I clever? My cleverness is a gift for which I can take no credit. Am I rich? It was God who gave me the power to get wealth.

Chastening. As a preventive against loathsome pride in His children, God lovingly disciplines them. Paul had this experience: "And lest I should be exalted above measure through the abundance of the revelations, there was given to me a thorn in the flesh...lest I should be exalted above measure" (2 Corinthians 12:7). Do we recognize, in some crippling limitation, some painful malady, some thwarted ambition, the gracious ministry of God to deliver us from something worse, the ascendancy of pride?

Mortification. A prudent farmer cuts down weeds when they are young lest they spread their seeds and multiply. So let us observe the proud thought, confess it, and put it away. Cherish the proud thought and you will find you have nursed a viper in your bosom. Pride is of the flesh, and the Spirit will help us in killing it. "If ye through the Spirit do mortify the deeds of the body, ye shall live" (Romans 8:13).

Comparison. We compare ourselves among ourselves and come off fairly well in the comparison. But let us compare ourselves with the perfect Christ, and if we are honest, we will be overwhelmed with the tawdriness and shabbiness or even the vileness of our characters. While the disciples in their pride wrangled to secure first place, the Lord of glory donned the slave's smock and washed their dirty feet. It is striking that Satan tempted Christ with the very sin that had caused his own downfall. But where he succumbed, Christ triumphed.

Contemplation. The final secret is the contemplation of Christ. Our best efforts of self-discovery and self-discipline will be inadequate alone to root out this cancer. It requires a radical and supernatural change of heart, and this is what is promised: "Beholding...the glory of the Lord, we are changed into the same image" (2 Corinthians 3:18). Pride shrivels and withers and shrinks away in the light of His humility. And again it is "by the Spirit of the Lord" that the transformation takes place. The Holy Spirit will always cooperate to the limit with anyone who comes to hate his pride and covets the humility of Christ.

Taken from *Spiritual Maturity* by J. Oswald Sanders. ©1994 by the Estate of J. Oswald Sanders. Used by permission. Available at your local Christian bookstore.

If pride has already ascended in your life, you may not even be aware of it. As we've said before, the first step to dealing with your pride is acknowledging it's there. If you aren't sure whether pride has raised its ugly head, ask a godly friend or church leader who knows you well enough and loves you enough to tell you the truth. If it indeed has manifested itself, reread this article and pay special attention to J. Oswald Sanders's cure for this potentially fatal disease. It will affect every relationship you have—including the one you have with the Lord. After that, read J. Oswald Sanders' book Spiritual Maturity. *It's one of the best ever written on the subject.*

EVALUATION QUESTIONS

1. Take some time and evaluate where you are in experiencing victory over pride. Where would you rate yourself on the following scale?

1_____5_____10

| Not even close to experiencing this breakthrough. | I've begun the journey, but I've got a ways to go. | I've experienced a breakthrough, and I'm living the abundant life. |

2. What would you consider to be the biggest hindrance to your experiencing victory over pride right now?

3. What one action should you take to experience victory over pride right now? I challenge you to do it.

"Before we can be filled with the Spirit, the desire to be filled must be all-consuming. It must be for the time the biggest thing in the life, so acute, so intrusive as to crowd out everything else. The degree of fullness in any life accords perfectly with the intensity of true desire. We have as much of God as we actually want."

A. W. TOZER (1897–1963)

"God commands us to be filled with the Spirit, and if we are not filled, it is because we are living beneath our privileges."

D. L. MOODY (1837–1899)

"God does not fill with his Holy Spirit those who believe in the fullness of the Spirit, or those who desire him, but those who obey him."

F. B. MEYER (1847–1929)

"Living one day in the Spirit is worth more than a thousand lived in the flesh."

RICHARD OWEN ROBERTS

"The Spirit's control will replace sin's control. His power is greater than the power of all your sin."

ERWIN W. LUTZER

And I, brethren, could not speak unto you as unto spiritual, but as unto carnal, even as unto babes in Christ.

1 CORINTHIANS 3:1, KJV

Live in the Power
of the Holy Spirit

J. I. PACKER

Too many people try to move from the Second Chair to the First by their own means. They work and work and work, but never seem to make any progress. They try to muster up the power of the Spirit in what they say and do. They might even take leadership positions in the church thinking that it will be the key to the First Chair. Sadly, they discover they're still in the Second Chair. Sounds very similar to the Israelites in the desert, doesn't it. Even though they just saw their God destroy the greatest power on earth through the ten plagues and by parting the Red Sea, they just couldn't believe that God had the ability to conquer the Land of Canaan by working His power in them. Are you walking in the power of the Spirit? If not, J .I. Packer has some insightful words that will challenge your very understanding of what it means to walk in power. Read on…

*A*t the turn of each year Time magazine looks back, looks ahead, and makes whatever comments it thinks fit. The first issue for 1990 contained a list of "Buzzwords Most Ready for Early Retirement," in which, after "upside potential, upscale marketing, fasttracker, bottom line, synergy, networking, streamlining, interfacing, prioritizing quality time, soft landing, hands-on manager" came "power player, power breakfast, power tie, power anything."

As I look at my bookshelves today, I see there items titled *Power Healing, Power Evangelism, Healing Power, Power Encounters, When the Spirit Comes with Power, Christianity with Power,* all published since 1985. Round go the wheels of the mind. Buzzword, eh? Fluffy, tiresome jargon, right? Overused among Christians, just as it is in the commercial world? Ripe for retirement? First thoughts might prompt us to say so, but second thoughts should give us pause.

For "power" is a very significant New Testament word. Where would I be if I imposed a self-denying ordinance on myself and declined to use it any longer? Where would the church be if we all acted that way? If we stopped talking about power we should soon stop thinking about it. If that happened we should be impoverished indeed. Hey, then, put on the brakes; stop being snide. For Christianity, at least, the word "power" is precious. Buzzword it may be, but we need it so that we can focus on what it refers to. This chapter will, I hope, make clear the importance of doing that.

The Power of God

The power that now concerns us is God's power—the energy exercised by Him in creation, providence, and grace. The usual word for it in the Greek New Testament is *dunamis,* from which comes our word "dynamite." Here we shall deal with just one segment of this tremendous topic, namely the power of God regenerating, sanctifying, and operating through us sinners.

To deal with this, however, means facing up to a problem, the recurring buzzword problem of passionately committed short sight. We may analyze the problem thus: a word presses buttons of interest, excitement, and desire to be in the swim and not be left behind. So people pick up the word and flash it as a kind of verbal badge, in order to show that they are fully up-to-date and know about the latest significant thing. But such use reflects little or no thought about this latest thing in itself. So the more the word is used this way, the woollier grows its meaning and the shorter the sight of its zealous users.

At the present time, more and more people are anxiously asking themselves and each other whether they have the power of God in their lives, with less and less certainty in their minds as to what that might mean. All they are sure of is that they want to identify with the folk who claim acquaintance with that power, since they do not want to be left out of any good thing that is happening. As in other instances, the buzzword problem thus opens out into a flock-of-sheep neurosis, an inclination to follow fashions blindly so long as one is part of a confident crowd. Where buzzwords buzz, you get notional fuzz! If we are to talk meaningfully about the power of God, we shall have to cut through some of that.

As a first step toward proper clarity on our theme, we need to see right at the outset that God does not give us His power as a possession of our own, a resource to use at our discretion. It should not be necessary to say that, but the amount of talk today about using the power of God shows that this misconception is common. God uses us, calling into play the powers He has given us, as channels through which His own power flows. But we are not storage units like batteries, or receptacles like buckets, in which the potential for power in action can be kept until needed. And we do not use God, or God's power, as we use electricity, switching it on or off as we like.

Wanting to possess divine power to use at his own discretion was the sin of Simon the sorcerer (Acts 8:18–24). His sin is recorded as a warning, not as an example to follow. The right desire at all times is to be "an instrument for noble purposes, made holy, useful to the Master and prepared to do any good work" (2 Timothy 2:21). The King James Version reads "a vessel unto honour, sanctified, and meet for the master's use," which is stronger and clearer.

Should Christians speak to us of using the power of God, red lights should flash before our mind. If however, the talk is of how to be usable and useful to God, we should be nodding our heads. Let us see to it that we do not go wrong here.

MANIFESTING GOD'S POWER

The power of God as seen in the New Testament leads us to look at ministries of various kinds. I am not speaking here of ordained or salaried ministry only, or even primarily.

Ministry means any form of service, and there are many such forms. Thus, being a faithful spouse and a conscientious parent is the form of ministry at home; discharging an office, fulfilling a role, and carrying a defined responsibility is the form of ministry (both ordained and lay) in the organized church; sustaining pastoral friendships that involve advising, interceding, and supporting is a further form of ministry in

Christ; and loving care for people at any level of need—physical or mental, material or spiritual—is the true form of ministry in the world.

Holiness is neither static nor passive. It is a state of increasing love to God and one's neighbor, and love is precisely a matter of doing what honors and benefits the loved one, out of a wish to raise that loved one high. Holy persons, therefore, show themselves such by praising God and helping others. They know they should, and in fact, they want to. God himself has made them want to, however self-absorbed they may have been before.

As their Christlikeness adds to their impact, credibility, and effectiveness for God when they serve their neighbors, so God uses their experiences in such ministry (success, failure, delight, frustration, learning patience and persistence, going the second mile, staying humble when appreciated, staying kind when attacked, holding steady under pressure, and so on) to advance the change "from glory to glory" in their own lives (2 Corinthians 3:18). He continues to make them more like Jesus than they were before.

It is noteworthy that most speakers and books on holiness say little about ministry, while most speakers and books on ministry say little about holiness. It has been this way for over a century, But to treat holiness and ministry as separate themes is an error. God has linked them, and what God joins man must not put asunder.

One regular result of ongoing sanctification is that concern for others, with recognition of what they lack, and wisdom that sees how to help them, is increased. Ministry blossoms naturally in holy lives. In effective ministry, God's power is channeled through God's servants into areas of human need. A saintly person of limited gifts is always likely to channel more of it than would a person who was more gifted but less godly. So God wants us all to seek holiness and usefulness together, and the former partly at least for the sake of the latter.

THE POWER OF GOD IS SHOWN MOST FULLY IN HUMAN WEAKNESS

There are many sorts of weakness. There is the bodily weakness of the invalid or cripple; there is the character weakness of the person with besetting shortcomings and vices; there is the intellectual weakness of the person with limited ability; there is the weakness brought on by exhaustion, depression, stress, strain, and emotional overload. God sanctifies all these forms of weakness by enabling the weak to be stronger (more patient, more outgoing, more affectionate, more tranquil, more joyful, and more resourceful) than seemed possible under the circumstances. This is a demonstration of his power that he delights to give.

Paul states the principle thus: "We have this treasure [knowledge of God in Christ] in jars of clay to show that this all-surpassing power is from God and not from us. We are hard pressed on every side, but not crushed; perplexed, but not in despair; persecuted, but not abandoned; struck down, but not destroyed. We always carry around in our body the death of Jesus, so that the life of Jesus may also be revealed in our body. So then, death is at work in us" (2 Corinthians 4:7–12). In a self-centered, pleasure-oriented, self-indulgent world like ours today, this sounds most brutal and chilling. But it is, in fact, the true meaning of the time-honored, much-applauded dictum, "Man's extremity is God's opportunity." Opportunity for what? to show his power, the power of his grace, now displayed for the praise of his glory.

Being weak, and feeling weak, is not in itself fun, nor can it be a condition of what the world would see as maximum efficiency. One might have expected God to use his power to eliminate such weakness from the lives of his servants. In fact, what he does again and again is to make his weak servants. into walking wonders—sometimes, of course, in the physical sense, immobilized wonders—of wisdom, love, and helpfulness to others despite their disability. It is thus that he loves to show his power. This is a truth that is vitally important to understand.

Paul himself learned this lesson very thoroughly through his interaction with the Corinthians. Paul was not a man for half measures, or self-effacement, or standoff relationships. He was naturally a "ball of fire," as we say, imperious, combative, brilliant, and passionate. Conscious of his apostolic authority and very sure that his teaching was definitive and healthgiving, he spent himself unstintingly in the discipling of his converts. He felt and expressed deep affection for them because they were Christ's, and naturally looked not only for obedience but also for affection in return.

In the case of the Corinthians, however, the obedience was wavering and grudging, and the affection was virtually nil. This, as Paul's letters to them illustrate, was partly because Paul did not come up to their conceited expectation that any teacher worth his salt would throw his intellectual weight about in order to impress them. It was partly too because other teachers, who did throw their weight about, had secured their loyalty, and partly also because they had embraced a triumphalist view of spiritual life that valued tonguespeaking and uninhibitedness above love, humility, and righteousness. They thought of Christians as persons set free by Christ to do just about anything, with no regard for the consequences. They looked down on Paul as "weak"—unimpressive in presence and in speech (2 Corinthians 10:10), and possibly wrong in some of his doctrinal and moral teaching. They were very critical of his personal style and behavior.

Anyone in Paul's position would find this painful to a degree, and it is clear from his letters to the Corinthians, with their expressions of anguished love and their alternations of pain, anger, disappointment, frustration, and sarcasm, that Paul himself did find it exceedingly painful. His response, however, was magnificent. He embraced weakness—not the weakness of ministry alleged by the Corinthians, but the weakness of a sick body, a servant role, and a hurting heart—as his calling here on earth. "If I must boast," he wrote, "I will boast of the things that show my weakness" (2 Corinthians 11:30). "I will not boast about myself, except about my weaknesses" (2 Corinthians 12:5). And he suited the action to the word:

> To keep me from becoming conceited...there was given me a thorn in my flesh, a messenger of Satan, to torment me. Three times I pleaded with the Lord to take it away from me. But he said to me, "My grace is sufficient for you, for my power is made perfect in weakness." Therefore I will boast all the more gladly about my weaknesses, so that Christ's power may rest on me. That is why, for Christ's sake, I delight in weaknesses, in insults, in hardships, in persecutions, in difficulties. For when I am weak, then I am strong.
> (2 Corinthians 12:7–10)

What was the thorn? We do not know. But it must have been a personal disability, some malfunctioning in his makeup, or he would not have said it was in his "flesh" (meaning his created humanity). And it must have been painful, or he would not have called it a "thorn."

Why was Paul given it (by God, in providence)? For discipline, as the apostle recognized, to keep him humble—no mean agenda, let it be said, when a man had such an enormous ego as did Paul.

In what sense was Paul's thorn a messenger of Satan? It sparked thoughts of resentment at God, pity for himself, and despair about the future of his ministry—the sort of thoughts that Satan specializes in stirring up within us all. Anything that prompts such thinking thereby becomes a messenger of Satan to our souls.

Why did Paul pray specifically to the Lord Jesus about his thorn? Because Jesus was the healer, who had wrought many miraculous cures in the days of his flesh and some through Paul during Paul's years of missionary ministry (see Acts 14:3, 8–10, 19:11). Now Paul needed Christ's healing power for himself, so in three solemn seasons of prayer he sought it.

Why was healing withheld? Not for lack of purehearted prayer on Paul's part, nor for lack of sovereign power on Christ's part, but because the Savior had something better in view for His servant. (God always reserves the right to answer our requests in a better way than we make them.) Jesus' response to Paul's prayer could be expanded like this: "Paul, I will tell you what I am going to do. I am going to display my strength in your continuing weakness, in such a way that the things you fear—the ending or enfeebling of your ministry, the loss of your credibility and usefulness—will not occur. Your ministry will go on in power and strength as before, though in greater weakness than before. You will carry this thorn in the flesh with you as long as you live. But in that condition of weakness, my strength will be made perfect. It will become more obvious than ever that it is I who keep you going." The implication was that this state of things would be more to Paul's personal blessing, more to the enriching of his ministry, and more to the glory of Christ the enabler, than an immediate cure would be.

What should we make of Paul's reaction? Clearly he understood and accepted what Christ had communicated to him as he prayed. Clearly he saw it as defining his own vocation. It is natural to suppose that one reason why he narrated it so fully was that he knew he was being made a model for others to imitate. His experience certainly is a model to which again and again we find ourselves required to conform.

CALLING ON GOD

The pattern is that the Lord first makes us conscious of our weakness, so that our heart cries out, "I can't handle this." We go to the Lord to ask him to remove the burden that we feel is crushing us. But Christ replies: "In my strength you *can* handle this, and in answer to your prayer, I will strengthen you to handle it." Thus in the end our testimony, like Paul's, is: "I can do everything through him who gives me strength" (Philippians 4:13); "The Lord stood at my side and *gave me strength*" (2 Timothy 4:17). And we find ourselves saying, with Paul: "Praise be to the God and Father of our Lord Jesus Christ, the Father of compassion and the God of all comfort, who comforts us in all our troubles, so that we can comfort those in any trouble with the comfort we ourselves have received from God. For just as the sufferings of Christ flow over into our lives, so also through Christ our comfort over-flows" (2 Corinthians 1:3–5).

By "comfort," Paul means the encouragement that invigorates, not the relaxation that enervates. It is in that sense that we join him in testifying to the comfort of God. We find ourselves living (if I may put it this way) baptismally, with resurrection-out-of-death as the recurring shape of our experience. And we realize with evergrowing clarity that this is the fullest and profoundest expression of the empowered Christian life.

It appears, then, that being divinely empowered so that one grows stronger in Christ has nothing necessarily to do with performing spectacularly or, by human standards, successfully (whether or not one performs so is for God to decide). It has everything to do, however, with knowing and feeling that one is weak. In this sense, we only grow stronger by growing weaker. The world means by strength (of character, mind, and will) a natural endowment, the ability to press ahead, undistracted and undiscouraged, toward one's goals. God-given strength or power is however a matter of being enabled by Christ himself through the Spirit to keep on keeping on in:

- personal holiness before God;
- personal communing with God;
- personal service of God; and
- personal action for God.

One keeps on however weak one feels. One keeps on even in situations where what is being asked for seems to be beyond one, and one does so in the confidence that this is how God means it to be. For only at the point where the insufficiency of natural strength is faced, felt, and admitted does divine empowering begin.

So the power path is humble dependence on God to channel his power to the depths of our being so as to make and keep us faithful to our calling in sanctity and service. With that we depend on him to channel his power through us into others' lives to help them move forward at their points of need. The power pitfall is self-reliance and failure to see that without Christ we can do nothing that is spiritually significant, however much we do quantitatively, in terms of energetic activity. The power principle—God's power scenario, we might call it—is that divine strength is perfected in conscious human weakness. The power perversions suppose that God's power is something we can possess and control, or that we may look to him to empower us for service when we are not looking to him to empower us for righteousness; but those ideas, as we have seen, are utterly wrong.

If I could remember, each day of my life, that the way to grow stronger is to grow weaker, if I would accept that each day's frustrations, obstacles, and accidents are God's ways of making me acknowledge my weakness, so that growing stronger might become a possibility for me, if I did not betray myself into relying on myself—my knowledge, my expertise, my position, my skill with words, and so on—so much of the time, what a difference it would make to me!

I wonder how many others, besides myself, need to concentrate on learning these lessons? I urge you to pause, and ask yourself how firmly they are anchored in your heart. They need to be anchored there very firmly indeed, and I fear that in many Christian hearts today they are not. May God in his great mercy weaken us all!

From *Rediscovering Holiness* ©1992 by J. I. Packer. Published by Servant Publications, Box 8617, Ann Arbor, Michigan 48107. Used with permission. Available through your local Christian Bookstore.

Very few Christians today would consider the word submission to be a key to living in power. But, as you've just read, it is impossible to exhibit God's power in your life without humble dependence on and absolute submission to God and His Word. If we could remember this day-in and day-out, we would experience a breakthrough that is truly powerful. In fact, this is one of the great habits of the First Chair Christian. Somewhere in his life he experienced a breakthrough that changed him forever. Isn't it time you experienced that breakthrough? In his book, Rediscovering Holiness, *J. I. Packer shows how living in holiness will bring about the power of the Holy Spirit like you've never experienced. Read it and discover a new power to your walk and a new passion for God.*

EVALUATION QUESTIONS

1. Take some time and evaluate where you are in experiencing this breakthrough. Where would you rate yourself on the following scale?

1	5	10
Not even close to experiencing this breakthrough.	I've begun the journey, but I've got a ways to go.	I've experienced a breakthrough, and I'm living the abundant life.

2. What would you consider to be the biggest hindrance to your experiencing this breakthrough right now?

3. What one action should you take to experience this breakthrough right now? I challenge you to do it.

God never destroys the work of his own hands,
he removes what would pervert it, that is all.
Maturity is the stage where the whole life has been brought
under the control of God."
OSWALD CHAMBERS (1874–1917)

"One of the marks of spiritual maturity is
the quiet confidence that God is in control…without
the need to understand why he does what he does."
CHARLES R. SWINDOLL

"He who believes himself to be far advanced in the spiritual life
has not even made a good beginning."
JEAN PIERRE CAMUS (1584–1652)

"It is right that you should begin again every day.
There is no better way to finish the spiritual life
than to be ever beginning."
SAINT FRANCIS OF SALES (1567–1622)

"Spirituality really means 'Holy Spirit at work.'"
LEON JOSEPH SUENENS

Let the Spirit Overcome Your Carnality

ANDREW MURRAY

Moving from the Second Chair to the First is not as easy as it might seem. In fact, if you're sitting in the Second Chair, you may not even understand much of the Scriptures that would help you get to the First Chair. But as you'll see after you've read Andrew Murray's words of wisdom, your spiritual life can move to the First Chair in a moment. Now that's a breakthrough! Becoming spiritually mature is a process, but becoming spiritually minded can happen quickly. Here's how.

The apostle commences the chapter (1 Corinthians 3) by telling these Corinthians that there are two stages of Christian experience. Some Christians are carnal; some are spiritual. By the discernment that God's Spirit gave the apostle, he saw that the Corinthians were carnal, and he wanted to tell them so. You will find the word carnal four times in these four verses.

The apostle felt that all his preaching would do no good if he talked about spiritual things to men who were unspiritual. They were Christians, real Christians, babes in Christ, but there was one deadly fault—they were carnal. So the apostle seems to say, "I cannot teach you spiritual truth about the spiritual life; you cannot take it in." But that was not because they were stupid. They were very clever and full of knowledge but unable to understand spiritual teaching. That teaches us this simple lesson: All the trouble in the Church of Christ, among Christians who sometimes get a blessing and lose it again, is just because they are carnal, and all that we need if we want to keep the blessing is to become spiritual.

How to Move from Carnal to Spiritual

Now come the very important and solemn questions, *Is it possible for a man to get out of the carnal and into the spiritual state? And how is it possible?* I think the first thing needed is that a man must have some sight of the spiritual life and some faith in it. Our hearts are so full of unbelief, without our knowing it, that we do not accept as a settled matter that we can become spiritual men. We do not believe it.

The Word speaks about two powers of life: the flesh and the Spirit. The flesh is our life under the power of sin; the Spirit, God's life coming to take the place of our life. What we need, and what the Bible tells us, is to give our whole life, with every idea of strength or power, away unto death, to become nothing, and to receive the life of Christ and of the Spirit to do all for us. Do believe that that can be.

I believe that it is possible for a man to live every day as led by the Holy Ghost. I have read in God's Word that God sheds abroad His love in the heart by the Holy Spirit. I have read in God's Word that as many as are led by the Spirit, they are the children of God. I have read in God's Word that if we are born again, we are to walk by the Spirit, or in the Spirit. Then it is possible; it is the life God calls us to and that Christ redeemed us for. As soon as He shed His blood, He went away to heaven to send the Spirit to His people. As soon as He was glorified, His first work was to give the Holy Spirit. If you will begin to believe in the power of Christ's blood to cleanse you and in the power of the glorified Christ to give His Spirit to you, you have taken the first step in the right direction.

But it is not enough that a man should have a vision of that spiritual life that is to be lived; it is also very needful that a man should be really convicted of his carnality. This is a difficult but needful lesson. There is a great difference between the sins of the unconverted man and the sins of the believer. As an unconverted man, you had to be convicted of sin and make confession of it. But what were you convicted of chiefly? Of the grossness of sin and very much of the guilt and punishment of sin. But there was very little conviction of inward, spiritual sins. You had no knowledge of them. There was very little conviction of inward sinfulness. God does not always give that in conversion or ordinarily. And so, how is a man to get rid of these two things: the more hidden sins and the deep inner sinfulness? In this way: after he has become a Christian, the man is convicted by the Holy Spirit of his carnal, fleshly life, and then the man begins to mourn over it, and be ashamed of it, and cry out like Paul, "Oh, wretched man that I am!" I am a believer, "but who shall deliver me from the body of this death?" (Romans 7:24) He begins to turn round for help and ask, Where am I to get deliverance? He seeks it in many ways, by struggling and resolve, but he does not get it until he is brought to cast himself absolutely at the feet of Jesus. Do not forget that if you are to become a spiritual man, if you are to be filled with the Holy Ghost, it must come from God in heaven. God alone can do it.

We can pass from the carnal to the spiritual condition in one moment of time. People want to grow out of the carnal into the spiritual, but they never can. They seek more preaching and teaching in order, they think, to grow out of the carnal into the spiritual. That child that I spoke of remained as a babe of six months; it had a disease, and it needed healing. Then growth would come. Now, the carnal state is a state of terrible disease. The carnal Christian is a babe in Christ. He is a child of God, Paul says, but he has this terrible disease, and consequently he cannot grow. How is the healing to come?

It must come through God, and God longs to give it you this very hour.

A man who becomes a spiritual man is not a man of spiritual maturity immediately. I cannot expect from a young Christian who has the Holy Spirit in His fullness what I can expect from a mature Christian who has been filled with the Spirit for twenty years. There is a great deal of growth and maturity in the spiritual life. But when I speak of one step, I mean this: you can change your place, and instead of standing in the carnal life, enter the spiritual life in one moment.

Note the reason why the two expressions are used. In the carnal man there is something of the spiritual nature, but you know that bodies get their names from that which is their most prominent element. A thing may be used for two or three objects, but it will likely get its name from that which is the most prominent. A thing may have several characteristics, but the name will be given according to that which is the most striking. So, Paul says, in other words, to those

Corinthians, "You babes in Christ are carnal; you are under the power of the flesh, giving way to temper and unloveliness, and not growing, or capable of receiving spiritual truth, with all your gifts."

And the spiritual man is a man who has not reached final perfection; there is abundant room for growth. But if you look at him, the chief mark of his nature and conduct is that he is a man given up to the Spirit of God. He is not perfect, but he is a man who has taken the right position and said, "Lord God, I have given myself to be led by Your Spirit. You have accepted me and blessed me, and the Holy Spirit now leads me."

You cannot save yourselves from the flesh or get rid of it, but Christ can lift you over into the new life. You belong to Christ, and He belongs to you. But what you need is just to cast yourself upon Him, and He will reveal the power of His crucifixion in you to give you victory over the flesh. Cast yourself, with the confession of sin and with utter helplessness, at the feet of the Lamb of God. He can give you deliverance.

A man must see the spiritual life; must be convicted of and confess his carnal state; must see that it is but one step from the one to the other; and then, lastly, he must take the decisive step in the faith that Christ is able to keep him. Yes, it is not a mere view; it is not a consecration in any sense of its being in our power; it is not a surrender by the strength of our will. No. These are elements that may be present, but the great thing is, we must look to Christ to keep us tomorrow, and next day, and always; we must have the life of God within us. We want a life that will stand against any temptation, a life that will last till death. We want, by the grace of God, to experience what the almighty indwelling and staying power of

Christ can do and all that God can do for us.

God is waiting, Christ is waiting, the Holy Spirit is waiting. Do you not see what has been wrong and why it is you have been wandering in the wilderness? Do you not see the good land, the land of promise, in which God is going to keep and bless you? Remember the story of Caleb and Joshua and the spies. Ten men said in effect: We can never conquer those people. Two said: We are able, for God has promised. Step out upon the promises of God. Listen to God's Word: "The law of the Spirit of Life in Christ Jesus hath made me free from the law of sin and death." Take a word like that, and claim that God shall do for you through His Holy Spirit what He has offered you.

Never mind, though, there be no new experience, and no feeling, and no excitement, and no light—but apparently darkness. Stand upon the Word of God, the everlasting God. God promises, as Father, His Holy Spirit to every hungering child. Will He then not give it to you? How shall He not give the Holy Spirit to them that ask Him? How could He not do it? For as truly as Christ was given for you on Calvary and you have believed in the blood, so truly the Holy Spirit has been given for you. Open your heart and be "filled with the Spirit." Trust the blood of Christ for the cleansing, confess the carnality of every sin, and cast it into the fountain of the blood, and then believe in the living Christ to bless you with the blessing of His Spirit.

Taken from *Absolute Surrender* by Andrew Murray. Published by Christian Literature Crusade. Available at your local Christian bookstore.

When it comes to being committed to Christ, you don't have to be a great theologian or an articulate preacher. You can be a nobody in the world's eyes and still be a giant in God's Kingdom! That's what is so wonderful about the Christian faith: "The first shall be last and the last shall be first" (Matthew 19:30). It's also why many people don't experience the spiritual breakthroughs so needed to live the abundant life. They try to get to the top of God's Kingdom the same way they get to the top of the business ladder. As Andrew Murray explained, it doesn't work that way. If you're having trouble experiencing the spiritual breakthrough of becoming spiritually minded, I recommend that you read Andrew Murray's book, Absolute Surrender. *It's one of my favorites and it will really help you make that move into the First Chair.*

Evaluation Questions

1. Take some time and evaluate where you are in experiencing this breakthrough. Where would you rate yourself on the following scale?

1	5	10
Not even close to experiencing this breakthrough.	I've begun the journey, but I've got a ways to go.	I've experienced a breakthrough, and I'm living the abundant life.

2. What would you consider to be the biggest hindrance to your experiencing this breakthrough right now?

3. What one action should you take to experience this breakthrough right now? I challenge you to do it.

SECTION TWO

Experiencing Spiritual Breakthroughs in Your Marriage

"A successful marriage is not a gift; it is an achievement."
ANN LANDERS

*"Chains do not hold a marriage together. It is threads, hundreds
of tiny threads that sew people together through the years."*
SIMONE SIGNORET (1921–1985)

*"Getting married is easy.
Staying married is more difficult.
Staying happily married for a lifetime
should rank among the fine arts."*
ROBERTA FLACK

"It is not marriage that fails, it is people that fail."
HARRY EMERSON FOSDICK (1878–1969)

*"It takes two to make a marriage a success and
only one to make it a failure."*
HERBERT SAMUEL

*"Successful marriage is always a triangle: a man,
a woman, and God."*
CECIL MYERS

Repair the Foundations of Your Marriage

JAMES DOBSON

Just about every marriage starts out in the First Chair—most people call it the honeymoon. But for some reason, it doesn't seem to take long for it to move to the Second Chair. The reason oftentimes is that the couple forgets (or never learned) the basics of a good relationship. What most of these couples fail to realize is that they don't have to settle for a Second Chair marriage! Simply going back to the basics of a biblical relationship in your marriage will move it into the Promised Land. Follow James Dobson as he shows us how to build a foundation that will weather the storms of life.

In an effort to draw on the experiences of those who have lived together successfully as husband and wife, we asked married couples to participate in an informal study. More than six hundred people agreed to speak candidly to the younger generation about the concepts and methods that have worked in their homes. They each wrote comments and recommendations, which were carefully analyzed and compared. The advice they offered is not new, but it certainly represents a great place to begin. In attempting to learn any task, one should start with the fundamentals—those initial steps from which everything else will later develop. In this spirit, our panel of six hundred offered three tried-and-tested, back-to-basics recommendations with which no committed Christian would likely disagree.

1. A CHRIST-CENTERED HOME

The panel first suggested that newlyweds should establish and maintain a Christ-centered home. Everything rests on that foundation. If a young husband and wife are deeply committed to Jesus Christ, they enjoy enormous advantages over the family with no spiritual dimension.

A meaningful prayer life is essential in maintaining a Christ-centered home. Of course, some people use prayer the way they follow their horoscopes, attempting to manipulate an unidentified "higher power" around them. One of my friends teasingly admits that he utters a prayer each morning on the way to work when he passes the donut shop. He knows it is unhealthy to eat the greasy pastries, but he loves them dearly. Therefore, he asks the Lord for permission to indulge himself each day.

He'll say, "If it is Your will that I have a donut this morning, let there be a parking space available somewhere as I circle the block." If no spot can be found for his car, he circles the block and prays again.

Shirley and I have taken our prayer life a bit more seriously. In fact, this communication between man and God has been the stabilizing factor throughout our thirty-plus years of married life. In good times, in hard times, in moments of anxiety, and in periods of praise, we have shared this wonderful privilege of talking directly to our heavenly Father. What a concept. No appointment is needed to enter into His presence. We don't have to go through His subordinates or bribe His secretaries. He is simply there, whenever we bow before Him. Some of the highlights of my life have occurred in these quiet sessions with the Lord.

I'll never forget the time some years ago when our daughter had just learned to drive. Danae had been enrolled in Kamikaze Driving School, and the moment finally arrived for her to take her first solo flight in the family car. Believe me, my anxiety level was climbing off the chart that day. Someday you will know how terrifying it is to hand the car keys to a sixteen-year-old kid who doesn't know what she doesn't know about driving. Shirley and I stood quaking in the front yard as Danae drove out of sight. We then turned to go back into the house, and I said, "Well, babe, the Lord giveth, and the Lord taketh away." Fortunately, Danae made it home safely in a few minutes and brought the car to a careful and controlled stop. That is the sweetest sound in the world to an anxious parent!

It was during this era that Shirley and I covenanted between us to pray for our son and daughter at the close of every day. Not only were we concerned about the risk of an automobile accident, but we were also aware of so many other dangers that lurk out there in a city like Los Angeles, where we lived at that time. That part of the world is known for its weirdos, kooks, nuts, ding-a-lings, and fruitcakes. That's one reason we found ourselves on our knees each evening, asking for divine protection for the teenagers whom we love so much.

One night we were particularly tired and collapsed into bed without our benedictory prayer. We were almost asleep before Shirley's voice pierced the night. "Jim," she said. "We haven't prayed for our kids yet today. Don't you think we should talk to the Lord?"

I admit it was very difficult for me to pull my 6'2" frame out of the warm bed that night. Nevertheless, we got on our knees and offered a prayer for our children's safety, placing them in the hands of the Father once more.

Later, we learned that Danae and a girlfriend had gone to a fast-food establishment and bought hamburgers and Cokes. They drove up the road a few miles and were sitting in the car eating the meal when a city policeman drove by, shining his spotlight in all directions. He was obviously looking for someone but gradually went past.

A few minutes later, Danae and her friend heard a clunk from under the car. They looked at one another nervously and felt another sharp bump. Before they could leave, a man crawled out from under the car and emerged on the passenger side. He was very hairy and looked like he had been on the street for weeks. The man immediately came over to the door and attempted to open it. Thank God, it was locked. Danae quickly started the car and drove off...no doubt at record speed.

Later, when we checked the timing of this incident, we realized that Shirley and I had been on our knees at the precise moment of danger. Our prayers were answered. Our daughter and her friend were safe!

It is impossible for me to overstate the need for prayer in the fabric of family life—not simply as a shield against danger, of course. A personal relationship with Jesus Christ is the cornerstone of marriage, giving meaning and purpose to every dimension of living. Being able to bow in prayer as the day begins or ends gives expression to the frustrations and concerns that might not otherwise be ventilated. On the other end of that prayer line is a loving heavenly Father, who has promised to hear and answer our petitions. In this day of disintegrating families on every side, we dare not try to make it on our own.

The couple who depends on Scripture for solutions to the stresses of living has a distinct advantage over the family with no faith.

By reading these holy Scriptures, we are given a window into the mind of the Father. What an incredible resource! The Creator, who began with nothingness and made beautiful mountains and streams and clouds and cuddly little babies, has elected to give us the inside story of the family. Marriage and parenthood were His ideas, and He tells us in His Word how to live together in peace and harmony. Everything from handling money to sexual attitudes is discussed in Scripture, with each prescription bearing the personal endorsement of the King of the Universe. Why would anyone disregard this ultimate resource?

Finally, the Christian way of life lends stability to marriage because its principles and values naturally produce harmony. When put into action, Christian teaching emphasizes giving to others, self-discipline, obedience to divine commandments, conformity to the laws of man, and love and fidelity between a husband and wife. It is a shield against addictions to alcohol, pornography, gambling, materialism, and other behaviors that could be damaging to the relationship. Is it any wonder that a Christ-centered relationship is the ground floor of a marriage?

2. COMMITTED LOVE

The second suggestion made by our panel of six hundred "experts" represented yet another back-to-basics concept. It focused on committed love that is braced against the inevitable storms of life. There are very few certainties that touch us all in this mortal existence, but one of the absolutes is that we will experience hardship and stress at some point. Nobody remains unscathed. Life will test each of us severely, if not during younger days, then through the events surrounding our final days. Jesus spoke of this inevitability when He said to His disciples, "In the world ye shall have tribulation: but be of good cheer; I have overcome the world" (John 16:33, KJV).

Dr. Richard Selzer is a surgeon who has written two outstanding books about his beloved patients, *Mortal Lessons* and *Letters to a Young Doctor.* In the first of these texts he describes the experience of horror that invades one's life sooner or later. When we're young, he says, we seem to be shielded from it the way the body is protected against bacterial infection. Microscopic organisms are all around us, yet our bodies' defenses effectually hold them at bay...at least for a season. Likewise, we walk in and through a world of horror each day as though surrounded by an impenetrable membrane of protection. We may even be unaware that distressing possibilities exist during the period of youthful good health. But then one day the membrane tears without warning, and horror seeps into our lives. Until that moment occurs, it was always someone else's misfortune—another man's tragedy—and not our own. The tearing of the membrane can be devastating, especially for those who do not know the "good cheer" that Jesus gives in times of tribulation.

Having served on a large medical-school faculty for fourteen years, I have watched husbands and wives in the hours when horror began to penetrate the protective membrane. All too commonly, their marital relationships were shattered by the new stresses that invaded their lives. Parents who produced a mentally retarded child, for example, often blamed one another for the tragedy that confronted them. Instead of clinging together in love and reassurance, they added to their sorrows by attacking each other. I do not condemn them for this human failing, but I do pity them for it. A basic ingredient was missing in their relationship, and it remained unrecognized until the membrane tore. That essential component is called commitment.

I heard the late Dr. Francis Schaeffer speak to this issue a number of years ago. He described the bridges that were built in Europe by the Romans in the first and second centuries A.D. They are still standing today, despite the unreinforced brick and mortar with which they were made. Why haven't they collapsed in this modern era of heavy trucks and equipment? They remain intact because they are used for nothing but foot traffic. If an eighteen-wheeler were driven across the historic structures, they would crumble in a great cloud of dust and debris.

Marriages that lack an iron-willed determination to hang together at all costs are like the fragile Roman bridges. They appear to be secure and may indeed remain upright...until they are put under heavy pressure. That's when the seams split and the foundation crumbles. It appears to me that the majority of young couples today, like some of those competing on those newlywed game shows, are in that incredibly vulnerable position. Their relationships are constructed of unreinforced mud, which will not withstand the weighty trials lying ahead. The determination to survive together is simply not there.

In stressing the importance of committed love, however, the panel of six hundred was referring not only to the great tragedies of life but also to the daily frustrations that wear and tear on a relationship. These minor irritants, when accumulated over time, may be even more threatening to a marriage than the catastrophic events that crash into our lives. And yes, Virginia, there are times in every good marriage when a husband and wife don't like each other very much. There are occasions when they feel as though they will never love their partner again. Emotions are like that. They flatten out occasionally like an automobile tire with a nail in the tread. Riding on the rim is a pretty bumpy experience for everyone on board.

The following classified ad, which appeared in the *Rocky Mountains News,* proves my point:

WILL TRADE
Will trade my noncooking and
nonshopping wife with attitude problem
for one Super Bowl
ticket.
No Indiangivers.
Call Jim, 762-1000.
Hurry.

Jim claimed that he wasn't kidding, although he was known to play practical jokes. He said the idea occurred to him the day after the AFC championship game, when it snowed heavily in Denver.

"She refused to go shopping," he said. "She said the roads were too slick, so she made me do it. I get tired of that stuff after a while. If I could get a Super Bowl ticket, it would be a one-way trip."

Sharon, his wife of eighteen years, was asked what she thought about his little advertisement.

"He's dead meat," she said.

The last time we checked, the couple had resolved their little misunderstanding and were still happily married. But this anecdote contains a message for newly married couples: Don't count on having a placid relationship. There will be times of conflict and disagreement. There will be periods of emotional blandness when you can generate nothing but a yawn for one another. That's life, as they say.

What will you do, then, when unexpected tornadoes blow through your home or when the doldrums leave your sails sagging and silent? Will you pack it in and go home to Mama? Will you pout and cry and seek ways to strike back? Or will your commitment hold you steady? These questions must be addressed now, before Satan has an opportunity to put his noose of discouragement around your neck. Set your jaw and clench your fists. Nothing short of death must ever be permitted to come between the two of you. Nothing!

This determined attitude is missing from so many marital relationships today. I read of a wedding ceremony in New York a few years ago where the bride and groom each pledged "to stay with you for as long as I shall love you." I doubt if their marriage lasted even to this time. The feeling of love is simply too ephemeral to hold a relationship together for very long. It comes and goes. That's why our panel of six hundred was adamant on this point. They have lived long enough to know that a weak marital commitment will inevitably end in divorce.

3. COMMUNICATION

The third recommendation by our panel of six hundred represents another basic ingredient of good marriages. Like the other two, it begins with the letter C. It focuses on good communication between husbands and wives. This topic has been beaten to death by writers of books on the subject of marriage, so I will hit it lightly. I would like to offer a few less overworked thoughts on marital communication, however, that might be useful.

First, research makes it clear that little girls are blessed with greater linguistic ability than little boys, and it remains a lifelong talent. Simply stated, she talks more than he.

The paradox is that a highly emotional, verbal woman is sometimes drawn to the strong, silent type. He seemed so secure and in control before they were married. She admired his unflappable nature and his coolness in a crisis. Then they were married and the flip side of his great strength became obvious. He wouldn't talk! She then gnashed her teeth for the next forty years because her husband couldn't give her what she needed from him. It just wasn't in him.

But what is the solution to such communicative problems at home? As always, it involves compromise. A man has a clear responsibility to "cheer up his wife which he hath taken" (Deuteronomy 24:5). He must press himself to open his heart and share his deeper feelings with his wife. Time must be reserved for meaningful conversations. Taking walks and going out to breakfast and riding bicycles on Saturday mornings are conversation inducers that keep love alive. Communication can occur even in families where the husband leans inward and the wife leans outward. In these instances, I believe, the primary responsibility for compromise lies with the husband.

On the other hand, women must understand and accept the fact that some men cannot be what their wife wants them to be. Some of the women who are reading this are married to men who will never be able to understand the feminine needs I have described. Their emotional structure makes it impossible for them to comprehend the feelings and frustrations of another—particularly those occurring in the opposite sex. They have never been required to "give" and have no idea how it is done. What, then, is to be the reaction of their wives?

My advice is that you change that which can be altered, explain that which can be understood, teach that which can be learned, revise that which can be improved, resolve that which can be settled, and negotiate that which is open to compromise. Create the best marriage possible from the raw materials brought by two imperfect human beings with two distinctly unique personalities. But for all the rough edges that can never be smoothed and the faults that can never be eradicated, try to develop the best possible perspective, and determine in your mind to accept reality exactly as it is. The first principle of mental health is to accept that which cannot be changed. You could easily go to pieces over the adverse circumstances beyond your control. You can hang tough, or you can yield to cowardice. Depression is often evidence of emotional surrender.

What can be done, then? A woman with a normal range of emotional needs cannot simply ignore them. They scream for fulfillment. Consequently, I have long recommended that women in this situation seek to supplement what their husbands can't give by cultivating meaningful female relationships. Having girlfriends with whom they can talk heart to heart, study the Scriptures, and share child-care techniques can be vital to mental health. Resist the temptation to pull into the walls of your home and wait for your husband to be all things to you. Stay involved as a family in a church that meets your needs and preaches the Word. Remember that you are surrounded by many other women with similar feelings. Find them. Care for them. Give to them. Then when you are content, your marriage will flourish. It sounds simplistic, but that's the way we are made. We are designed to love God and to love one another. Deprivation of either function can be devastating.

Taken from *Love for a Lifetime* by James Dobson. ©1987, 1993, 1996, 1998 by James Dobson. Used by permission of Multnomah Publishers, Inc. Available at your local Christian bookstore.

I learned a long time ago that the basics always rule. And you've just read three simple steps that will help you experience a breakthrough in the very basics of how your marriage operates. Some of your marriages aren't Christ-centered—they're self-centered: a surefire way to tempt you to look for the divorce lawyer's office. Some of you aren't committed to loving your mate regardless of what her or she does. Instead you're committed to pleasing yourself. And some of you are so full of yourselves that the only conversation you're willing to have with your spouse is, "What's for dinner?" or "What's on TV?" If any of these describe your marriage, it's time for a change. Time for a breakthrough. And to further encourage and help your marriage, James Dobson's book, Love for a Lifetime, *is must reading. Every couple should read it after they get engaged, after they're married, and again every five years after that. It's that good! It's that important!*

EVALUATION QUESTIONS

1. Take some time and evaluate where you are in experiencing this breakthrough. Where would you rate yourself on the following scale?

1_____5_____10

Not even close to experiencing this breakthrough.	I've begun the journey, but I've got a ways to go.	I've experienced a breakthrough, and I'm living the abundant life.

2. What would you consider to be the biggest hindrance to your experiencing this breakthrough right now?

3. What one action should you take to experience this breakthrough right now? I challenge you to do it.

*"Let the wife make her husband glad to come home
and let him make her sorry to see him leave."*
MARTIN LUTHER (1483–1546)

*"Marriage cannot make anyone happier who does not bring
the ingredients for happiness into it."*
SYDNEY J. HARRIS (1917–1986)

"Marriage is adventure, not an achievement."
DAVID A. SEAMANDS

*"Married life offers no panacea—if
it is going to reach its potential, it will require an all-out
investment by both husband and wife."*
JAMES C. DOBSON

*"Success in marriage is more than finding the right person:
it is being the right person."*
ROBERT BROWNING (1812–1889)

*"You'll never see perfection in your mate, nor
will he or she find it in you."*
JAMES C. DOBSON

Destroy the Common Marriage Myths

GARY CHAPMAN

After you've established some solid foundations, it's important that you build your marriage on truth—not a bunch of myths or old wives' tales. Remember the Israelites in the book of Exodus? One of the reasons they continued to wander in the desert was because they believed lie after lie after lie. If they would have simply believed the truth God was giving them, they could have seen the Promised Land a lot sooner. The same holds true for your marriage. If you've bought into some of the myths of marriage, you're about to experience an incredible breakthrough in your marriage.

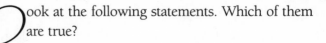

ook at the following statements. Which of them are true?

1. My state of mind is determined by my environment.
2. People cannot change.

3. When you are in a bad marriage, there are only two options: resign yourself to a life of misery or get out.

4. Some situations are hopeless.

If you answered "true" to any of these, please read on. In fact, all four statements are false; they are commonly held myths.

Unfortunately, many people in troubled marriages base their lives upon commonly held myths. If you or someone you love has a troubled marriage, it's time to practice "reality living."

Reality living refuses to believe these myths and chooses rather to face life with a far more positive spirit. What are the postulates of reality living as they apply to troubled marriages? Let me share six truths that can give direction to any troubled marriage.

REALITY NUMBER ONE:
I Am Responsible for My Own Attitude

Reality living approaches life with the assumption that I am responsible for my own state of mind. Trouble is inevitable, but misery is optional. Attitude has to do with the way I choose to think about things. It has to do with one's focus. Two men looked through prison bars—one saw the mud, the other saw the stars. Two people were in a troubled marriage—one cursed, the other prayed. The difference always is attitude.

Wendy said, "My husband hasn't had a full-time job in three years. The good part is not being able to afford cable TV. We've done a lot more talking on Monday nights." She went on to say, "These three years have been tough, but we have learned a lot. Our philosophy has been 'Let's see how many things we can do without that everybody else thinks they have to have.' It's amazing how many things you can do without. It's been a challenge, but we are going to make the most of it."

Three weeks after I met Wendy, I encountered Lou Ann. She was at the point of mental and physical exhaustion. Her husband had been out of work for ten months and was working a part-time job while looking for full-time employment. However, Lou Ann had been biting her nails for ten months. She was certain that they would lose everything they owned. She complained that they could not afford cable television and talked about how difficult it was to operate with only one car. Every day she lived on the cutting edge of despair.

The difference between Wendy and Lou Ann was basically a matter of attitude. Their problems were very similar, but their attitudes were very different, and that difference had a profound impact upon their physical and emotional well-being.

The challenge to maintain a positive mental attitude is not a contemporary idea. It is found clearly in the first-century writings of Saul of Tarsus:

> Do not be anxious about anything, but in everything, by prayer and petition, with thanksgiving, present your requests to God. And the peace of God, which transcends all understanding, will guard your hearts and minds.... Finally, brothers, whatever is true, whatever is noble, whatever is right, whatever is pure, whatever is lovely, whatever is admirable—if anything is excellent or praiseworthy—think about such things. (Philippians 4:6–8, NIV)

REALITY NUMBER TWO:
Attitude Affects Actions

The reason attitudes are so important is that they affect my actions, behavior, and words. If I have a pessimistic, defeatist, negative attitude, it will be expressed in negative words and behavior. At that point, I become a part of the problem rather than a part of the solution. The reality is that I may not be able to control my environment—sickness, an alcoholic spouse, a teenager on drugs, a mother who abandoned me, a father who abused me, a spouse who is irresponsible, aging parents, etc.—but I am responsible for what I do within my environment. My attitude will greatly influence my behavior.

Clearly Wendy and Lou Ann demonstrated this reality. With her positive attitude, Wendy had done several things over the past three years to enhance the climate of her marriage. She had given her husband affirming words when he got discouraged in his job search. She had assured him that the right job would come and in the meantime, they would make it on his part-time job and her part-time job. She had suggested that they collect aluminum cans to obtain "fun" money. At first her husband had resisted the idea, thinking it humiliating. Eventually, though, he liked the idea, and they enthusiastically collected cans not only on the highways when they took their evening walk but also through several local establishments with whom they arranged to pick up their cans. Within three months, they had built up their volume so that every week, they could go out to eat and attend a movie or some other recreational activity. Neither of them felt guilty about spending this money to have fun because they had created it for that purpose. Wendy's attitude had led her to positive creative actions.

On the other hand, Lou Ann had been verbally critical of

her husband for ten months. When he came home without a job, she asked him, "What did you do wrong this time?" She had told all her friends how disappointed she was in her husband. He often overheard her on the telephone saying such things as, "I don't know what we're going to do if he doesn't get a job soon." Her husband had a part-time job, but she did not. Her reasoning was "We can't make a living on part-time jobs, so why bother?" She spent most of her time sleeping, watching television, and visiting with her friends. Her marriage was in serious trouble. Her negative attitudes led to negative actions that compounded the problem. Attitude affects actions, and actions influence others. Which brings us to the third reality.

REALITY NUMBER THREE:
I Cannot Change Others, but I Can Influence Others

The two parts of this reality must never be separated. That I cannot change my spouse is an often-recited truth, but that I can and do influence my spouse is a truth often overlooked. Because we are individuals and because we are free, no one can force us to change our thoughts or behavior. On the other hand, because people are relational creatures, they are influenced by all to whom they relate. Advertisers make millions of dollars each year because of this reality. They do not make us buy their product, but they do influence us. Otherwise, they would drop their advertisements.

This reality has profound implications for marriage. I must acknowledge that I cannot change my spouse. I cannot make her stop certain behaviors or start certain behaviors (though she may change herself). I can neither control the words that come from her mouth, nor can I control the way she thinks or feels. I can make requests of my spouse, but I cannot be assured that she will respond positively to my requests.

When we fail to understand this reality, we are likely to fall into the trap of seeking to manipulate our spouse. The idea behind manipulation is that if I will do this, my spouse will be forced to do that. Manipulation may involve positive stimuli as well as negative stimuli. If I can make her (or him) happy enough, she will respond to my request. Or if I can make her miserable enough, she will respond to my request. All efforts at manipulation will ultimately fail for one simple reason. We are free. The moment we realize the individual—including our spouse—is controlling us by manipulation, we will rebel. None of us wants to be controlled by our spouse.

However, our inability to change our spouse must be laid alongside our ability to influence him or her—for better or for worse. All married couples influence each other every day. This is done by our attitudes and actions. This influence is exerted every time we encounter each other throughout the day. Your spouse walks in the room in the afternoon, gives you a hug and kiss, and says, "I love you. I've missed you today." With those simple actions and words, he has influenced you in a positive way. On the other hand, if your spouse walks into the house, goes straight to his computer room or walks out on the patio to drink a Coke, and fails to acknowledge your appearance or behavior, he has influenced you in a negative way. Chances are your response to those two encounters will be vastly different. One tends to influence you to respond positively; the other influences you to respond negatively.

Over the years, I have tested this reality with numerous individuals in troubled marriages. When an individual is willing to choose a positive attitude that leads to positive actions, the change in his or her spouse has often been radical. One lady said, "I can't believe what has happened to my husband. I never dreamed that he could be as loving and kind as he has been for the last two months. This is more change than I ever anticipated." The reality of the power of positive influence holds tremendous potential for troubled marriages.

REALITY NUMBER FOUR:
My Actions Are Not Controlled by My Emotions

In the last three decades with the rise of popular psychology, especially through the mass media, Western society has given an undue emphasis to human emotions. In fact, emotions have become our guiding star. Our songs and movies are filled with such themes as "If it feels good, do it," "I must be true to my emotions," "When I'm with you, I feel so good," and "I just don't love her anymore." The search for self-understanding has led us to the conclusion that you are what you feel and that authentic living is being true to your feelings.

When applied to a troubled marriage, this philosophy advises, "If you don't have love feelings for your spouse any longer, admit it and get out of the marriage. If you feel hurt and angry, you would be hypocritical to say or do something kind to your spouse." This philosophy fails to reckon with the reality that man is more than his emotions.

The reality is that our actions are far more important than our emotions, and in fact, our actions will affect our emotions. I may feel depressed. Life seems heavy. A friend calls and asks if I'd like to join him for a Coke float at Mayberry's. My emotions are negative; my desire is to lie on the couch and forget the world, but I choose to say yes. Two hours later, my emotions have changed and the world looks much brighter.

I am not suggesting that emotions are unimportant. They

are indicators that things are going well or not so well in our relationship. Positive emotions encourage me to positive actions. Negative emotions conversely encourage me toward negative actions. But if I understand that negative actions will make things worse and that positive actions hold the potential for making things better, I will always choose the high road. I am always influenced by my emotions, but I need not be controlled by them.

This reality has profound implications for a troubled marriage. It means that I can do and say positive things to my spouse in spite of the fact that I have strong negative emotions. To take such positive action does not deny that our marriage is in serious trouble. It does not overlook the problems, but it chooses to take steps that hold potential for positive change rather than allowing negative behavior to escalate.

REALITY NUMBER FIVE:
Admitting My Imperfections Does Not Mean That I Am a Failure

Most troubled marriages include a stone wall between husband and wife, built over many years. Each stone represents an event in the past where one of them has failed the other. These are the things about which people talk when they sit in the counseling office. The husband complains, "She has been critical of my performance on the job or as a father.... She has failed to give me any words of appreciation and affirmation for my hard work.... She has put me down in front of the children." On the other hand, she gripes, "He is married to his job and has no time for me.... He often ignores me when he comes home, and he expects me to be a slave around the house while he watches football on television."

Demolishing this emotional wall is essential for rebuilding a troubled marriage. Destroying the wall requires both individuals to admit that they are imperfect and have failed each other. I am not implying that the responsibility for the wall is equally distributed between the husband and the wife; many times, one is more at fault than the other. But the fact is that neither has been perfect.

To acknowledge your imperfections does not mean you're a failure; it is rather to admit that you're human. As humans, you and I have the potential for loving, kind, and good behavior, but we also have the potential for self-centered, destructive behavior. For all of us, our marital history is a mixed bag of good and bad behavior. Admitting our past failures and asking for forgiveness is one of the most liberating of all human experiences. The fact is your spouse knows that you have failed, and you know that you have failed.

When I admit my failure and request forgiveness, I am tearing the wall down on my side. My spouse may readily forgive me or may be reluctant to do so, but I have done the most positive thing I can do about past failures. I cannot remove them, nor can I remove all of their results, but I can acknowledge them and request forgiveness.

Many people have found the following statements to be helpful in verbalizing their confession of past failures:

"I've been thinking about us, and I realize that in the past, I have not been the perfect husband/wife. In many ways I have failed you and hurt you. I am sincerely sorry for these failures. I hope that you will be able to forgive me for these. I sincerely want to be a better husband/wife. And with God's help, I want to make the future different."

Whether your spouse verbalizes forgiveness or has some less enthusiastic response, you have taken the first step in tearing the wall down between the two of you. If the hurt has been deep, your spouse may question your sincerity. He or she may even say, "I've heard that line before," or, "I'm not sure that I can forgive you." Whatever the response, you have planted in his or her mind the idea that the future is going to be different. If, in fact, you begin to make positive changes as a spouse, the day may come when your partner will freely forgive past failures. Until then, concentrate on making positive changes.

REALITY NUMBER SIX:
Love Is the Most Powerful Weapon for Good in the World

The French novelist Victor Hugo once wrote, "The supreme happiness of life is the conviction that we are loved."

Many agree with the novelist. Sigmund Freud said, "Love is the first requirement of mental health." William James said, "The deepest principle in human nature is the craving to be appreciated." Religious and secular leaders today agree that love holds a central place in a person's search for meaning. It is unfortunate that in the modern world the focus has been more on receiving love than giving love.

Most of the couples who sit in my office talk about the lack of love, affection, and appreciation they have received from their spouse through the years. Their emotional love tanks are empty, and they are pleading for love. I am deeply sympathetic with this need. I believe love is a person's deepest emotional need. The difficulty in a troubled marriage is that we are focusing on receiving love rather than giving love. Many husbands say, "If she would just be a little more affectionate, then I could be responsive to her. But when she gives me no affection, I just want to stay away from her." He is waiting for love before he loves. However, someone must take the initiative. Why must it be the other person?

The final principle for reality living declares love to be the most powerful weapon for good, and that especially applies in marriage. The problem for many husbands and wives is that we have thought of love as an emotion. In reality, love is an attitude with appropriate behavior. It affects the emotions, but it is not in itself an emotion. Love is the attitude that says, "I choose to look out for your interests. How may I help you?" Then love is expressed in behavior.

When we understand that love is basically a way of thinking and behaving, we can then love our spouse, even when we have negative emotions toward him or her. Our loving actions tend to stimulate positive emotions in our spouse. These emotions encourage our mate to reciprocate. When our spouse expresses loving actions to us, our emotions respond and we begin to feel warmly toward them. Thus the emotion of love grows out of loving actions.

Emotional warmth can be reborn in a marriage, but it is the result of loving actions. If we simply wait for warm emotions to return, we fail to set in motion the cycle that stimulates warm emotions.

Taken from *Loving Solutions* by Gary Chapman. ©1998 by Gary Chapman. Used by permission of Moody Press. Available at your local Christian bookstore.

Many couples have experienced breakthroughs in their marriage by becoming aware of these six realities. They realized that building their marriage on truth rather than myth is the only way to go. One leads to life, and life more abundantly; the other leads to destruction. The First Chair person puts into action these six realities. The Second Chair person, on the other hand, still buys into the myths and lies Satan likes to throw. If you're living in a Second Chair marriage, it's time you exchanged the lies for the truth and experienced the spiritual breakthrough that will follow. If you'd like to read more about this topic, I encourage you to check out Gary Chapman's book Loving Solutions.

EVALUATION QUESTIONS

1. Take some time and evaluate where you are in experiencing this breakthrough. Where would you rate yourself on the following scale?

1	5	10
Not even close to experiencing this breakthrough.	I've begun the journey, but I've got a ways to go.	I've experienced a breakthrough, and I'm living the abundant life.

2. What would you consider to be the biggest hindrance to your experiencing this breakthrough right now?

3. What one action should you take to experience this breakthrough right now? I challenge you to do it.

*"Christians are supposed not merely to endure change,
nor even to profit by it, but to cause it."*
HARRY EMERSON FOSDICK (1878–1969)

*"Everyone thinks of changing the world,
but no one thinks of changing himself."*
LEO TOLSTOY (1828–1910)

*"Be not afraid of growing slowly;
be afraid only of standing still."*
CHINESE PROVERB

*"A successful marriage is an edifice
that must be rebuilt every day."*
ANDRÉ MAUROIS (1885–1967)

Chase Away the Marriage Predators

JOHN TRENT

Regular maintenance on your marriage is a must. Why? Because time has a way of breaking down even the strongest of marriages if they are not maintained properly. You say you've built your marriage on a good foundation and built its walls with solid truth? Great! Now it's time to make sure nothing gets in that would cause your home to crumble. If you've ever had termite damage to your home, you know how devastating the little things can be. So it is with marriage. Most of the breakthroughs in this book deal with major problem areas, but not this one. This is a breakthrough in the details—the areas that are often overlooked. But don't think that just because we're working with the details that this chapter is trivial. In fact, this chapter could hold one of the biggest breakthroughs you'll experience. You see, people who have First Chair marriages have made dealing with the details a habit. They're downright good at making sure all the bases are covered. If this doesn't describe you, let John Trent show you how it's done.

*S*abotage! That's what it had to be—sabotage.

U.S. airplanes, desperately needed to fight the Nazi war machine, were grounded during World War II as their engines were proving defective, again and again. All the evidence pointed to sabotage. The Air Force's Eighth Division had lost as many as forty planes a day in the daylight raids over France. Many more returned to base with one or more engines shot to pieces. The need for engine parts was urgent and rated an A-plus priority. But many replacement parts were flawed.

My aunt Dovie had joined thousands of other women like Rosie the Riveter and pitched in to do what she could for the war effort. In her case, that meant working double shifts to make replacement aircraft-engine parts for the B-17 Flying Fortresses. Dovie, her coworkers, and her bosses all knew that if the enemy wanted to keep bombers from flying combat missions, one way would be to sabotage desperately needed engine parts. And even though the Nazis were an ocean away from the United States and security was tightened, that's just what was happening! Somehow, a saboteur was loose—and they'd narrowed his or her actions down to Aunt Dovie's department.

My aunt was working in the GM engine division near Indianapolis and was assigned to an assembly line that did the final packing and crating of massive silver-plated pistons. When the pistons left Building 5, they looked flawless. But after they arrived overseas and were uncrated, the silver plating had countless pinsized pits and holes that rendered them unsafe and unusable. Intelligence agents backtracked the parts and suspected that some Nazi sympathizer was splashing acid or some other solvent on the pistons before they were crated. But during every shift and through each step of manufacturing, supervisors, armed security guards, and G-men posing as workers watched every step. It had to be someone in the final act of packing, they concluded. Someone Aunt Dovie might have worked alongside day after day! The problem persisted, and the security and spot-checks remained constant. Everyone was suspicious of everyone else.

Then, it happened. One day my aunt walked into the lunchroom and suddenly froze in her tracks. At barely five feet tall and one hundred pounds, my aunt did not look like a spy-killer. But she recognized the enemy. There the spy stood, standing right near the cafeteria entrance. She knew it! And soon she made sure her supervisors and everyone else in the plant did as well.

Security personnel quickly captured the traitor and then smashed it for good measure. "Smashed" it because the traitor was the peanut machine that stood just outside the cafeteria door.

Every day it had dispensed tasty salted peanuts at just a nickel a handful. Here was the perfect snack to take in your hands and munch on as you walked back to the packing department. And the perfect snack to ruin engine parts. Many of the men and women who had stopped by the peanut machine were failing to wash their hands before picking up and crating the silver pistons. That small amount of salt being transferred from skin to silver plating may have seemed insignificant, yet, allowed to remain and given time to do its destructive work, it caused incredible damage.

Who would have thought that something so small could have caused such a big problem? Though it's only speculation, I think that Solomon's bride would have recognized the dangers of little things wreaking major havoc.[1] She sure did during her approaching marriage to Solomon, and she asked his help to capture "the little foxes" that could undermine their marriage.

She saw clearly how little things, left unchecked or unnoticed, can lead to unbelievable damage. This principle urges couples to take note of problems while they're small, before they have time to eat away at a couple's commitment and finally destroy the relationship. Solomon's bride-to-be knows they have a good thing, and she wisely wants to protect it. That's why, in poetic fashion, she makes a pointed request of Solomon:

> Catch the foxes for us, the little foxes that are ruining the vineyards, while our vineyards are in blossom. (Song of Songs 2:15, NASB)

"CATCH THE FOXES FOR US..."

Her picture of foxes is clever and appropriate. Foxes were rampant in Solomon's day, and while they are beautiful animals, farmers knew they were cunning predators capable of doing much damage. As a shepherdess, the future bride no doubt had heard stories about or seen firsthand what a fox could do.

There is so much wisdom in the words of Solomon's bride. She draws a picture of protective love for each of us who would guard his or her home. Yet we must admit that it's a challenge to deal with issues at the "fox" level before they turn into ravaging "lions." For one thing, they seem like annoyances, not fundamental issues. "Small" things like bouncing a check, procrastinating on a chore, skipping church to sleep in on Sunday, or sniping at each other. Yet these "little foxes" can quickly grow into patterns of behavior or personal problems that become irritants and then genuine threats to the health and stability of our relationship. How can we deal with these issues while they're still at the fox level?

FOX HUNTING

Here is a proven plan for avoiding or reducing problems. To hunt down and capture those loose foxes before they become major problems, I recommend the following five steps.

1. Recognize the Need to Do Some Things Differently.

Zach and Diane had an unhealthy motto they lived by: If It Doesn't Work…Keep Doing It. Though they didn't have that motto nailed on the kitchen wall, they lived it out through their actions. Diane had gotten down on herself after their third child was born. She had gone through the normal post-partum mood swings, and a significant amount of weight gained from the pregnancy wasn't coming off like before, making her feel even more depressed.

Zach had the best of intentions when he told her, "Honey, you can lose that weight. I know you can!" But he simply did not listen to Diane's frustrations; instead, he gave her pep talks. When she didn't seem to respond, Zach redoubled his efforts, paying for membership in a health club for her and lecturing her on the dangers to her and the kids of her pessimism. When she still didn't respond, he urged her to "pray about her nega-tive attitude," bought her a shelf full of health-store vitamins, and insisted that she go to the doctor for a physical checkup.

Nothing worked. In fact, very soon the solution he was trying so hard to force on his wife was actually a major part of the problem! He loved her too much to just watch her "become fat and unhappy," but he wasn't willing to realize that what he was doing daily wasn't helping bring any change. He needed to do more of something different, not more of the same. He could have become more vulnerable himself—drawing out her nurturing side—or acknowledged her feelings or asked her what she felt might help or a number of other things. Instead, he did more of the same, even though it brought fewer results.

Without exaggeration, I cannot think of a counseling session when I haven't said to an individual or couple who felt stuck in a problem, "More of the same doesn't bring change." So if a single-shot solution won't work, what will? We begin by recognizing our strengths in the relationship.

2. Focus on Your Strengths.

When the church at Ephesus had gotten off track, the resurrected Lord Jesus Himself told believers there, "I know your deeds and your toil and perseverance" and named a number of other positive qualities. "But I have this against you, that you have left your first love" (Revelation 2:2–4, NASB).

The remedy for a dwindling love, the Lord Jesus said, was to first look at what they'd done right. "Remember," He says, "from where you've fallen." In other words, they needed to remember the times they were "on top of things," serving Him with their whole hearts and walking closely with their Savior. The same principle is extremely important to apply for married couples who would see their love light stay bright and shining. If you're facing a problem today, take time together to look at your relationship strengths. As you look at your relationship (even going back to your courtship if you have to), what have you done well as a couple? Were there times when you've been sensitive to each other's needs? Have there been times when you've worked through a problem or made a decision together where both of you walked away feeling closer than before?

Couples who are struggling today, often are husbands and wives who have forgotten that back a few miles in their journey were successes and genuine strengths. Going back to times in your relationship where things worked well, even if those periods were only a short period of time, can give you an important platform to face current issues.

3. State a Clear Goal.

Time and again, I'll ask a couple who seems stuck, "Where would you like to be in your relationship?" Most of the time, they are experts at attacking each other and telling me what's wrong with their relationship. But they stop and stumble when you ask them what their goals are as a couple.

You begin to move past a problem when you clearly express a goal. Goal setting is a serious and important part of dealing with problems. It doesn't trivialize a problem to break it down into concrete, action-oriented steps. It's helpful! Notice that in His advice to the Ephesus church in Revelation 2, the Lord tells the Ephesian believers to do three things to rekindle their love for Him: "Remember from where you have fallen, and repent and do the things you did at first" (v. 5). To "repent" means to turn around and begin walking toward God's best. And to "do the things you did at first" is a call to get with a program that's brought success. Call them steps, principles, pictures, or points—just do them!

How does this actually work in real life? First, come up with a written goal for dealing with an issue. For example, a husband is very frustrated with his wife, who often breaks their budget by buying something unexpected; he is frustrated even if she buys when the item is on sale. Spending differences can certainly be foxes that turn into lions. To head off the problem while it's still small (or make it smaller if it's already roaring out of control), they first set a goal. They come up with a written goal: "Neither of us can spend more than fifty dollars that isn't budgeted for without calling the other person first." That stops the rationalization "It's easier to ask forgiveness than permission!" and it gives them a specific goal that, if needed, can be broken down into specific steps.

Clear goals take a negative problem and start you on the way to constructive change.

4. Divide the Goal into Measurable Behaviors.

Carl and Heather face a fox of their own: Heather doesn't feel listened to. Together, they agree to look at the problem, break it down, and propose specific actions for a solution. They express that solution as a multipart goal. Such steps help husbands and wives answer a powerful question: How will you know when things are better in this area? It's amazing how some couples can make legitimate, even significant changes, but somehow miss or discount them because no standard has been set!

Couples can capture little foxes if they take their concern, set a goal, and then break it into concrete steps. Carl and Heather, for example, developed three specific steps:

1. When he walks in the door, he'll spend the first ten minutes talking to me before going over to watch the news.
2. I'll know he's listening when he asks me two follow-up questions after I've shared something important. (A follow-up question would be something like, "Then how did that make you feel?" or "What do you think that means?")
3. He will have a videotape in the VCR when he's watching a football game, ready to record the action, so that

if I do ask him a question, he can look at me and give me his full attention instead of looking around me at the television.

With these steps, Carl knew specific things to do, and Heather could measure progress in the problem area. Reaching the goal by setting up concrete steps not only gives a man the ability to aim his "hunter" instinct at specific problems, but it helps the wife crystallize what she really wants to be different in the relationship. This leads to step five in hunting for problem foxes.

5. Stay Open to Change through All Seasons.

One final step in keeping the fences up and the foxes out is to try different activities to keep your relationship strong and healthy. Come up with your own list of things that "color outside the lines." Here are a few ideas:

- If it's been a while since the two of you went out to breakfast, schedule a breakfast date.
- If you haven't seen a movie in two years, start watching for something redeeming to see together.
- If you've never gone on a weekend missions outreach, sign up!
- If you've never been on a three-day Christian cruise, start saving up for one.
- If your church has a Saturday-evening service you haven't yet attended, make it your church service that week.

Being open to new things is important in solving problems and keeping your love strong. One of the greatest examples of someone who continues to find vitality and new life in his ministry and marriage is my friend and fellow author Chuck Swindoll. When Cindy and I were at a booksellers' banquet a few years ago, Chuck and his wife, Cynthia, greeted us. With twinkling eyes, he told me, "Trent, just say yes to what I'm about to ask you."

"What's that?" I asked.

"I want you and Cindy to join Cynthia and me on a motorcycle trip. We're taking our Harley and going from Portland all the way down the coast to L.A. It's going to be great! You guys *gotta* come!"

Not having the days available or our own Harley, we couldn't join them on their motorcycle trip. But Cindy and I are committed to building in times of refreshment in our marriage.

My prayer for you, dear reader, is that you'll act purposefully and persistently to catch those little foxes that come with any relationship.

Taken from *Love for All Seasons* by John Trent. ©1996 by John Trent. Used by permission of Moody Press. Available at your local Christian bookstore.

I don't think I know of any marriage that couldn't benefit from these words of wisdom. In fact, if you've ever heard the words "We don't need to work on our marriage because we're doing just fine" come out of your mouth, it's time to be worried. Every marriage can be better than it is—even the best ones. But pride says, "We've got it all together." The couples who stay together the longest and remain the happiest work on their marriage even when it doesn't seem like it needs work. If you would like to read about more ways to keep your marriage strong through all the seasons of life, consider adding John Trent's book Love for All Seasons *to your library. You'll be glad you did.*

EVALUATION QUESTIONS

1. Take some time and evaluate where you are in experiencing this breakthrough. Where would you rate yourself on the following scale?

1	5	10
Not even close to experiencing this breakthrough.	I've begun the journey, but I've got a ways to go.	I've experienced a breakthrough, and I'm living the abundant life.

2. What would you consider to be the biggest hindrance to your experiencing this breakthrough right now?

3. What one action should you take to experience this breakthrough right now? I challenge you to do it.

1. And I think she would have liked Aunt Dovie! My precious, godly aunt passed away several years ago, but along with my mother and grandmother, she helped raise me. I used an elaborated version of this story to praise her incredible attention to detail in *The Two Sides of Love* (Pomona, Calif.: Focus on the Family, 1990).

*"The Christian is supposed to love his neighbor,
and since his wife is his nearest neighbor,
she should be his deepest love."*
MARTIN LUTHER (1483–1546)

"Try praising your wife even if it does frighten her at first."
BILLY SUNDAY (1862–1935)

*"Can there be a love
which does not make demands on its object?"*
CONFUCIUS (551–479 B.C.)

*"Duty does not have to be dull.
Love can make it beautiful and fill it with life."*
THOMAS MERTON (1915–1968)

*"Forgetting oneself is not a refinement of love.
It is a first condition of love."*
LEON JOSEPH SUENENS

Husbands, Love Your Wives

TONY EVANS

Husbands often believe that their biggest role in marriage is to be the provider and protector. While it is true that these are important aspects of the husband's role, they are but a manifestation of his greater role—loving his wife. You see, if you make loving your wife your primary role, then providing for her is natural, as is protecting her—and a lot of other things. But if you make providing for her your primary role, you may spend too much time working and not enough time loving her. This, unfortunately, is the tragic scenario we see unfolding before our eyes in this country. Work is king! And wives are ignored. Husband, it's time to put a stop to this trend and make loving your wife your primary role in marriage.

One of the first things mamas teach their little kids is, "It's not polite to point." Adam didn't have a mama, but he sure needed to learn that lesson. The first thing Adam did when God confronted him about his sin was point at Eve and say, "She gave me the fruit and told me to eat it; it's her fault" (see Genesis 3:12). Men have been tempted to blame their wives ever since.

But if there is any area where we as Christian men need to move beyond excusing and blaming to loving and blessing, it's in our marriages. This is where most of the enemy's attacks will come, because Satan's long-term goal is to destroy the whole human race, not just men.

Satan didn't bother Adam before Eve was created. But as soon as Eve came on the scene, the attack was launched. Satan focuses his attacks on the husband-wife relationship because by destroying that, he destroys children and families too. He who controls the family controls the future.

What that means, my brother, is that if we can learn to relate to our wives with love and sensitivity while providing the godly leadership we're responsible to provide, we'll start winning a lot of spiritual battles that Christian men are now losing. And we'll be happier and more fulfilled in the process.

WHAT GOD EXPECTS

In Genesis 2:15, God made His will clear to Adam right up front when He put Adam in the garden and appointed him to "work it and take care of it." Then God told him to enjoy all the fruit of the garden, with one famous exception—the tree of the knowledge of good and evil (vv. 16–17).

In other words, God taught Adam about work and following instructions before He ever created a mate for him. But these verses point out a major weakness in many homes today: husbands who don't know what God has said. Ask the average man what God has said about his responsibility to his wife, to his children, and to himself as the head of the home and he will either admit he doesn't know or give an answer that reveals he doesn't know.

And instead of looking to God for answers as to who they are, many men adopt the standards of the culture and base their identity on clothes, cars, cash, or romantic conquests. That reduces manhood to a primitive and degrading level.

But God's definition of manhood is the ability to put divine truth into action at home and on the job. No amount of strength, good looks, or liquid assets can improve a man's performance—not from God's perspective.

So God didn't bring a woman into Adam's life until he had a job and divine insight. Only when Adam had met those two requirements was he ready for marriage. Only then did God say, "It is not good for the man to be alone. I will make a helper suitable for him" (Genesis 2:18, NIV).

Creating a mate for Adam was God's idea, not Adam's. That reminds us that all of God's plans are perfect. If you're in a bad marriage, it's not because God had a bad idea. Marriage is His ideal. It's the partners in a marriage who turn it from an ideal into an ordeal, causing them to look for a new deal.

So Adam was a responsible, godly man when the Creator brought him Eve to be his helper. That word *helper* gives you a woman's basic responsibility. She was created to come alongside the man to assist him. She was never meant to bear the burden of responsibility for the home and family.

God laid the responsibility for the home on Adam, not Eve. That's why, even though it was Eve who plucked the forbidden fruit and gave it to her husband, God came looking for Adam. And when Adam tried to pass the blame to Eve, God wasn't buying it.

Whenever a husband shifts the burden of leadership to his wife, he makes a serious mistake. Generally speaking, that gives the wife a level of responsibility God never planned for her to have. God intended and still intends for the husband to carry the weight of the responsibility for his home.

By now you may be saying, "Boy, Tony, you sure are hard on men." You're right. But that's only because men are to be the leaders. As leaders, we are held accountable for our marriages in the same way that Adam was called to account for Eve's surrender to the serpent.

We are also commanded to love our wives the way Christ loves the church. Paul writes:

> Husbands, love your wives, just as Christ loved the church and gave himself up for her to make her holy, cleansing her by the washing with water through the word, and to present her to himself as a radiant church, without stain or wrinkle or any other blemish, but holy and blameless. (Ephesians 5:25–27, NIV)

Why does God command men to love their wives? Because we are to take the lead in demonstrating the nature and power of unconditional love, the kind of love Christ demonstrated for His church. A husband's love is meant to be so powerful that it transforms his wife into what she should be, just as Christ's love for the church transforms us into what we should be.

That means if our wives have blemishes, it is our job to correct them. But because we men don't understand the theology of marriage, we want to bail out when the going gets tough. However, the weaknesses of our wives provide the perfect context for revealing the reality of God and how powerful the Holy Spirit can be in transforming people. When we demonstrate this kind of sacrificial, servant love, we will see our wives transformed from what they were into what they should be.

A lot of men don't realize that when they married their wives, they married their wives' histories as well. Some women enter marriage deeply bruised and broken from abuse or neglect from previous relationships. Although these scars may be hidden, they are there, and sooner or later they will reveal themselves. Drawing on the analogy of Ephesians 5, it is the husband's job to be his wife's "savior" and sanctifier; to bring deliverance that frees her from the pain of the past and leads her into the joy of a glorious new future, just as Christ does for us.

Now make no mistake—this kind of love is tough for many men to pull off. One man said to me, "Man, this stuff is so hard. My wife is crucifying me." To which I responded, "You said you wanted to be like Jesus, didn't you?" Remember that after the crucifixion comes the resurrection.

None of this absolves women from responsibility. God did not command women to love their husbands, maybe because that seems to come naturally to them. But God did command women to respect their husbands (Ephesians 5:33).

Just as women have a need to be loved, men have a need to be respected. That is why Peter tells wives not to use their tongues to turn disobedient husbands around but rather to use reverence (1 Peter 3:1–2). If each spouse follows the command God gave specifically for the male and female, a couple can become the unit He intended.

Respect is particularly needed by men in the black community. Often black males don't receive respect at their jobs. In a society where many black men are still regarded as "boys" no matter what their age, there needs to be a place where they know they are respected. That place should be the home.

The mate God gave you was created to fit together with you in marriage. When God created Adam, He knew that the man was in need of someone similar to himself. Eve was created to make Adam complete, to help him fulfill God's intentions for his life.

Whenever a man says, "I have achieved so much," he ought always to include, "because I have a wife who has enabled me." A godly man will acknowledge his wife's contribution to his success. On every rung of the ladder of success, there is ample room for two sets of feet!

How to Love Your Wife

In 1 Peter 3:7, the apostle gives husbands some very important insight into their wives and how to treat them:

> Husbands, in the same way, be considerate as you live with your wives, and treat them with respect as the weaker partner and as heirs with you of the gracious gift of life, so that nothing will hinder your prayers. (NIV)

Whenever the Bible says "in the same way" or "likewise," you know the writer is building off of something that came before. Peter does the same thing in 3:1 when he says to wives, "In the same way be submissive to your husbands." What Peter is referring to is the end of chapter 2, where he paints a magnificent portrait of Christ as our suffering Redeemer.

Notice especially how relevant these verses are to the marriage relationship. "Christ suffered for you, leaving you an example, that you should follow in his steps" (2:21, NIV). So husbands who are suffering with their wives can't go around thinking, "Yeah, well, that's Jesus. If I were Jesus I could live with her too."

No, no, my brother. We are to follow "in his steps." It gets even better in verse 23: "When they hurled their insults at him, he did not retaliate; when he suffered, he made no threats."

Jesus could have said, "I'm not going to have any human beings talking to Me this way. I'm not going to have them treating Me this way. Don't they know who I am? I could take them out with a word." Jesus could have done that, but when He was messed over, He didn't retaliate or make threats.

Instead, He "bore our sins in his body on the tree...by his wounds you have been healed" (3:24, NIV). Notice that He got the wounds, or stripes, but we get the healing.

SACRIFICE, SACRIFICE

Now when you put this all together in relation to the way a husband is to treat his wife, what you get is an incredible picture of an amazing sacrificial, selfless, and gracious love.

Could it be that the only way some husbands will win back their wives is by the stripes these husbands are willing to bear? When you are willing to bear stripes for someone else, that's when you start to understand the meaning of love.

Now, you are not going to hear that on the street, I guarantee you. No one is going to go on a TV talk show and tell about how he was willing to suffer in order to love and nurture his wife. The word on the streets to men is, "You give the stripes—you don't take them."

TO KNOW HER IS TO LOVE HER

Peter also says we are to be understanding toward our wives (1 Peter 3:7). What he means is that we should study them. The Bible tells men to study the Word and their wives. Both can be difficult to interpret and understand, but both richly repay the effort! I'm afraid we give very little time to really getting to know our wives.

Women are very complicated and often hard to understand. When they are experiencing the emotions and mood swings that come with changes in their bodies, it's easy for a husband to react with irritation and anger, especially when his wife doesn't respond the way he thinks she should. I'm not saying it's easy to deal with that, but then it's not easy for your wife either. You'll get a lot further with understanding than you will with the kind of irritation that pushes her away and says, "I don't want anything to do with you when you're like this." Peter says to study your wife, to learn to read her movements and emotions so you can respond with understanding instead of rejection.

LOVE, HONOR, AND CHERISH

Peter continues by saying we husbands are to grant our wives honor. That means lifting them up, pampering them the way we did when we were dating. Notice that Peter doesn't say, "Work at changing your wife." If you are trying to change your wife instead of honoring her, you are messing up.

You may be saying, "Oh, I get the deal. I'm to honor my wife so she will change into the person I want her to be."

No, that's not the deal. True love, agape love, does what is needed for the person loved whether or not the one doing the loving receives anything in return. Besides, our ultimate goal should be to help our wives become what God wants them to be, not what we want them to be.

Now if you truly love and honor your wife, it will change her. But don't expect it to happen in a week. If it took you five years to mess up your marriage, it may take you five years of pampering to fix it. I don't know.

What I am saying is that you need to be willing to love your wife the way Christ loved you, and that may involve taking some stripes and some abuse in order to put things back on track.

Peter calls the wife the "weaker partner" or the "weaker vessel." When she has to work and then come home and cook and take care of you and the kids, her emotional circuits get overloaded. Then you get mad because she is not loving and available to you at bedtime.

But that's saying your desires and needs are more important than hers, which is not treating her as an equal, as a fellow heir of the grace of life. You are the leader in the home, but your wife is every bit your equal in essence and in worth before God.

One reason we are to live with our wives in a loving, understanding, and sacrificial way is so that "nothing will hinder [our] prayers" (1 Peter 3:7, NIV). If we are not honoring our wives, if we are not willing to take stripes for them, if we are not loving them as Christ loves the church, then we may as well get off our knees.

But what a reward we have when we learn to love our wives as our own bodies. Remember, God doesn't take our love and give us nothing in return. As we love and honor our wives, they will blossom and develop into women of grace and true beauty. Then we will experience the kind of fulfilling love that a lot of married people think is beyond their grasp,

A PERFECT UNION

The Trinity is made up of three coequal persons. One God who makes Himself known to us as God the Father, God the Son, and God the Holy Spirit. Marriage is an earthly replica of this divine trinity, three persons who are "three-in-one": a man, a woman, and God. You cannot leave God at the altar and expect to have a happy marriage.

Christ's resurrection power operating in your life is the only power that can save your life, your marriage, and your home. When Christ rose from the dead, He gave you access to the power of His resurrection. That power can enable you and your wife to love one another, trust each other, and share life together until death parts you. God alone can give you the ability to do that.

It's the power of God operating in your life that makes marriage work. If you haven't made that personal decision to turn the totality of your life—including your marriage—over to Jesus Christ, you don't have that resurrection power.

But you can have that power if you believe Christ rose from the dead to help you be the kind of husband He has called you to be. When you give Him your life, then you will experience marriage as God intended it to be. He made marriage, and He can make it work.

I challenge you, as one brother to another, to commit yourself without reservation to the Lord. Give Him your marriage, and let Him remake it in His image. Then you won't need any more excuses.

Taken from *No More Excuses* by Tony Evans. ©1996 by Tony Evans. Used by permission of Crossway Books. Available at your local Christian bookstore.

The Bible warns husbands not to deal treacherously with their wives. Is your marriage suffering? Are you unfulfilled in your marriage? If the answer to either of these questions is yes, is it possible that the reason is because of your lack of love for your wife? Philippians 2:3 tells us to "consider others better than yourselves."

Do you consider your wife to be more important than you? If not, you've dealt treacherously with her. Those are strong words, but considering her to be better than you is what true love is all about. This is definitely a breakthrough that could revolutionize the way your marriage works—the way you and your wife relate. If you're reading all this and saying, "Yes, but...," then you need to read Tony Evans's book No More Excuses. *If you're making excuses here, you're probably making them elsewhere as well.*

EVALUATION QUESTIONS

1. Take some time and evaluate where you are in experiencing this breakthrough. Where would you rate yourself on the following scale?

1	5	10
Not even close to experiencing this breakthrough.	I've begun the journey, but I've got a ways to go.	I've experienced a breakthrough, and I'm living the abundant life.

2. What would you consider to be the biggest hindrance to your experiencing this breakthrough right now?

3. What one action should you take to experience this breakthrough right now? I challenge you to do it.

"A candle loses nothing by lighting another candle."
PROVERB

"Dedicate some of your life to others.
Your dedication will not be a sacrifice;
it will be an exhilarating experience."
THOMAS DOOLEY

"You give but little when you give of your possessions.
It is when you give of yourself that you truly give."
KAHLIL GIBRAN (1883–1931)

"The service that counts is the service that costs."
HOWARD HENDRICKS

Wives,
Help Your Husbands

ELIZABETH GEORGE

"I will make him a helper."
GENESIS 2:18, NKJV

There are two ways that a Christian woman can have a dramatic impact on her family—and the world as a whole—serving and submitting to her husband. Why these two? Because they are what God created her to do within the family structure. Unfortunately, service and submission have been tossed out the window by most women today. These women have bought into the idea that they can have a bigger impact on the world and those around them by climbing the corporate ladder. If this would describe you, then God wants you to experience a breakthrough that may be difficult for you to undergo. But if you'll let Elizabeth George explain and then let the Lord work in your heart, I can assure you, the end result will be truly amazing!

*I*t was a bright autumn day at the University of Oklahoma. As I hurried toward my first class after lunch, I noticed him again. He was smiling as he came my way. Every Monday, Wednesday, and Friday our paths seemed to cross as he, too, rushed to class. His name—Jim George—was unknown to me at the time, but he looked extremely nice, he was cute, and I loved his smile! Well, evidently he noticed me, too, because soon a mutual friend set up a blind date for us.

That was in November 1964. On Valentine's Day we were engaged, and our wedding took place the first weekend school was out, June 1, 1965. That was thirty-one years ago—and I wish I could say, "That was thirty-one wonderful, blissful, happy years ago," but I can't. You see, Jim and I began our marriage without God, and that meant rough times. From the beginning we fumbled, we argued, and we let each other down. Because we didn't find fulfillment in our marriage, we poured our lives into causes, friends, hobbies, and intellectual pursuits. Having two children also didn't fill the emptiness we each felt. Our married life droned on for eight frustrating years until, by an act of God's grace, we became a Christian family, a family centered on Jesus Christ as the head, a family with the Bible to guide us.

Giving our lives to Jesus Christ made a tremendous difference inside our hearts, but how would Christ change our marriage? We each had been given new life in Christ, but what were we going to do about the tension in our marriage and therefore in our home?

I had much to learn about being a woman, a wife, a mother who pleased God. And thankfully—soon after naming Jesus as my Lord and Savior—I had in my hands a calendar for reading through the Bible. On January 1, 1974, I began to follow that schedule, and as I read I did something that I recommend you do, too. I marked every passage that spoke to me as a woman with a pink highlighter.

Well, God went to work on my makeover that very day. On January 1, my first day of reading, I came across the first aspect of my job assignment as a Christian wife: I was to serve Jim. I marked these words in pink: "It is not good that man should be alone; I will make him a helper comparable to him" (Genesis 2:18, NKJV).

CALLED TO SERVE

A woman after God's own heart is a woman who carefully cultivates a servant spirit, whether she is married or not. Following in the steps of Jesus, who "did not come to be served, but to serve" (Matthew 20:28), calls for lifelong attention to the heart attitude of serving. And that attitude and service starts at home with your family—specifically, if you're married, with your husband. God has designed the wife to be her husband's helper. So the first step on my journey of a thousand miles to becoming a godly wife was beginning to understand that *I am on assignment from God to help my husband.*

And just what is this "helper" from Genesis 2:18? Borrowing a few of Jim's Bible-study books, I learned that a helper is one who shares man's responsibilities, responds to his nature with understanding and love, and wholeheartedly cooperates with him in working out the plan of God.[1] Anne Ortlund talks about becoming a team with your husband, pointing out that being a team eliminates any sense of competition between spouses. Writing about this partnership of marriage, she describes a wife being solidly behind and supportive of her husband. She declares, "I have no desire to run parallel to Ray, sprinting down the track in competition. I want to be behind him, encouraging him."[2]

I can honestly say that I became a better wife—and a better Christian—when I became a better helper. Realizing I am on assignment from God to help my husband opened my eyes. According to God's plan, I was not to compete with Jim. Instead, I am to be solidly behind him and supportive of him. He is the one who is supposed to win, and I am supposed to help make his victory possible.

Reading about Mamie Eisenhower, the wife of former president Dwight D. Eisenhower, gave me further insight into being a helper. Julie Nixon Eisenhower explained, "Mamie had seen her role as one of emotional support for her husband.... She had no interest in promoting herself. Most of all, she was the woman behind the man, the woman who proudly proclaimed, 'Ike was my career.'"[3]

As God impressed on my heart the importance of a servant spirit, especially in my role as a helper to my husband, I wrote out a prayer of commitment. As I did, I stepped back a few paces to ensure that, in my own heart, Jim was clearly in front and I was definitely stationed behind him to help. On that day—and in that prayer to God—I began a life of serving Jim that has continued for more than two decades. Oh, I have many things to do, but my primary purpose and role each day is to help Jim, to share his responsibilities, to respond to his nature, and to wholeheartedly cooperate with him in God's plan for our life together. This mind-set, this servant spirit, helps me be more like Christ as I esteem others—especially my husband—as better than myself (Philippians 2:3) and commit myself to service.

A HEART THAT SUBMITS

Having started down the road toward becoming my husband's helper, I kept reading my Bible. As I did so, I discovered more to my role of wife, and I saw other qualities I needed if I was to be the kind of wife God wants me to be. In fact, the number of times my pink marker hit the pages showed me I had a lot of work to do. The next big item I noticed was *I am on assignment from God to submit to my husband.*

As a new Christian, I found submission a foreign concept, and I had to do some research. When I did, I learned that, in the Bible, *submission (hupotasso)* is primarily a military term meaning to rank oneself under someone else. This heart attitude is lived out by subjection and obedience,[4] by leaving things to the judgment of another person and yielding or deferring to the opinion or authority of someone else.[5]

As I said, the concept was foreign, and I felt my heart hesitating. But I kept studying and praying to be a woman and wife after God's own heart, and some insights from the Bible helped flesh out the heart attitude of submission that God desires in His women.

THE FACT OF SUBMISSION

First, the fact is that the Christian lifestyle—for men as well as women—is one of submission. You and I are called to be "submitting to one another" (Ephesians 5:21). God's desire for us—married or single, young or old—is to honor, serve, and subject ourselves to one another. We reflect Christ's character as we move away from selfishness and, acting out of honor for other people, defer to them. A heart willing to submit, dedicated to honoring and yielding to others, is to be the heart of God's people, His women, His church.

When it comes to marriage, God arranged for the sake of order that the husband lead and the wife follow. For marriage to run smoothly, God has said, "The head of every man is Christ, the head of woman is man, and the head of Christ is

God" (1 Corinthians 11:3, NKJV).

Now don't be alarmed. The husband's headship doesn't mean we wives can't offer wise input (Proverbs 31:26) or ask questions for clarification during the decision-making process. But the husband's headship does mean that he is responsible for the final decision. Author Elisabeth Elliot describes her father's headship in her childhood home: "'Head of the house' did not mean that our father barked out orders, threw his weight around, and demanded submission from his wife. It simply meant that he was the one finally responsible."[6] In the end, the husband is accountable to God for his leadership decisions, and we as wives are accountable to God for how we submit to that leadership. Our husband answers to God for leading, and we answer to Him for following. Now I ask you, which responsibility would you rather have?

God's instruction that the man lead and the woman follow results in beauty as well as order. I remember as a child seeing the stuffed "head" of a goat in a museum—only it had two heads. It was abnormal, grotesque, a freak attraction, a curiosity. And so is a marriage with two heads! But God, the perfect Artist, designed marriage to be beautiful, natural, and functional by giving it a single head, the husband. Thank You, Lord, that marriage is Your work of art!

THE WHO OF SUBMISSION

The who of submission is clear in Ephesians 5:22: "Wives, submit to your own husbands," not to other people we admire and respect. And this is an important distinction.

A Christian woman married to a man who was not a believer came to me for some counsel. Sue wanted to quit her job and attend Bible college for four years in preparation for entering full-time Christian work. After telling me her heart's longings, I asked her, "Well, Sue, what does your husband say about this?" She quickly answered, "Oh, he doesn't want me to do it."

"Why, Sue," I exclaimed, "God has spoken!" You see, God's plan for marriage is that each wife honor and submit to her husband. When Sue had talked about her dream with her pastor and her Christian employer, both of them had told her to go ahead with her plans. She was all too ready to honor the guidance of others. But the Bible is clear: We are to submit to our own husband—not to a church leader, not to other people we respect, not even to our father.

Sometimes we're tempted to dismiss God's plan, saying, "My husband isn't walking with God, so I don't have to submit to him," or, "My husband isn't a Christian, so I don't have to submit to him." The apostle Peter wrote the following words to help women in those exact situations, women with unbelieving and/or disobedient husbands: "Wives...be submissive to your own husbands, that even if some do not obey the word, they, without a word [from their wives], may be won by the conduct of their wives" (1 Peter 3:1, NKJV). In other words, our submission to our husband—whether or not he is a Christian, whether or not he is obeying God—preaches a lovelier and more powerful sermon than our mouth ever could!

It's important to mention here the one exception to following your husband's advice, and that is if he asks you to violate some teaching from God's Word. If he's asking you to do something illegal or immoral, go to a trusted pastor and follow the counsel you receive there.

THE HOW OF SUBMISSION

Besides clarifying the who, Ephesians 5:22 also gives us the how of submission: "Wives, submit yourselves unto your own husbands, *as unto the Lord*" (KJV, emphasis added). As soon as I stopped thinking about submitting to Jim and started thinking about submitting to the Lord, my struggle to submit slowly began to abate. I sort of mentally set Jim to one side, and that left me staring straight into the Lord's face. Suddenly the how of submission became much simpler—and easier! My submission had nothing to do with Jim and everything to do with the Lord. As a familiar Scripture says, "Whatever you do [including submitting to your husband!], do it heartily, *as to the Lord* and not to men" (Colossians 3:23, NKJV, emphasis added). What a blessing to apply this Scripture to honoring, submitting to, and following Jim!

THE MOTIVE FOR SUBMISSION

Perhaps the Scripture that reached deepest into my heart when God's call to submission was taking root there was this one: "Admonish the young women to [be] obedient to their own husbands, that the word of God may not be blasphemed [discredited, dishonored]" (Titus 2:45, NKJV). As I pondered this verse, the idea of submitting to my husband suddenly leaped into the heavenly realm, rising far above all my earthly, petty, selfish, and fleshly excuses for not wanting to submit to Jim.

Once again it became clear to me that my submission had nothing to do with Jim and everything to do with God! God has instituted submission, commanded submission, and given me the faith in Him to be able to submit—and He is honored when I do! My obedience to my husband testifies to all who are watching that God's Word and His way are right. This call to submit is indeed a high calling!

STEPS TO SUBMISSION

How does a wife submit to her husband? Here are some steps I have taken.

Dedicate your heart to honoring your husband. Change requires a decision, and that's definitely the case with submission. You and I have to decide to submit to our husband, make up our mind to practice submission, and dedicate our heart to honoring God and our husband in this way.

Remember to respect. Submission flows from the basic heart attitude of respect. God states, "Let the wife see that she respects her husband" (Ephesians 5:33, NKJV). God isn't telling us *to feel* respect, but to show respect, to act with respect. A good way to measure our respect for our husband is to answer the question, Am I treating my husband as I would treat Christ Himself?

You reveal your respect for your husband in little daily instances. Do you, for instance, ask your husband to do something, or do you tell him? Do you stop, look, and listen to him when he's talking? Do you speak about him with respect?

Respond to your husband's words and actions positively. Ooooh, submission came hard for me! I was a student in the sixties, a decade of protest against all authority, and I was a part of the women's liberation movement in the seventies. So when I first became a believer I had much to learn from God and the lovely women I met at my church.

Yet old ways die hard. I would buck, snort, kick, and fight with Jim about everything—which lane he should drive in, whether or not we got donuts on the way to church on Sunday morning, his method of disciplining the children versus mine, how he should handle his ministry. On and on our struggles went. I knew what Scripture said (I'd even memorized the passages we've been considering!), but I still couldn't submit. For me the breakthrough came with developing a positive response. I trained—yes, *trained*—myself to respond positively to anything and everything my husband said or did. And the training was a two-phase process.

Phase One: Say nothing! Have you ever been in the presence of a woman who doesn't respect her husband? She nags at him, picks on him, and disagrees with him in public. She corrects him, struggling with him over every little thing ("No, Harry, it wasn't eight years ago; it was seven years ago"). Or she cuts him off, interrupts, or, worse, finishes his sentences for him.

Clearly, saying nothing is a great improvement over that kind of behavior. Saying nothing is also a giant step toward submission! All we have to do to give a positive response is keep our mouth closed and say nothing! It took me some time, but I finally realized that my mouth doesn't always have to be moving. I don't always have to express my opinions, especially after Jim has made a decision. Why speak thoughts I'll later regret?

Phase Two: Respond with a single positive word. After I had pretty well mastered saying nothing in Phase One, I graduated to Phase Two and started to respond with one posi-tive word. I chose the word *sure!* (and that's with an exclamation mark behind it and melody in my voice). And I began to use this positive response and say, "Sure!" on the small things.

My dear friend Dixie also chose the word, *sure!*—and let me tell you something that happened in her family as a result. Dixie's husband loved to go to Price Club, a crowded and noisy discount warehouse. Many times he would announce after dinner, "Hey, let's all go to Price Club!" Well, Dixie— with three children, one of them a baby at the time—could have presented a watertight case against dragging the entire family out to Price Club on a school night after dark, but she didn't. She also never challenged Doug's leadership in front of her little family. Instead, she just smiled, responded "Sure!" and got everyone into the car for another trip to Price Club.

Many years later as, one by one, Dixie's family members shared around the Thanksgiving dinner table about their favorite thing to do as a family, all three of her grown-up children said, "Going to Price Club as a family!" Family unity, fun, and memories came because of Dixie's sweet heart—and word—of submission.

Once you've begun to respond positively to the small things, you'll quickly find it becoming easier and even natural to respond positively to larger and larger issues, like car purchases, job changes, and household moves. I amazed myself one morning at 5:30 A.M. when the phone rang. Jim was calling from Singapore, where he was traveling with our missions pastor. He didn't say, "Hello, how are you? How are the children? I miss you so much, I love you so much, and I can't wait to see you." Instead he blurted, "Hey, how would you like to move to Singapore and minister?" And out of my mouth blooped, "Sure," followed by, "Where is it?"

Maybe it was the early hour or my loneliness for Jim or the surprise. Or maybe it was because, in the preceding ten years, I had grown in the area of submission. Whatever the reason, my training in submission and in responding positively paid off. God gave me the grace to say, "Sure!" (We did go to Singapore and served there for a year. It was a wonderful experience for our ten and eleven-year-old daughters as well as for Jim and me. The four of us loved it so much we wanted to spend the rest of our lives there!)

Ask of each word, act, and attitude, "Am I bending or bucking?" Whenever tension wells up in your heart and you're resisting or questioning your husband's direction, ask,

"Am I bending or bucking?" Your answer will point to the problem. Enough said!

Wow! These are some tough words! But if you'll let them work on your heart, you'll find that these are some life-changing, marriage-changing words. These very principles changed my marriage, and I know they can change yours. If you want to be A Woman after God's Own Heart, *then I'd highly recommend you read Elizabeth George's book by that name. There's a lot more to being a godly woman than serving and submitting, but it's a great place to start. In fact, it's a breakthrough you'll want to experience over and over again as you serve and submit to your husband daily.*

EVALUATION QUESTIONS

1. Take some time and evaluate where you are in experiencing this breakthrough. Where would you rate yourself on the following scale?

1	5	10
Not even close to experiencing this breakthrough.	I've begun the journey, but I've got a ways to go.	I've experienced a breakthrough, and I'm living the abundant life.

2. What would you consider to be the biggest hindrance to your experiencing this breakthrough right now?

3. What one action should you take to experience this breakthrough right now? I challenge you to do it.

1. Charles F. Pfeiffer and Everett F. Harrison, eds., *The Wycliffe Bible Commentary* (Chicago: Moody Press, 1973), 5.

2. Ray and Anne Ortlund, *The Best Half of Life* (Glendale, Calif.: Regal Books, 1976), 97.

3. Julie Nixon Eisenhower, *Special People* (New York: Ballantine Books, 1977), 199.

4. W. E. Vine, *An Expository Dictionary of New Testament Words* (Old Tappan, N.J.: Fleming H. Revell Company, 1966), 86.

5. *Webster's New Collegiate Dictionary* (Springfield, Mass.: G. & C. Merriam Co., Publishers, 1961), 845.

6. Elisabeth Elliot, *The Shaping of a Christian Family* (Nashville: Thomas Nelson Publishers, 1992), 75.

"Married life is a marathon....
It is not enough to make a great start toward long-term marriage.
You will need the determination to keep plugging....
Only then will you make it to the end."
JAMES C. DOBSON

"Regret is an appalling waste of energy; you can't build on it;
it's only good for wallowing in."
KATHERINE MANSFIELD (1888–1923)

"Most divorces are not bad marriages,
just poorly prepared marriages."
JIM TALLEY

"So many persons who think divorce a panacea for every ill
find out when they try it that the remedy
is worse than the disease."
DOROTHY DIX (1870–1951)

"A slip of the foot you may soon recover.
But a slip of the tongue you may never get over."
BENJAMIN FRANKLIN (1706–1790)

"The great test of a man's character is his tongue."
OSWALD CHAMBERS (1874–1917)

Bring Happiness to Your Spouse

ROBERT JEFFRESS

It never seems like I have enough time." If you're like most Americans, you've probably said this once or twice—possibly even in the past twenty-four hours! The question is, what do you need more time to do? Work? Play? Spend time with your spouse and kids? Or is it all three of these as well as about twenty others? The Scriptures tell us to "number our days." Our days on earth may be short; none of us is given any assurance that our marriage will work out or that our spouse or kids will live to see another day. If you lost your spouse tomorrow (either by divorce or death), would you have any regrets about how you used the time you had with him or her? If so, this breakthrough is for you.

A few Saturdays ago, I took my two daughters to a local park to enjoy an afternoon of hiking, in-line skating, and just general goofing off. While sitting on the edge of the sandpile in which my five-year-old was entertaining herself, I noticed one of the young families from our church that had apparently come to the park for the same reason. But they did not appear to be having nearly as much fun as we were. And I knew why. The husband, an Air Force pilot, was preparing to be transferred to Korea for one year, during which time he would be separated from his wife and two young children. As I watched them, I knew what they were trying to do: cram in a few more minutes of togetherness before his quickly approaching departure. (Have you ever noticed how impossible it is to try to have a good time?) I imagined that the family had experienced about all of the togetherness they could stand during the last few days. Nevertheless, they did not dare waste their final hours together and regret not having spent more time with one another.

When the dad's eyes caught mine, he walked over to talk to me.

"How are things going?" I asked, already knowing the answer.

"To be honest, Robert, it's kind of rough. My children seem to be adjusting to the idea of my leaving, but it is really rough on Sharon—and on me."

After talking about all the challenges that lay ahead for both him and his family, I asked him if he would mind sharing some of his thoughts with me on paper. "As you face this separation, what will you miss most about your family?" I normally would not have asked such a potentially painful question, but I knew he was already an avid journaler. Perhaps this catharsis would help him.

The following week he dropped by my office on his way out of town to leave the pages he had penned. The first pages of his thoughts dealt with some of the regrets he knew he would face concerning his kids. But then he wrote about his wife.

If only I had paced myself in my flying job, then I would have a gazillion more minutes with Sharon than I actually have in reserve. I thought what I was doing was important, and it was, but most things I did could have waited until tomorrow, and I could have come home just to be with her. I was saving time to do that by getting ahead, but I got so far ahead, I met myself on the backside leaving as I was showing up again to start. Bad choice to waste time away from God's chosen mate for me.

Work is important, but I have never thought for one second that I should have spent more time at work. In contrast, I have thought on countless occasions that I should have spent more time at home. If only I had helped with dinner more, then Sharon wouldn't have ever thought she was the only cook for our family. If only I had bathed the kids more, then Sharon wouldn't think that she was the bathroom monitor. If only I had gone to the grocery store with her, she wouldn't have had to guess at what treats I would most like to eat.

I was too busy or too noncommittal to go with her. We could have had a lot of fun picking out things together and trying out new stuff, but she got into a routine of going, and I got into a routine of getting out of it any way I possibly could.

It was weird that while on temporary duty assignment, I would go to the grocery store, wash clothes, and cook for myself.

I made the time to do those things because they had to be done by me. They had to be done at home, too, but I rarely invested the time to do the same necessities with my wife. That could have been some valuable time together, but I missed the chance to spend time with her. Now, as I took forward, those decisions to miss out being with her were just plain dumb.

You need to know that the guy who penned these words is not the stereotypical couch potato who sits in a greasy undershirt, belching in front of the TV set. Most people would consider him to be a model husband, father, and Christian leader. Nevertheless, as he faces temporary separation from his wife, he is filled with regrets. Without any effort, he is able to rattle off a number of things he wished he had done differently in his marriage. And I have a hunch that when he returns from his yearlong assignment overseas, he will be a regular at the local supermarket.

Unfortunately, many husbands and wives never have the "luxury" of a prolonged, temporary separation to reorder their priorities. Instead, they are ambushed by illness, divorce, or death and left to spend the remainder of their lives drowning in a sea of "if only's":

If only I had told him more often how much I love him.
If only we had taken that trip together.
If only I had said no to that affair.
If only I had chosen to forgive her.
If only I had built him up instead of always tearing him down.
If only I could take back those hurtful words.
If only we had not divorced.

However, I believe that one way to lessen the pain of the inevitable separation from our mate that we will all experience is to remove as many of the regrets as possible. In this chapter we will examine four important resolves that will help you to experience a regret-free marriage.

1. REFUSE TO DIVORCE.

In a survey I conducted with men in my church about regrets in life, divorce was at the top of the list of the regrets they had in their marriages. Why? Many of them realized that divorce (and even remarriage) did not solve problems; it only created new ones.

That is why I am convinced that the most foundational resolve we can make to experience a regret-free marriage is to remain with our mate.

Our mates are tailor-made by God to complement us, not irritate us.

Occasionally I will open my dresser drawer and discover that my socks have been mismatched or that the dryer has mysteriously sent one sock to the twilight zone, never to be seen again. I have a whole collection of single socks in my drawer that have lost their mates. Matching my socks correctly is quite a challenge because I have so many socks of different colors and materials. However, if I had only one pair of socks, it wouldn't be too difficult to keep them together.

When God created Adam and Eve, there were no spares. He created them "male and female," not "males and females." No Adam, Eve, Jack, Janet, Steve, or Laura, in case things did not work out between the First Couple. No, Adam and Eve were created for one another.

God had promised Adam that He would make "a helper suitable for him" (Genesis 2:18, NIV). The word translated "suitable" could be translated "opposite." God's plan was for the first woman to complement, not duplicate, the first man. Their gifts, their temperaments, their needs would balance one another. And so God "built" Eve (that is what the Hebrew word translated "made" in Genesis 2:22 means) according to some very precise specifications. Given the foreknowledge of

God, I believe God also created Adam to complement his future wife, Eve.

Do you view your mate as God's unique creation for you and you alone? Do you understand that there is no one out there better suited to meet your needs than that husband or wife living under your roof? Only when you truly appreciate God's customized job in creating your spouse does the sometimes murky issue of divorce become more clear.

Every marriage relationship is orchestrated by God.

It is obvious that God arranged the union between Adam and Eve. Moses tells us that God "brought her [Eve] to the man" (Genesis 2:22, NIV). Just as God joined together Adam and Eve, He is still in the business of bringing men and women together today.

I like to recall the unique set of circumstances that God used to bring my wife and me together. Amy was living in Illinois and I was living in Texas when we were in the sixth grade. That summer, Amy's father was given two choices: remain in Illinois or transfer to Texas. He chose Texas. They purchased a home one street over from my parents' home. That meant Amy and I would attend the same junior high school. There were several different seventh-grade math classes, but Amy ended up in mine. There were thirty seats in the classroom. She was assigned to the one in front of me.

Guess what? By "chance" I was the first person she met on her first day in school. And out of the endless possibilities for class assignments in a school of three thousand students, we had every class scheduled together (except P.E.). We immediately began a friendship in that seventh-grade math class that lasted through college and resulted in our marriage.

I imagine you and your mate have a similar story to tell. In fact, I encourage you to sit down some evening with your mate and review all the circumstances that led you two together. No doubt you will see the sovereign hand of God guiding you to your mate.

A commitment to remain together is the first step in experiencing a regret-free marriage, but it is not the only step.

2. MAKE YOUR MATE'S HAPPINESS A PRIORITY.

There are many couples who refuse to divorce yet continue a miserable existence together. I remember reading one amazing study that claimed only 17 percent of marriages could be classified as "happy." Why is that? In a word: selfishness. Whenever you have people with separate agendas, watch out! Friction will result and sparks will fly. You see that in many churches today. The bottom-line cause of practically every conflict in a church is individuals demanding their way in order to satisfy their desires. Bob likes traditional music; Mary wants contemporary music. Jim thinks it is too warm in the sanctuary; Susan believes it is too cold. Joe thinks we need more doctrinal messages; Sara desires more application-oriented studies. Selfishness produces schisms.

James, the half brother of Jesus, explained it this way:

What is the source of quarrels and conflicts among you? Is not the source your pleasures that wage war in your members? (James 4:1, NASB)

Reduce every conflict between people down to its essence, James says, and you will always end up with the same common denominator: selfishness. I want it my way. For just a moment think about the last major argument you had with your mate (and don't play like you never have arguments—I know better). It may have involved money, sex, a decision about how to spend leisure time, or maybe an issue concerning your in-laws. Regardless of the subject, the spark that ignited the conflict was selfishness. You wanted your way; your mate wanted his or her way.

Now, if indeed most marriages are unhappy because of conflict and if the chief reason for unhappiness in marriages is selfishness, it seems that the answer to most unhappiness is placing your mate's interests above your own. And that is exactly what Paul commands in Philippians 2:

> Do nothing from selfishness or empty conceit, but with humility of mind let each of you regard one another as more important than himself, do not merely look out for your own personal interests, but also for the interests of others. (Philippians 2:3–4, NASB)

However, before you can put your mate's interests above your own, you first have to know what his or her interests are. Do you know what is really important to your mate? Maybe it is spending thirty minutes each evening talking without the television blaring in the background. Possibly it's getting to spend some time alone each week engaging in a favorite hobby. Your mate might need a nice vacation every year, even though you can think of many better ways to spend the money. Getting together with other couples might be important to your spouse, even though you would rather spend time alone.

Here's the irony: Consistently placing your desires above your mate's will only produce conflict and unhappiness in your marriage. On the other hand, making your mate's happiness a priority not only brings him or her happiness, but ensures a regret-free marriage for you, as well.

3. AVOID HURTFUL WORDS WITH YOUR MATE.

I heard somewhere that for every hurtful remark made to a family member, it takes four positive statements to counteract the damage. I doubt the validity of that statement. I'm not sure it is ever possible to counteract the emotional damage inflicted by our words. Words are like nails driven into a wall. Even though you may remove the nail, the hole remains. James used another image to communicate the power of our speech:

> And the tongue is a fire, the very world of iniquity; the tongue is set among our members as that which defiles the entire body, and sets on fire the course of our life, and is set on fire by hell. (James 3:6, NASB)

Just as one careless spark can destroy an entire forest, so a careless word can destroy the spirit of a marriage. Many times I have been in counseling sessions where the husband or wife will recall a comment made by their mate years or even decades earlier. Although the perpetrator does not remember the conversation, the wounded party can recall it verbatim.

Paul gives us a wonderful filter through which to pour all of our words to our mate: "Let no unwholesome word proceed from your mouth, but only such a word as is good for edification according to the need of the moment, that it may give grace to those who hear" (Ephesians 4:29, NASB). Using an acrostic originally developed by Alan Redpath, let me share five questions to ask yourself before you make a remark to your spouse:

> **T** Is it True? Earlier in Ephesians 4 Paul says that we need to lay aside all falsehood and speak truth to our mates.

H Is it Helpful? Our goal should be to help, not hinder, our mate.

I Is it Inspiring? Paul says our speech should "edify," literally "build up" our mate, not tear him or her down.

N Is it Necessary? Not every thought needs to be expressed. Paul says only to speak "according to the need of the moment."

K Is it Kind? Even when confrontation is necessary in a marriage, our words should communicate grace to our mate. Paul writes later, "Be kind to one another, tender-hearted, forgiving each other, just as God in Christ also has forgiven you" (Ephesians 4:32, NASB).

4. BUILD MEMORIES WITH YOUR MATE.

An obviously happily married couple was asked to what they owed their successful marriage of thirty years. The husband replied, "We dine out twice a week: candlelight, violins, champagne, the works! Her night is Tuesday; mine is Thursday." Chuckle, chuckle. Yet for many couples that formula is more the rule than the exception. Many couples can identify with comedian Rodney Dangerfield's quip: "My wife and I sleep in separate rooms, we have dinner apart, we take separate vacations. We're doing everything we can to keep our marriage together!"

I will admit that it is necessary, and sometimes helpful, to spend some time apart as a couple. I think that one of the greatest myths about marriage is that when we marry we must become like our mate to have a successful relationship. If he likes to play golf, she should enjoy swinging a nine iron; if she enjoys the opera, he should salivate over *Madame Butterfly*. But the Bible teaches that God gave us a mate to complement us, not to duplicate us (see Genesis 2:18). Don't try to become like your mate, and don't expect your mate to morph into a clone of you. It won't happen. And it shouldn't happen. As we discussed in the previous section, putting your mate's interests before your own means that you need to give them the freedom to pursue those God-given interests that bring pleasure to them.

Nevertheless, don't forget that the primary purpose of marriage was companionship. After God created the plants, the animals, and even Adam, He pronounced His work as "good." But the only thing in God's creation that was labeled "not good" was Adam's loneliness. "It is not good for the man to be alone; I will make him a helper suitable for him" (Genesis 2:18, NASB). Although God gives some people the ability to live without a companion, His plan for most of us includes a mate who will provide companionship, comfort, and affection. Our mate is a gift from God, a gift He wants us to enjoy, not merely endure. Listen to the advice of Solomon, the wisest man who ever lived:

> Enjoy life with the woman whom you love all the days of your fleeting life which He has given to you under the sun; for this is your reward in life and in your toil in which you have labored under the sun. (Ecclesiastes 9:9, NASB)

I see a lot of couples marking time in their marriages. Waiting for the kids to get out of diapers, waiting for the last child to graduate from college, waiting for their children to marry, waiting until the mortgage is paid, waiting to retire, waiting…waiting…waiting. For what? Solomon is saying, "Wake up! Life is quickly passing you by. You don't have to wait to enjoy life." That husband or wife is God's gift for you to enjoy now. Do you have a hobby you both would enjoy? Why not start one today? Do you have a trip you've dreamed of taking together? Borrow the money if you have to and go. There's no guarantee that there will be a tomorrow. As a pastor I deal with many people who have lost their mate. Without exception, those who are able to cope best are those who have a storehouse of memories with their mate from which to draw.

As I write these words I have just returned from conducting the funeral service of a man in our church who suddenly dropped dead from a heart attack. Tears flooded my eyes as I stood at the head of the casket and watched his wife look into the face of her husband one last time, and listened to the uncontrollable sobs of anguish that come at the end of a half century of togetherness. I know that I should have been thinking about her grief, but I could not help but imagine myself in her situation. What would it feel like, what *will* it feel like, to stare at the lifeless body of my mate? I cannot begin to imagine the grief I will feel. But I am determined not to compound that pain with regrets that can be eliminated today by these resolves.

Taken from *Say Good-bye to Regrets* by Robert Jeffress. ©1998 by Robert Jeffress. Used by permission of Multnomah Publishers, Inc. Available at your local Christian bookstore.

What are you waiting for? Too many couples are missing the time of their lives. Grab your spouse and get busy living life to its fullest.

But regrets don't just happen when we fail in our marriages. They happen in every area we don't set our priorities right. This could include our job, our children, our parents, our church, and many other areas of life. Today you've experienced a breakthrough with your marriage. What will it be next? If you're having trouble making that next step, Robert Jeffress's book Say Good-bye to

Regrets *is a great place to start. This is definitely a breakthrough you won't regret experiencing.*

Evaluation Questions

1. Take some time and evaluate where you are in experiencing this breakthrough. Where would you rate yourself on the following scale?

1	5	10
Not even close to experiencing this breakthrough.	I've begun the journey, but I've got a ways to go.	I've experienced a breakthrough, and I'm living the abundant life.

2. What would you consider to be the biggest hindrance to your experiencing this breakthrough right now?

3. What one action should you take to experience this breakthrough right now? I challenge you to do it.

*"Husbands and wives should constantly guard
against overcommitment.
Even worthwhile and enjoyable activities become damaging
when they consume the last ounce of energy or
the remaining free moments in the day."*
JAMES C. DOBSON

"It takes a great man to make a good listener."
ARTHUR HELPS (1813–1875)

*"One of the best ways to demonstrate God's love
is to listen to people."*
BRUCE LARSEN

Rekindle Your Romance

DAVID AND CLAUDIA ARP

I thought the fire was out in my fireplace. I stirred the ashes, and I burned my hands.

ANTONIO MACHADO[1]

Romance between a husband and wife is one of the greatest "symptoms" of a First Chair marriage. It's a symptom because very rarely does romance take place on a regular basis if the rest of the breakthroughs in this section have not been experienced. Does that mean you have to be perfect in order to have romance? Absolutely not! In fact, romance oftentimes burns the hottest after forgiveness has been given by one spouse to another for wrongdoing. But, obviously, we don't want that to be the only time romance shows its beauty in our marriage. We want romance to be a regular part of our married life—day in and day out. If the fires in your marriage aren't stoked on a regular basis, it's a good sign that you're sitting in the Second Chair. Let's read how David and Claudia Arp suggest we move to the First Chair.

*O*ur favorite getaway place in the whole world is a little chalet in the Austrian Alps. That's where we are as we write this chapter. Sometimes we come with no agenda. It's a great place to relax, and in the summer and autumn we take long walks. In the winter, we ski when we have the energy. It's wintertime now. We're not skiing. We're writing. But it helps that we are snowed in. One thing we love about this chalet is the wonderful open fireplace. It has lit our fires more than once. But we're here to work—to write this book. Of course, we do have to work on this chapter on love, and what's a chapter on love without a little research?

Back to our fireplace. It is rather small and the wood burns fast, so we usually burn one log at a time and watch it like a hawk. Yesterday when Dave lit the fire, the log he chose was too long to fit, so he turned it perpendicular to the fireplace and lit it. A bit later Claudia saw the log hanging out of the fireplace and rearranged it so it would continue to burn. Since it had burned for a while, it fit snugly in the fireplace the right way.

Dave walked back into the room, looked at the fire, and said, "Wow! Look how that log moved!"

Logs don't move on their own. If a fire is to keep going, someone has to stoke it. The same is true in our love life— especially in the second half of marriage. If you have a great love life, it's because you fan the flames and stoke the fire! It takes effort, but it gets chilly in a long-term marriage if the coals of passion and love have gone out! We know from time to time our fires have burned uncomfortably low.

It usually happens when we are on overload, like the time we were in Toronto. It started with a call from one of our publishers, asking if we would be willing to do media interviews while we were in Chicago leading our Marriage Alive seminar. What would authors say but, "Yes, we'd love to"?

Another publisher called and wanted us to tack a day of meetings on the front of our trip. They were only a short distance from Chicago. "Sure," we said. "That makes sense." Then the other publisher called back. They had a great opportunity for us to do several TV programs after the ones in Chicago. It would just require a short flight to Toronto. Our aim is to please, so we said, "Of course we can do that. No problem."

We used the extra day we had in Chicago between all these varied activities to do some footwork for our youngest son's impending wedding in Wheaton.

Why do plans sound so good before we live them? Unfortunately, this plan was a killer—and the victim was our love life. Oh, we had good meetings, a great Marriage Alive seminar, and media interviews that all seemed to go well. We found a wonderful place for the wedding rehearsal dinner. At the end of that six-day marathon, we were exhausted but thought we were over the hump. So that night we went out to celebrate.

Claudia, the day lark, needed toothpicks to hold her eyes open, but right in the middle of dinner, Dave, who doesn't always choose the best moments, commented to Claudia, "Now that we are beyond this rush of interviews, we need to work on our love life. Lately we seem to be ignoring that part of our marriage, and I'm concerned."

Claudia, who'd had one more interview than Dave that day, broke into tears. Surely this wasn't happening to the "marriage doctors" who wrote *The Love Book*! Wasn't this the empty nest we'd waited and planned for? Time for each other, time for loving. And why couldn't Dave understand how completely tired Claudia was? Why was he bringing this up? The night was ruined.

Both of us were shocked at our behavior. It was a wake-up call! We loved each other and we loved making love. Yet our schedule was crowding out our intimate times together. What could we do to change this scenario? We had no instant answers, but we had a commitment to each other to find some.

Later that spring, we were on assignment in Vienna, Austria, for three months. We used this time to work on getting control of our life. You don't fix in one day what has taken years to create. And it was more than our love life that needed repairing. We needed to retool our lifestyle and find time for healthy living and for us. We were enthusiastic about the second half of our marriage, and we wanted to be healthy enough to enjoy it.

During our three months in Europe, we slowed down and found more time for each other, and we rediscovered some simple principles for building a creative love life—principles that, frankly, we had been too busy to personally apply. Following are some of our discoveries.

SIX SECRETS OF REKINDLING ROMANCE

Working on your love life has no age barrier. During one of our Marriage Alive seminars, Elizabeth, who had been married for forty years, told us about the struggles in the sexual relationship she shared with her husband: "We were older when we got married. I was twenty-nine and Alfred was thirty-two. We weren't so good in our love life. We tried a number of things that didn't work. I remember reading a book that was supposed to tell us what we needed, and I just wasn't like that. If Alfred had followed that book, he would have been all wrong.

"We were committed to each other, and at one point we gave up watching TV. It was taking up all our free time. As we began to explore different possibilities, I discovered I really liked to cuddle. Then we got a nice stereo system, and that helped put us in the mood and blocked outside noises. Sometimes it's the simple little things that actually made a difference in our love life."

As we work on "romancing" our own marriage and talk to other couples like Elizabeth and Alfred who are in the second half of marriage, we've discovered several key ingredients for rekindling romance in long-term marriages. Hopefully, they will help you stoke your marital fires.

SECRET #1: BE AFFECTIONATE

During a Sweetheart's Banquet at which we were speaking, an elderly couple came up after our talk, and sheepishly the wife told us, "When we were first married, someone suggested we shower together. We tried it and it was so much fun, we've been showering together every morning since."

"Now that we aren't so agile," her husband added, "we can steady each other and prevent falls. Plus, after all the years it's still fun to wash each other's hair and back. The shower is a great place to be affectionate!"

Romance isn't reserved just for the young, and neither is it reserved for the bedroom. Being affectionate, thoughtful, and kind at other times will spill over into your love life. We all like to be nurtured and cherished. Phone calls, notes that say "I love you," cooking your mate's favorite dish, giving a bouquet of flowers, holding hands, a peck on the cheek, a wink across the room, and saying loving and endearing things to each other will add romance to your relationship.

SECRET #2: BE A LISTENER

Two of the most important lovemaking skills and romance enhancers are listening with your heart and talking to your spouse while you are loving each other. Your love life may be active, but if it is all action and no talk, you're missing an added dimension of romance. Tell your mate what you like. Use a little body language. Nobody is a mind reader!

If you find it difficult to talk about the intimate side of your relationship, start by reading a book together. You may find that this is less threatening, and it may open the door for conversation—and who knows what doors conversation may open!

SECRET #3: BE ADVENTURESOME

Add some adventure. Try a little spontaneity. If you always make love in the evening, try mornings. Call in late for work (if your boss will let you) and grab a couple of hours with each other while you are fresh. Plan a middle-of-the-day rendezvous. One couple, both of whom work downtown, took a picnic basket to work and met at a downtown motel on their lunch break. Another couple, on a more austere budget, met during their afternoon break in their car in the parking garage for hugs and kisses. Go on and brainstorm. You're only limited by your imagination! Try some variety in when and where you make love. Remember, variety can be the spice of life. Be explorers.

SECRET #4: BE PLAYFUL

Our friends Dave and Jeanne love rabbits and have four (the stuffed variety) that always travel with them. When we visited them recently, we personally met all their rabbits and discovered rabbit decorating themes all over their house! The rabbits were usually in pairs, just like Dave and Jeanne, who in retirement are usually together. They may be older, but their playful spirit and love of romance have blossomed with years. Romance depends on your attitude and perspective. For instance, Jeanne laughingly said, "What might be considered sexual harassment at work can bring enjoyment and pleasure at home!"

The empty nest is a great time to enter our second childhood. Too often we take our mates and ourselves too seriously. Or we always hurry. Remember, whatever you do to promote romance, getting there is half the fun. Making time for love will help you be good to each other. Take time to unwind from your busy day; make the transition slowly. Go for a walk and hold hands. Stop along the way for a kiss or two. Taking time to kiss and cuddle and laugh and share intimate thoughts during your lovemaking will add romance.

SECRET #5: BE IN SHAPE

In our forties, we realized we weren't as agile as we thought. Stress, teenagers, and yard work had taken their toll. This was about the time Claudia injured her back, requiring several months of therapy. Part of her therapy program was to work out with light weights and do numerous exercises. Not only did this benefit her back, it helped her general physical condition so much that Dave decided (under duress) to join her.

Having lived on overload for so long, it seemed strange to take time to work out together. But it has had great benefits—even in the bedroom!

Sometimes romance in the empty nest is zapped by the battle of the bulge. As we age, it's natural, regardless of what the TV ads say, to put on a little padding. Thin may be "in" in our culture, but for the older population, being too thin can be a health hazard. Whatever our scales register, we can improve our fitness and firmness by regular exercise. Fitness walking several times each week gives us energy and helps us stay in shape. Face it, when you feel good about your body, you feel better about romance! So we encourage you to keep physically fit. Walk and exercise for your love life. You won't regret it!

Note: Not everything is cured by walking and exercise. If you have a medical problem or take medication that interferes with your love life, talk with your physician. There may be a simple solution, and it's certainly to your benefit to check it out! A yearly physical is a good investment in the health of your marriage.

SECRET #6: BE A LITTLE WACKY

What can you do to jolt your own established patterns? What can you do that is a little out of character? A fun getaway at Shakertown in Kentucky was a little out of character for us. To appreciate this romantic interlude, you need to know your history. Shakertown is basically a museum because the population has totally died out. You see, they practiced celibacy. Each house had separate doors for the women and for the men. Everything was separate. Just walking through the old houses and buildings in the town gave us a real feeling of history. As we stood for some time in the little graveyard, we wondered what kinds of lives those people experienced. Did they have romantic feelings for each other? Did they fall in love? Did they slip away and break the celibacy rules?

Later that evening, as we broke the rules, we thought, *What a great location for empty-nest couples who want to do something creative that is just a little off the wall.* If you live near Kentucky, we recommend Shakertown, but wherever you live, we recommend a weekend getaway. Nothing helps revive romance like focused time away together.

If your budget is limited, be creative. Our friends Joseph and Linda love camping getaways. Other couples trade houses and condos. Maybe you have adult children who would loan you their homes when they are away. When our oldest son and daughter-in-law lived in Williamsburg, Virginia, they offered us their apartment when they were going to be away for several weeks. Imagine our surprise when we arrived to find the table romantically set for two, with candles and their best china! Go on and think creatively. Plan a getaway for yourselves!

LEARN TO PACE YOURSELF

We look forward to growing old together and loving each other along the way, but we are learning that if that is going to happen, we must pace ourselves. We try to control our schedule instead of having it control us, as in our Toronto experience. But there are still times we must fly a lot or make multiple trips. Recently we knew it was time to regroup when we got on the hotel elevator and punched the number for the floor our room was on in the previous city! But even though we still get in hectic situations, we are handling them with a little more savvy. For example, on a recent business trip to Grand Rapids, Michigan, we set our alarm and got up early, and before our long, hectic day of meetings, we took time for us. Making personal time for ourselves before we started made the whole day go better.

The next city, we continued to invest time in us. That Saturday morning in Minneapolis, we took a long walk. We mean a really long walk! As we walked, we talked and forgot how far we were walking. Exhausted but relaxed, we got back to our room about noon to get ready for our afternoon meeting. We had left the Do Not Disturb sign on our door all morning, because we wanted to shower and freshen up before the maid cleaned our room.

At about 1:00 P.M. we left our room and took the sign off our door. As we were walking down the hall, Dave was still talking about how far we had walked when he said, "Claudia, you wore me out! We overdid it! You did me in!"

"Well," Claudia responded, "I feel great! I feel invigorated!"

We ran into the maid, so Dave told her, "We're out of room 401 for a little while. You can clean it now."

The maid's funny look clued us in that she had heard our entire conversation. Guess she wondered what this older couple had been doing in their room all morning! We laughed all the way to our car.

As we reflected on our trip to Toronto and then on our trip to Grand Rapids and Minneapolis, we thought, two stressful trips but two completely different experiences. What made the difference? We had learned to pace ourselves, to make personal time a priority, and to find time for loving each other.

We hope you will find time to pace yourself, to stoke your own fire, and to make your love relationship a priority. Take it from our friends Dave and Jeanne: It can just keep getting better and better as the years go by. "Romance doesn't have to die out," said Dave. "It can grow and blossom through all your married years if you continue to show your love in physical ways plus loving words and deeds. God designed man and woman to enjoy each other in marriage, and we find that enjoyment still growing after forty-five years of marriage."

Let us encourage you to fan the fires of romance. You never know where it might lead. Go on and take the risk. Stoke your own fire, and enjoy marriage with your lover and your best friend!

Taken from *The Second Half of Marriage* by Dave and Claudia Arp. ©1996 by Dave and Claudia Arp. Used by permission of Zondervan Publishing House. Available at your local Christian bookstore.

Do you see some things you can begin doing right now to encourage romance in your marriage? But now the tough part begins—*actually doing it. If it's been a while since romance has been seen in your home, it might be tough to bring it back around at first. But keep going. Soon you'll find that romance keeps getting easier and easier. If it doesn't, go back through this section and see if you experienced these breakthroughs. They will go a long way toward reestablishing romance in your marriage. If you're just now experiencing that empty-nest feeling, you may have been more focused on the kids for the last twenty years than on romance with your spouse. If that's where you are, I suggest you take a look at the Arps' book* The Second Half of Marriage. *It will help you stoke those flames of romance even after the kids are gone.*

EVALUATION QUESTIONS

1. Take some time and evaluate where you are in experiencing this breakthrough. Where would you rate yourself on the following scale?

1	5	10
Not even close to experiencing this breakthrough.	I've begun the journey, but I've got a ways to go.	I've experienced a breakthrough, and I'm living the abundant life.

2. What would you consider to be the biggest hindrance to your experiencing this breakthrough right now?

3. What one action should you take to experience this breakthrough right now? I challenge you to do it.

1. Gabriel Calvo, *Face to Face* (St. Paul, Minn.: Int. Marriage Encounter, 1988), 19.

Experiencing Spiritual Breakthroughs in Your Family

"In no order of things is adolescence the simple time of life."
JOAN ERSKINE STEWART

"Honor is a gift we give to others.
It isn't purchased by their actions or contingent on our emotions."
GARY SMALLEY

"Fifty years from now it will not matter
what kind of car you drove, what kind of house you lived in,
how much you had in your bank account, or
what your clothes looked like.
But the world may be a little better because you were
important in the life of a child."
ANONYMOUS

Honor Your Children as Priceless Treasures

GARY AND GREG SMALLEY

This is perhaps the most difficult yet rewarding breakthrough a parent can experience. For many parents, their teenagers seem to be in a different world. There's the old generation-gap problem, but it seems to be deeper than that. And, to be honest with you, it probably is. Many teenagers are angry. You've probably tried many different ways to get through to them, all to no avail. That's why we've decided to deal with this parental breakthrough first. For those parents whose children aren't teenagers yet, I suggest you apply these principles now—don't wait until they're teenagers. You might just be able to avoid the problems many families experience during the teen years.

*D*uring several summers of the Smalley kids' high school years, they attended an outstanding sports camp called Kanakuk Kamp in Branson, Missouri. Their time at camp transformed their lives. And the reason Kanakuk had such an impact is that the staff and counselors are prime examples of honor. Everything they did helped the Smalley teenagers feel highly valued. All the children who attend camp win awards and ribbons, and the hugs and encouragement they receive are works of art.

In addition to demonstrating honor, the counselors teach lessons about things like spirituality, good sportsmanship, and the consequences of premarital sex. The Smalley teens' favorite lesson, however—the one that had the most profound impact on their lives—was about the "I'm Third" principle. The camp staff and counselors all strive to demonstrate this principle, which is exemplified by the heroic story they recount of an Air National Guard pilot named Johnny Ferrier.

The following is an account of a day Johnny Ferrier had been preparing for all his life. The story was originally featured in the *Denver Post* in the late 1950s.

Out of the sun, packed in a diamond formation and flying as one that day, the Minute Men dove at nearly the speed of sound toward a tiny emerald patch on Ohio's unwrinkled crazy quilt below. It was a little after nine in the morning of June 7, 1958, and the target of the Air National Guard's jet precision team was the famed Wright Patterson Air Force Base, just outside Dayton.

On the ground, thousands of faces looked upward as Colonel Wait Williams, leader of the Denver-based Sabre-jet team, gauged the high-speed pullout. For the Minute Men pilots—Colonel Wait Williams, Captain Bob Cherry, Lieutenant Bob Odle, Captain John Ferrier, and Major Win Coomer—the maneuver was routine, for they had given their show hundreds of times before millions of people.

Low across the fresh, green grass the jet team streaked, far ahead of the noise of the planes' own screaming engines. Judging his pull-up, Colonel Williams pressed the microphone button on top of his throttle: "Smoke on...now!" The diamond of planes pulled straight up into the turquoise sky, a bush tail of white smoke pluming out behind. The crowd gasped as the four ships suddenly split apart, rolling to the four points of the compass and leaving a beautiful, smoky fleur-de-lis inscribed on the heavens. This was the Minute Men's famed "flower burst" maneuver. For a minute the crowd relaxed, gazing at the tranquil beauty of the huge, white flower that had grown from the lush Ohio grasslands to fill the great bowl of sky.

Out on the end of his arm of the flower, Colonel Williams turned his Sabre hard, cut off the smoke trail, and dropped the nose of his F-86 to pick up speed for the low-altitude crossover maneuver. Then, glancing back over his shoulder, he froze in terror. Far across the sky to the east, John Ferrier's plane was rolling. He was in trouble. And his plane was headed right for the small town of Fairborn, on the edge of Patterson Field. In a moment, the lovely morning had turned to horror. Everyone saw; everyone understood. One of the planes was out of control.

Steering his jet in the direction of the crippled plane to race after it, Williams radioed urgently, "Bail out, John! Get out of there!" Johnny still had plenty of time and room to eject safely. Twice more Williams issued the command: "Bail out, Johnny! Bail out!"

Each time, Williams was answered only by a blip of smoke.

He understood immediately. John Ferrier couldn't reach the mike button on the throttle because both hands were tugging on a control stick locked in full-throw right. But the smoke button was on the stick, so he was answering the only way he could—squeezing it to tell Walt he thought he could keep his plane under enough control to avoid crashing into the houses of Fairborn.

Suddenly, a terrible explosion shook the earth. Then came a haunting silence. Walt Williams continued to call through the radio, "Johnny? Are you there? Captain. Answer me!"

No response.

Captain John T. Ferrier's Sabre jet had hit the ground midway between four houses, in a backyard garden. It was the only place where he could have crashed without killing people. The explosion had knocked a woman and several children to the ground, but no one had been hurt with the exception of Johnny Ferrier. He had been killed instantly.

Major Win Coomer, who had flown with Ferrier for years, both in the Air National Guard and on United Airlines, and had served a combat tour with him in Korea, was the first Minute Man to land. He raced to the crash scene, hoping to find his friend alive.

Instead, he found a neighborhood in shock from the awful thing that had happened. But then Coomer realized that the people felt no resentment, as is ordinarily the case when a peaceful community is torn by a crash. A steady stream of people began coming to him as he stood in his flying suit beside the smoking, gaping hole in the ground where his best friend had just died.

"A bunch of us were standing together, watching the show," an elderly man with tears in his eyes told Coomer. "When the pilot started to roll, he was headed straight for us. For a second, we looked right at each other. Then he pulled up right over us and put it in there." And in deep humility the old man whispered, "This man died for us."

It had been a bold and courageous last act. But it was not an act alien to the nature of John Ferrier. He had been awarded one of the nation's highest medals for risking his life "beyond the call of duty" in Korea. An although he hadn't known it, he'd been preparing for this tragic day for years by practicing this most important principle:

"'You shall love the Lord your God with all your heart, and with all your soul, and with all your mind.' This is the great and foremost commandment. 'The second is like it, You shall love your neighbor as yourself.'" (Matthew 22:37–39, NASB)

A few days after Johnny's death, his wife, Tulle, wrote the founder of Kanakuk Kamp, Coach Bill Lantz, this letter:

> Coach, I went through my husband's billfold last night and found the old worn card which he always carried— "I'M THIRD." He told me once he got it from you. He said that you stressed it at one of your camp sermons. Johnny may have had faults, though they were few and minor, but he followed that creed to the very end. God is first, the other fellow second, and "I'm third." Not just on June 7, 1958, but long before that—certainly as long as I've known him. I'm going to carry that same card with me from now on and see if it won't serve as a reminder. I shouldn't need it, but I'm sure I do as I have many more faults than Johnny.

The principle by which Johnny Ferrier lived and died is also the greatest lesson you can teach your teenager. At the heart of making others feel valuable, loved, and accepted is a decision to honor them, even above ourselves. To teach honor, however, we must have a clear, concrete understanding of what it means to honor someone.

WHAT IS HONOR?

When you think of honoring someone, you may envision attending your teen's award dinner, asking a famous celebrity for an autograph, or cheering for your favorite team. You may also think of honor as a feeling of respect that goes in only one direction—usually toward a superior or someone who has "earned" or "deserves" it. But honor can be passed on to loved ones regardless of whether they deserve it, because, like love, it's an act of the will

Honor simply means deciding to place high value, worth, and importance on another person by viewing him or her as a priceless gift and granting him or her a position in our lives worthy of great respect.

In other words, honor is a gift we give to others. It isn't purchased by their actions or contingent on our emotions. It may carry strong emotional feelings, but it doesn't depend on them. Rather, it's a decision we make daily toward someone who is special and valuable to us.

As with genuine love, honor is one of the greatest gifts we can provide. In fact, honor is genuine love in action. To honor a person involves choosing to highly value him or her even before we put love into action. In many cases, love often begins to flow once we've decided to honor that person.

THREE WAYS TO HONOR TEENAGERS

One way to communicate honor is to grant each child a high place in our lives and the loving respect that accompanies it. A second is to look upon each teen as a priceless treasure. The third is to understand that to help teenagers develop honor, they must see us demonstrate it. Let's consider each of these methods in detail.

1. Place your teenager in a highly respected position.

One time when I (Greg) was in junior high, Mom and Dad made a simple decision that would have a far greater positive impact on me than they realized at the time. They decided that Dad would take me along to a conference of professional athletes at which he was speaking. At one point in our time there, while we were walking through the hotel, a football landed nearby. When I turned around, my jaw dropped and I almost fell over. Standing in front of me was my favorite football star, number 80 for the Seattle Seahawks, Steve Largent, who was later inducted into the NFL Hall of Fame.

It was like a fantasy come true. And as if that weren't exciting enough, Steve then talked and played catch with me for about an hour. Finally, to top off the perfect day, Steve gave me an autographed picture. Before I went to bed that night, I vowed to wear the number 80 if I ever got to play organized football.

Dad's taking me with him to the conference and introducing me to all the players was an act of honor. He was placing me—literally, in this case—in a highly respected position. Hearing my name coming from Dad's lips when meeting Steve Largent and others communicated that he thought enough of me to use my name with them and that I was worth their taking the time to meet me.

Early one summer morning a few years later, Mom woke me up at 5:30, just as I had begged her to do. The first day of freshman football practice had arrived, and it was terribly important for me to be first in line to get my equipment. I knew I was about to be assigned the number that would identify me forever (or at least through my high school football career). I had dreamed about this day for months, because only Steve Largent's number 80 would do. I had to get that number.

Practice started at 7:00 sharp, and I was standing in front of the equipment shed by 6:00. Fortunately, number 80 was still available, and my dream came true. Throughout my high school days, I would be identified with the hero I had met years before because my mom and dad had chosen to put me in a position of high respect.

Even if you've unknowingly been in the habit of dishonoring your teen, you can choose today to stop the devastating effects of dishonor—even reverse them—by giving your teen the gift of honor.

2. See your teenager as a priceless treasure.

A second way to communicate honor to our teens is to see and treat each of them as a priceless treasure. We honor God by recognizing that His worth is beyond any price. Similarly, we honor our teenagers by considering them to be special gifts God has entrusted to us, as the Scriptures declare (Psalm 127:3).

We encourage you to remind your teenagers daily how valuable they are. If possible, give them a ring, a wall plaque, or something else that will remind them daily of their high value in your eyes.

Why is it so important to view our teens as special treasures? Because "where your treasure is, there your heart will be also" (Matthew 6:21). Whatever we highly value naturally attracts our affections, desires, and enthusiasm. Likewise, when we learn to treasure our teenagers, our positive feelings for them go up as well.

To get a better handle on what we mean by treasuring someone, imagine that you owned a priceless painting. You would make it the center of attention in your home. You would protect it by making sure it was hung securely and away from direct exposure to the sun. You would highlight it with indirect lighting and a subtle yet elegant frame. You would certainly brag about it to your friends and family because it meant so much to you. You would constantly feel grateful for the opportunity to possess something so marvelous and valuable. Just coming home from work and looking at it would raise your spirits.

Parents who treasure their teenagers respond to them in many of the same ways. When you treasure a person, you want to protect her. You'll go out of your way to see that she succeeds. You'll highlight her best points, mentioning her frequently in conversations. The thought of coming home to see her after a long day at work will give you energy.

Isn't it interesting how inanimate objects such as paintings tend to keep their value over the years, whereas living objects like teenagers often see their value drop? The decision to treat teens as priceless treasures sometimes has to be made hourly. But it pays rich dividends.

We've looked at placing teens in a highly respected place and treating them as priceless treasure. Now let's turn our attention to a third way to communicate honor. We've saved the most important for last.

3. Demonstrate honor in your actions.

As we seek to communicate and teach honor to our teenagers, it's vital for us to understand that honor can't really be taught with words. Our kids must see it demonstrated in our actions. Thus, modeling is the best way to communicate honor.

Teenagers are incredibly perceptive about what we parents do. When it looks as if we value the house, job, car, or poodle more than them, our actions speak much louder than our words of love and honor.

I (Gary) had to continually remember the importance of modeling when my children were teenagers. They watched me all the time to see if my actions matched my words. One day while I was trying to take a nap, I learned a valuable lesson in this regard. I didn't want to be disturbed, so I had instructed my two boys to leave me alone. Looking back, that probably wasn't the best choice of words. It had the same effect as throwing fresh meat on the floor and instructing two puppies to stay. The problem was that my boys had seen me play plenty of practical jokes on others. I was in real trouble!

As I was sleeping comfortably in my chair, Greg and Michael determined this would be an excellent opportunity to give me a taste of my own medicine. They sneaked up behind me and poured warm water down my throat as I lay snoring. As I started to choke and gag, the boys ducked behind my chair. Dazed from being forced out of deep sleep, I was confused about what I had just swallowed. Then it hit me. I was hemorrhaging! I must be having a massive nosebleed!

To keep from dripping blood all over the floor, I cupped my hand over my face and ran toward the bathroom. After crashing into the coffee table and tripping over our dog on the way, I finally made it to the sink. Because I didn't want to faint at the sight of all my blood, I slowly removed my hands and exposed…nothing.

Where's all the blood? I thought as I carefully surveyed my body. I was sure I had felt a large amount of liquid gushing down my throat, so I had anticipated seeing quarts of blood flowing from my nose.

"What's going on?" I yelled.

Then it dawned on me. "Where are Michael and Greg?"

When I returned from the bathroom, I heard snickering coming from behind the chair. "Get out here!" I ordered. "Do you have any idea how dangerous that was?" I challenged after they had moved into the open.

My first instinct was to ground the boys for a year, yell at them for being so irresponsible, and finally shame them with a few choice words. After all, they'd almost given me a heart attack! But as I stood there facing them, I suddenly remembered all the times I had played jokes on them. It was fair turnabout.

As I was reminded that day, what we do as parents has a tremendous influence on our kids. In areas both trivial and vitally important, they imitate our behavior. Thus, if we want to help our teens learn how to honor God, others, and themselves, we must first demonstrate it. Before I really started to learn the significance of honor, I had to ask for forgiveness so many times. Finally, I realized that honoring my kids right off kept me from constantly needing to ask for forgiveness.

If your teenagers are to develop a Johnny Ferrier-like appreciation of honor, they first need to see it in you. We're not saying they shouldn't honor people unless they're honored first. But it's a fact of life that teens (or any children) rarely do something they haven't first seen done by their parents. Common sense tells us this, as well as the research literature. For example, the aggression children observe in their families while growing up influences the amount and type of aggression in their own marriages.[1] Similarly, how people handle pain seems to be influenced by how important people in their lives have dealt with it.[2]

Since what parents do has such an impact on their children, we encourage you to teach by example. Provide your teenagers with a model of how others are to be honored.

Bound by Honor by Gary and Greg Smalley, a Focus on the Family book published by Tyndale House Publishers. ©1998 by Gary Smalley and Greg Smalley. All rights reserved. International copyright secured. Used by permission. Available at your local Christian bookstore.

Many people interpret the second greatest command (to "love your neighbor as yourself") to mean that they have to love themselves before they can properly love others. But think about what Johnny Ferrier would have done if he loved himself first! Those people on the ground who saw his plane coming straight for them were very thankful Johnny loved himself last.

In the early stages, raising children is often a selfless job. But as the kids get older, we are tempted to return to our selfish ways. It's time to put ourselves third. What would it say to your spouse and children if you made a point of coming home on time from work? It would say they are more important than work and money. You don't have to set aside your responsibilities as a parent to honor your family. You just have to set aside your selfish ambition. We desperately need all parents to experience this breakthrough. If you'd like to read more about working with your teenagers, I recommend Greg and Gary Smalley's book Bound by Honor. *It will help you experience even more breakthroughs in your relationships with your teens.*

EVALUATION QUESTIONS

1. Take some time and evaluate where you are in experiencing this breakthrough. Where would you rate yourself on the following scale?

1	5	10
Not even close to experiencing this breakthrough.	I've begun the journey, but I've got a ways to go.	I've experienced a breakthrough, and I'm living the abundant life.

2. What would you consider to be the biggest hindrance to your experiencing this breakthrough right now?

3. What one action should you take to experience this breakthrough right now? I challenge you to do it.

1. D. Kalmuss, "The Intergenerational Transmission of Marital Aggression," *Journal of Marriage and the Family* 46 (1984), 11–19.

2. K. D. Craig, "Social Modeling Influences: Pain in Context," in *The Psychology of Pain,* ed. R. A. Sternbach (New York: Raven Press, 1986), 67–95.

"All the Christian virtues are locked up in the word prayer.*"*
CHARLES HADDON SPURGEON (1834–1892)

*"Give me the children until they are seven and
anyone may have them afterward."*
SAINT FRANCIS XAVIER (1506–1552)

*"Children want their parents more than they want the junk we
buy them."*
JAMES C. DOBSON

*"Don't panic even during the storms of adolescence.
Better times are ahead."*
JAMES C. DOBSON

"Give a little love to a child and you get a great deal back."
JOHN RUSKIN (1819–1900)

*"Many children are afraid to go to their parents for counsel.
Parents many times treat children as children when they often
need to be talked to like grown-ups."*
BILLY GRAHAM

Persevere as a Proactive Parent

DENNIS AND BARBARA RAINEY

There are a lot of books out there about how to become an effective parent. Some of them are quite good, but many of them miss the mark. Just what does it take to be effective in our parenting? How do we produce godly offspring? Well, we can't just hope that it happens; if that's all we do, it won't happen. Your first priority must be to follow the Bible: instruct and "tell them what the Lord has done." Tell them what He's done in your life; tell them what He's done in the Bible; have friends tell them what He's done in their lives. Soon they'll start to understand that God really does affect our lives, and they will want to have those things happen in their lives. But that's only the first step. Our good friends Dennis and Barbara Rainey share seven priorities of parenthood that will help you experience a breakthrough in becoming an effective parent.

Let's pretend we are old friends who, after years apart, have just bumped into each other while making connections at O'Hare International Airport in Chicago. After exchanging greetings, you tell us your oldest child will soon be a teenager. We nod and smile. "Been there. Done that. Several times."

"Say, what can you tell us about successfully raising teenagers?" you ask with a nervous laugh. "Some of our friends tell us it's horrible."

We all look at our watches—thirty minutes until you board your flight for Hawaii and we head back to Little Rock. You offer to buy the Starbucks coffee.

Here's our best shot—seven guiding priorities to embrace every day of your child's preadolescent and adolescent years.

The coffee is hot, your pen and notepad are ready, here goes.

PRIORITY 1: PRAYER

This one probably does not surprise you. But before you glance at your watch and start tapping your foot, please consider carefully what we have gleaned from parenting six teens.

The sobering news about raising children is that we really have no ultimate control over whether our child will choose the narrow gate "that leads to life" (Matthew 7:14, NIV) or the wide gate that leads to destruction. If other experiences in life have not humbled us and shown us how dependent we are on God, then parenting a preadolescent or teenager will.

But understanding our desperate need to depend on God is the good news. Once we give up the naive idea that we parents can dictate the choices our children will make and the spiritual gate—narrow or broad—they will walk through, then we are ready to slip on the knee pads and get serious about prayer.

What have we learned about prayer for our children as they prepare for and enter adolescence?

Pray regularly. Bring every concern, dream, desire about your child to God in fervent, persistent prayer. (Luke 18:1–8 contains a great parable on persistent prayer that must have been told just for parents of teenagers.)

Two of the best times to pray with your child are on the way to school (assuming you drive him or her) and at bedtime—regardless of age. We live about five miles from our school. Every morning we would pray about things most important to our children: tests, friends, teachers, activities. As the car topped the hill right before the school building, we always concluded with the same request: "And, Lord, we ask that you would keep Rebecca, Deborah, and Laura from harm, evil, and temptation this day. That they would experience You at work in their lives and be used by You to influence others for Your Kingdom. Amen."

Now that our teenagers drive themselves to school, we use breakfast for this prayer time.

Bedtime prayers can be more personal for each child. Pray for his or her future mate, relationships, activities, challenges, temptations, and heart for God. Don't assume that even a teenager is too big for you to kneel beside the bed and stroke his or her face and pray.

Pray offensively. Before your child hits adolescence, pray for his peer group, that he or she will have at least one strong Christian buddy for the teenage years. Ask God to protect your child daily from others who would be an evil influence. Also consider asking God to help you spot your child doing things right so that you can encourage him or her in making right choices.

Pray defensively. On more than one occasion we have sought the Lord's help in removing a friend of questionable character from a child's life.

From time to time we have felt that one of our teens might be deceiving us, but we could never be absolutely certain. In those situations we have asked God to help us catch him if he's doing something wrong. God seems to feel sorry for parents who pray this prayer!

Pray intensely. One of the most misunderstood spiritual disciplines of the Christian life is prayer accompanied with fasting (the giving up of food for a prescribed period of time). Although fasting does not earn points with God, He nonetheless assumes in Scripture that we will fast and pray (see Matthew 6:16–18) and promises to reward us if we do it correctly. We know a couple who have set aside each Monday to fast—sunup until sundown—and pray for their struggling fourteen-year-old child.

Pray when God brings your child to mind and burdens you. It may be at that very moment your child is facing a circumstance of critical importance. Some friends of ours were burdened one night to pray for their daughter. At the very time they slipped out of bed and to their knees, a police car was driving by their daughter's car on a remote mountain road where she and a girlfriend had gone to look at the city lights, eat a sandwich, and talk. Unknown to them, an escaped prisoner was hiding underneath the car. The girls drove off unharmed, and the prisoner was apprehended.

Pray with your child. It's easy for prayer to become an exclusive dialogue: you and God. Why not do what one mom, Nina, did with her teenage daughter, Natalie, and become prayer partners. Natalie's teenage years were filled with special moments where she and her mom knelt together and prayed over Natalie's struggles and challenges.

Pray together as a couple. For more than twenty-six years of marriage we have ended every day we're together in prayer. No spiritual discipline has protected our marriage and our family more than this daily time of communion together with God.

Three of our six children have made it through adolescence. With that behind us, you might think we are tempted to coast to the finish line. Hardly. We've been humbled so many times that we know how impossible it is for us to shape the hearts of our children. We pray more than ever for our children—all of them.

God wants the same thing for you and your child. Talk to Him. "The effective prayer of a righteous man can accomplish much" (James 5:16, NASB).[1]

PRIORITY 2: STANDARDS

We are amazed at how many moms and dads have never had a focused conversation on what the specific boundaries and standards will be for their child during the preadolescent and teen years. Regularly in our sixth-grade Sunday school class we were shocked by the choices children were making. One Sunday over half the class of sixty eleven- and twelve-year-olds admitted that they had viewed an R-rated movie in the last three months. Many watched the movie with their parents.

Have you and your spouse talked about dating, driving, jobs, grades, curfews, friends, and after-school activities? The list seems endless at times. We promise this: If you don't nail down your own convictions ahead of time, your teenager and his peer group will establish their own!

If you have not agreed as a couple upon guidelines, your child will soon hit you with the divide-and-conquer strategy. Children are experts on whether Dad or Mom has the easy touch on certain issues.

Even when you know you should be united as a couple

and clear on the rules, you may still stumble. I took one of our daughters shopping for some shorts. As I waited outside the dressing room at the department store, another child, who looked to be about thirteen, came out to model shorts for her mom. Those shorts were aptly named—they looked incredibly short to me. Then our daughter came out. Compared to what I had just witnessed, her pair seemed acceptable.

When we got home, our daughter modeled her new outfit for the rest of the family. One of our sons said, "Dad! I can't believe you let her buy those. They're too short!"

Barbara agreed. In the area of clothing, we have a policy: a particular piece of clothing must pass the approval of both parents (an opinion of a brother or sister is appreciated usually, but is not a binding vote) before it goes into the permanent wardrobe. I had blown it but was saved by our shared conviction. Amid frowns and protests, the shorts went back to the store.

PRIORITY 3: INVOLVEMENT

We are not suggesting that you become the ultimate soccer mom. That's not bad—being there at all of your child's activities—but involvement means much more than driving the car pool and never missing a dance recital.

Involvement means crawling inside your child's head and heart. Involvement is moving from the exterior to the interior of an adolescent's life. Involvement means diving into the turbulent currents caused by emotions—the child's and the parent's. Soul to soul. Heart to heart. This can be scary and uncomfortable.

The sobering truth is that you can be in the same house, the same gym, but be clueless about what's really going on in your child's life. Although it's a humbling thought, consider beginning with this assumption: "I'm not involved in my child's life. I don't really know what's going on."

It may mean trying to get into your child's life and being thwarted by the child. Pushed out. Locked out. The child, emotionally confused, doesn't know what he or she wants or needs. We've been there.

You may have to endure a time or two when your child is screaming at you, when you just want to say, "You're grounded for a month," and run from the messy details of a relationship. This is hard, and it's why so many parents give up.

Involvement also means not losing heart when you don't see immediate results. When a child is not living according to what's acceptable, many parents surrender. They settle for less. Lower their standards. And stop pressing the child. They end up compromising, shrugging their shoulders, and saying with a sigh, "Maybe my goals and standards for my teenager were unrealistic. I guess what he's doing is not that bad."

Connecting with your teenager may be one of the most demanding challenges of your life. Even after raising three adolescents, I still struggle with involvement. Just recently, after Barbara told me I was too busy, I sensed my relationship with a daughter was slipping away. I was losing touch. I've had to commit myself to reconnection. I overhauled my schedule. I'm back doing things she wants to do, like taking her fishing, having date nights, and just hanging out talking.

Reconnecting can be something as simple as walking into your child's bedroom and just sitting there, asking a few questions, and then listening. Really listening. Like recently when Barbara went on a date with Rebecca: They sat at a Sonic drive-in, munching on fries, and Rebecca soaked up the one-on-one time. She needed the attention.

Pursuing a heart-to-heart relationship is usually rewarding. Although some of the information may be unsettling, you will know your child. And in knowing, you will be able to pray with power and minister to your preteen's or teen's needs.

PRIORITY 4: TRAINING

The best parenting is proactive, not reactive.

The reactive parent stays in a defensive posture, continually reacting to a child's mistakes. A proactive parent goes on the offensive and does what is necessary to become the child's trainer.

Effective training involves at least three parts.

First, parents need to see the goal clearly. They need to know what they are trying to achieve. Most parents have never written a mission statement for what they are trying to build into their children. It's no wonder so many parents feel like failures or don't really know if they've succeeded or not.

Shortly after we started our family, I recall how I began to develop a list of everything I wanted to teach our children. I started with a list of twenty-five things that soon ballooned to more than fifty. It was a good exercise, but it was overwhelming. In addition, Barbara was frustrated with me because I had developed the list and she hadn't really been involved in shaping it.

Months later we went away for a weekend and wrote down separately what each of us wanted to build into our children. Both of us ended up with a prioritized top-ten values list. We then got together and worked our way through a unified list of our top five values. That list has proved to be the North Star for our parenting.

Second, effective training involves repetition. A Green

Beret once told me, "As Green Berets we train to learn what to do, in every conceivable circumstance, over and over and over again. Then in times of battle we know what to do. It's just second nature to us."

That is a picture of what we parents should do. We train our children and instruct them in making the right choices in the circumstances they will face. And we do it over and over.

Repeated training situations should begin early in your preteen's life. Seize the window of opportunity—the eighteen months or so when your child is between ten and twelve—to run your own boot camp to prepare him for the traps. Do not underestimate the capability of a child this age to understand truth and develop personal convictions.

Continue training all the way through the adolescent years. There's a danger in assuming that the standards don't need to be revisited often as your child advances through high school. You may need to find fresh ways of repackaging what you teach, but don't stop teaching.

Finally, training involves accountability. One of the major mistakes made is giving our children too much freedom without appropriate oversight. This is especially true if a family has more than two children. We tend to overcontrol our firstborn child and release the younger children prematurely.

My mom was the master at accountability during my teenage years. She demanded to know where I was and what I was doing. I can still hear her saying, "Where are you going? Who will be there? What time will you be home?" And my dad was right in there with her. The first night that I was allowed to go out alone in the car, he wrote down the mileage on the odometer and gave me a five-mile maximum limit.

There is an old saying: You cannot expect that which you

do not inspect. One of our biggest regrets as parents is not doing a better job of inspecting what we expected with each of our preteens and teenagers.

PRIORITY 5: COMMUNITY

We have become increasingly convinced and alarmed that one of the most damaging changes that has occurred in recent years is the loss of community in raising our children. We used to look out for the children of others far more than we do now.

I remember when I was growing up in Ozark, Missouri, population thirteen hundred, in the 1960s that if I peeled out from a stop sign at 8:00 P.M. any night of the week, month, or year, by 9:30 P.M. when I parked in the driveway, I could expect my parents to know about it. One night I got into a fight at the Dairy Queen. Fifteen minutes later, when I walked through the door at home, they already knew what had happened.

This type of involvement is rare today. Humorist Garrison Keillor has said, "Adults no longer dare to influence other people's children. You should be able to discipline another person's child, up to a point. Children are supposed to be raised by all sorts of people."[2]

Keillor uses a key phase, "adults no longer dare." We have developed the philosophy that we have no right to tell another parent about a concern we have about his or her child. And children suffer from our failure to be involved in the lives of others.

We've called parents about behavior we have observed in their children and had them tell us they "didn't want to hear it." They didn't want to know. One parent angrily chewed me out for calling about something his son had done that was clearly wrong.

We need to drop our defensiveness and fear, and encourage others to offer observations to us about how our children are doing when we're not there to see for ourselves. Take the initiative by telling the parents of friends of your child, "If you see my teenager doing anything questionable, you have the freedom to tell me. I want to know."

It took us several adolescent projects in our own family to learn how much we needed the help of others to monitor and correct our children. Friends, true friends, have cared enough to courageously call and express a concern about something they've seen one of our children doing that they knew we wouldn't approve of. Those are tough phone calls to make. And tough to receive. But in each and every case we've seen God use these circumstances to help us keep a child out of a threatening trap.

There is a natural community that we need to do a better job of tapping into for our children's accountability: our church. Certainly this group of folks ought to have the right perspective on the value and worth our children possess. We are in this thing together, and that should pertain especially to raising the generation that is the future of the church. Why not call a meeting of all the parents, say fifth through twelfth grade? Give everyone the challenge and freedom to look out for one another's children.

PRIORITY 6: DIRECTION

We have found that most Christian parents desire more than anything else to raise children who will grow up to love Jesus Christ and walk with Him. With that overall objective in mind, we have searched the Scriptures to discern what biblical goals we should aim for with our children. The four qualities we developed give us four clear goals to pursue as we craft our children. Nearly every issue or trap our children will encounter can be linked to a young person's need in one of four areas.

Identity: The Scripture records the story of God giving man and woman an identity. The nation of Israel was selected, adopted, and set apart by God to be His people. Every person is born with a unique, divinely imprinted identity. If we want to properly guide our children to a healthy self-identity, we must acknowledge and support the Creator's design in three key areas: spiritual identity, emotional identity, and sexual identity. We must also communicate with them one of the most important messages they will ever receive: "You are made in the image of God. You are an incredibly valuable child."

Character: From Genesis to Revelation, character development is a major theme of God's work in people. And it's one of the major assignments God gives us as parents. Character is how your child responds to authority and life's circumstances. It is responsibility and comes as a result of training our children to submit to God and His Word.

Relationships: None of us was intended to make a journey through life alone. We need the strength, comfort, encouragement, resources, and power provided by God and others. Try teaching truth without having a relationship with your child. It produces rebellion. Similarly, relationships without truth can result in a self-indulgent teen, one who is spoiled.

Children also need parents who will build into them the ability to love others. And this training can occur quite naturally in the context of family relationships. The best school to learn about relationships and resolving conflict is in the University of Family, where the professors teach and train their students for more than eighteen years.

Mission: Every person needs a reason to live, a driving passion or calling that provides meaning and motivation. This is a person's mission.

We need to ask ourselves, "Have I more passion for the values of this world than for the things of God? What are my goals in life? Are they ones I want my child to copy?"

Every child should be helped to understand that life is a dynamic relationship with God that overflows in love for other people—a love that the Holy Spirit uses to reconcile the lost to God. Everything else, as good or innocuous as it may be, is only a prop to facilitating this mission.

PRIORITY 7: PERSEVERANCE

Winston Churchill could have been talking to parents when he said, "Never give in, never give in, never, never, never, never—in nothing, great or small, large or petty—never give in except to convictions of honor and good sense."[3]

Parenting is not a weekend project. We're talking years—the rest of your life, actually. Fortunately, adolescence does have a time limit, but we'll never make it if we have to see immediate results for our efforts.

In fact, so often during the teen years, it may seem like you're losing ground. You may be working hard, pouring truth and your heart into a child, and yet one foolish choice follows another. The temptation is to feel that you have failed. It's over. Hang it up. Toss in the towel.

Don't. Don't. Don't. If your parenting boat seems to be leaking like a sieve, keep bailing with one arm and rowing with the other. Perseverance is the parenting quality that helps you keep doing all the other important things—praying, training, staying involved, setting standards, developing community, and establishing direction.

You will get tired. You will experience pain. The ones we are sacrificing for—our children—will sometimes say and do things that hurt us deeply. They do that because they are still children, and "Foolishness is bound up in the heart of a child" (Proverbs 22:15, NASB).

At times we may have to endure even a broken heart, but

we must not lose heart: "And let us not lose heart in doing good, for in due time we shall reap if we do not grow weary" (Galations 6:9, NASB).

In thinking about the perseverance needed by parents, we smile and take heart at the pithy quote by the great English preacher Charles Haddon Spurgeon: "It was by perseverance that the snail reached the ark."

There you have it, our thirty-minute summary, with probably a minute or two to spare. Before you run to catch that plane, here's the list of priorities one more time:

Prayer
Standards
Involvement
Training
Community
Direction
Perseverance

These seven big ideas can make the difference between frustration and fruit in parenting preadolescents and teenagers.

Taken from *Parenting Today's Adolescent,* copyright © 1998 by Dennis and Barbara Rainey. Published by Thomas Nelson Publishers, Inc.. Used by permission. Available at your local Christian bookstore.

What's the common denominator in all of these things we've just read about? You. That's right! You are the one living the Christian life. You are the one telling your children what the Christian life is all about. You are the one expecting your children to live the Christian life. The things you do on a daily basis will impact your children's lives more than your pastor, more than your youth minister, more than anyone. The only way others become a bigger influence in your child's life is if you take yourself out of the equation! When Jesus was preparing to leave, he said, "I will never leave you or forsake you." Jesus told us that he would always be there for us. What a reassuring truth. We as parents are to be emulators of Christ, even in being there. Granted, we can't be there all the time. But in principle, we can always be there—and we can show them what Christ was talking about. Do your kids see Jesus in you? If you would like more help in becoming an effective parent, read the Raineys' book Parenting Today's Adolescent. *Many of the principles they discuss apply to any parent with children of any age.*

EVALUATION QUESTIONS

1. Take some time and evaluate where you are in experiencing this breakthrough. Where would you rate yourself on the following scale?

1	5	10
Not even close to experiencing this breakthrough.	I've begun the journey, but I've got a ways to go.	I've experienced a breakthrough, and I'm living the abundant life.

2. What would you consider to be the biggest hindrance to your experiencing this breakthrough right now?

3. What one action should you take to experience this breakthrough right now? I challenge you to do it.

1. The book *Watchmen on the Walls* by Anne Arkins and Gary Harrell is a great resource when you don't know what to pray for your child.

2. Jeffrey Zaslow, "Straight Talk," *USA Weekend*, Nov. 14–16, 1997, 23.

3. Winston Churchill, address at Harrow School, Oct. 29, 1941. Cited in *Bartlett's Familiar Quotations*, 16th edition (Boston: Little, Brown and Company, 1992), 621.

"Children have more need of models than of critics."
FRENCH PROVERB

*"Direct your efforts more to preparing youth for the path
and less to preparing the path for youth."*
BENJAMIN BARR LINDSEY (1869–1943)

*"The school will teach children how to read, but the environment
of the home must teach them what to read. The school can teach
them how to think, but the home must teach them what to believe."*
CHARLES A. WELLS

*"God is each virtue's goal, its impulse and its crown.
He is its only why, reward, and sole renown."*
ANGELUS SILESIUS (1624–1677)

Day 18

Experiencing Spiritual Breakthroughs in Your Family

Prepare Your Children to Be Sexually Pure

TIM AND BEVERLY LAHAYE

If you've read the papers lately, you're fully aware of the escalating teenage pregnancy rates. Given how passive parents are these days, it's really not too surprising. But it is no less tragic. It is so imperative that Christian parents in particular experience a breakthrough in this area that I ask you to pay special attention to this chapter. Read it two, three, even four times if you need to. Then review it periodically. Your children need guidance in this area, and they don't need to get it from a class at school. They need to get it from you.

$\mathcal{N}$ ext to leading your children to Christ for salvation and teaching them to walk in the Spirit so they will live in the will of God, the best thing you can do for them is to raise them to be chaste. Sexual purity saves them from a lot of heartache, guilt, and even physically destructive diseases.

But admittedly, that is easier said than done, for you cannot make life's decisions for them. You can do everything right in preparing them to make the right choices, but in the final analysis they will make their own decisions. That is what free will is all about. At best you can only help them prepare for the inevitable moments of temptation. When the lights are low, the music sweet, and their feelings hot, the final decision rests with them. They will have to live by the decisions they make. In many cases, so will you!

The following suggestions are some of the most important things you can do to prepare your children for those adult temptations that threaten to destroy them. Study them carefully.

LOVE THEM

The best preparation you can give your children for life in an adult world is the assurance of your love. Everyone can afford that! As children grow up it is not uncommon for them to have strong feelings of inadequacy. That is why public educators talk so much about their need for self-acceptance. What teens fail to understand is that such feelings are almost universal among children. They are little people in a big world, where to them it seems everyone else can do things, but they are inept.

The best antidote for a child's feelings of ineptness is genuine love from his or her mother and father. When children grow up conscious of the fact that they are important because the two people most important in their world take time to love them, it gives them the realization of self-worth. We have found that children (particularly girls) who come from homes where they are loved usually make easy adjustments to marriage. Girls who were exposed to normal father-daughter love and were able to climb up on their father's lap anytime they chose and find his heart's door open, seldom have sexual hang-ups in marriage. Girls who were rejected by their fathers in childhood often show signs of frigidity within six to eighteen months of marriage or after the birth of their first child.

PROVIDE THEM TWO LOVING ROLE MODELS

The first two people of the opposite sex that children observe showing love to each other are their mother and father. They do not have to know the details about what their parents do in the sanctity of their love; in fact, it is better if they do not know. But they do need to pick up the signals from their parents that they genuinely love each other.

A case could be made for that kind of love model being the best sex education there is. Millions of couples have gotten married without any knowledge of the opposite sex and went on to learn to experience a great love life. The key was their mental attitude toward the experience, and usually that was learned by watching the way their parents treated each other.

We also believe, based on our experience in counseling many married couples, that one of the reasons God gave human beings their powerful attraction toward the opposite sex is not only to propagate the race but to help smooth their otherwise irritating personal differences. When properly consummated in marriage, sexual expression is so exciting, fulfilling, and enriching that it draws the two lovers ever closer together despite those differences that would otherwise drive them apart. Children can feel that love, and it makes them look forward to marriage with positive anticipation. It also stands in sharp contrast to the cheap and tawdry view of sex that is exhibited by Broadway and Hollywood.

Parents need to cultivate their love not just for themselves but also for their children. For years we have encouraged couples to take minihoneymoons as often as possible (preferably every three months). This is a time for them to get away from the children for a night or two and just enjoy each other emotionally, socially, and physically. When children see their parents going away just to be together, it reassures them that their parents still love each other, and it keeps the marriage mystique alive.

The Power of a Moral Example. The best insurance against immorality in a marriage is a warm love relationship between partners and the serious commitment to sexual exclusivity they made to each other and God on their wedding day. It is devastating to the moral practices of Christian youth when their parents are immoral. Many a girl has traded her virtue more out of revenge for her father's unfaithfulness to her mother than as an act of passion.

START EARLY TEACHING YOUR CHILDREN ABOUT SEX

Sex is both the most exciting experience in the world and the most difficult to talk about. One reason it is the source of crude jokes with some people is because it is difficult for them to discuss on a serious level—so difficult that some couples rarely discuss it between themselves. We have found that usually couples who do not enjoy good sexual relationships are the ones who find it difficult to discuss sex with each other and with their children. As a general rule, the better the love life a couple has the easier it is to discuss it privately.

The reason sex is difficult to talk about even between loving partners is that it is intrinsically private. God intended it so! The normal instinct for modesty was given to us by God to protect our sexual body parts and activities. Sex was meant to be private.

It should not surprise us then that sex is difficult to talk about with our children. They instinctively want to keep it private, and so do we. In this day and age, it is extremely important to talk to our children about sex. If we do not, someone who probably does not share our values will.

TEACH THEM WHO THEY ARE

We hear a lot from public educators today about self-image or self-acceptance. It is a problem for children because public educators reject or omit all references to God and teach children they are biological accidents—the result of random chance as products of evolution. We know better. Our children are creatures of God! They need to know that. Talk about improving their self-image! Children who know they are creatures of God have much less trouble understanding "Who am I?" or "Where did I come from?" than those children who mistakenly think they evolved. You should assure them of the following:

1. *They are children of God and coheirs with Jesus Christ* (John 1:12; Romans 8:17). If they have received Christ personally, they have been born again into the family of God. Somewhere between the ages of six and twelve, you should make sure your child has received Christ personally. Then make sure they understand that God loves them and has a wonderful plan for their life. Teach them that their body is not their own but is "the temple of God" and should be kept holy.

2. *They are your children.* It is reassuring to children to know they were wanted by their parents and are loved by them. Let them know that although you may not approve of everything they do, you do approve of them and love them. They are important to you and should know it. What they do

in life is important to you, and their decisions will affect not only them but their whole family.

Their stand for virtue and integrity is a testimony for them, for their Lord, and for their family. Similarly, if they squander their integrity and lose their reputation by sexual promiscuity, it is a reproach to the whole family.

HELP YOUR CHILDREN SELECT THEIR FRIENDS

Peer pressure today is strong, and it has the most influence on our young between the ages of fourteen and twenty-four. If there is ever a time your children need positive Christian friends, it is during those formative years.

Note these words of Scripture: "Bad company corrupts good character" (1 Corinthians 15:33, NIV). That verse is probably the main reason I am in the ministry today. When I was seventeen, my godly mother forced me to break off my close friendship with four boys I had played sports with, ran around with, and double-dated with for five years. However, she had noticed changes in me she did not like. Then God brought that verse to her attention one morning during her devotions and she saw it "as a message from God."

I did not welcome that announcement and at first balked. But in her lovingly stern way, she said with tears in her eyes, "Young man, as long as you park your feet under my table, you will abide by my rules!" Naturally, I thought she was intolerant, mean-spirited, and unloving, but today I rise up to call her blessed! One of those friends has spent sixteen years in a federal penitentiary, and two have been divorced three times. I am still in love with my first and only wife and have what to me is the most fulfilling of all vocations. My mother and that verse saved my life. Your children, at the most important time in their lives (and probably when they least want it), will need your help in screening their friends. Don't fail them!

WARN THEM OF THE DANGERS OF SEXUALLY TRANSMITTED DISEASES

In this promiscuous society of ours where fornication is called casual sex or sexual activity, equating it almost to the level of sporting events, three million people contract sexually transmitted diseases each year. According to the Centers for Disease Control's latest report, "86% of all STDs occur among persons aged 15–29 years." Obviously, our youth need to know about their vulnerability to these diseases. It is one more reason you have to encourage them to remain virtuous until marriage.

PROVIDE THEM WITH CLEAR GUIDELINES FOR DATING

It was surprising to us to find that many of the Christian young people who attended our discussion groups had no clearly defined rules for dating. Interestingly enough, the importance of such rules was not lost on the teens themselves, for many of them responded to the question, What suggestions would you like to see offered to parents? by saying, "Give kids strict rules for dating." Many of these young people felt parents were too lax. One sixteen-year-old commented, "My parents are so naive," yet both her parents were dedicated Christians and leaders in the church. Please develop your own dating rules, share them with your child, and lovingly enforce them. If you do not, someday you may wish you had.

TEACH THEM TO BE THE MORAL COP

Our macho society has bred the false notion that on a date a boy can go as far as a girl will let him. That, together with the usual male aggression complex and their growing sex drive, often makes girls a target of sexual conquest. That is, of course, morally wrong and should have no place in a Christian teen's attitude. After all, we are accountable to God for our behavior. Both the boy and the girl should be taught to be the moral police officer, the person who decides what is right or wrong, while on a date. This protects them both and helps them maintain their virtue regardless of sexual temptation.

HELP THEM MAKE A FORMAL COMMITMENT TO VIRTUE

During the last few years, popular child psychologist Dr. James Dobson and others have developed the idea of a formal commitment to virtue before marriage, which we heartily recommend. It is an expansion of the idea my friend and youth evangelist Ken Poure popularized many years ago. After taking his sixteen-year-old daughter out for a formal dinner in a fancy restaurant, he had an intimate father-daughter talk and formally introduced her to the wonderful world of dating. That night she made a commitment to God and her dad to be a virgin on her wedding day.

One writer added the idea of presenting the teen with a ring or key that symbolized their virtue. The young person, either a boy or girl, made a formal commitment to remain virtuous until marriage, and then both parent and child prayed and made that commitment to God. Then the child was given the ring or key to present to their marriage partner on their wedding night.

TEACH THEM TO PURIFY THEIR MINDS

All sin begins in the mind. If a person never sins in his mind, he will never sin with his body. That may be one of the reasons our Lord raised the moral level of adultery from the physical act of sex to the mental act of lust: "But I tell you that anyone who looks at a woman lustfully has already committed adultery with her in his heart" (Matthew 5:28). Note how different that is from the humanistic philosophy that dominates our society and encourages fantasies even for school-age children.

Today, parents who would protect their children adequately must teach them how to and how not to use their minds. From the onset of puberty and the new exciting hormonal changes in their bodies, young people begin to have sexual thoughts that need to be resisted not cultivated. The last thing they need is to cultivate these thoughts through fantasy trips. They need to bring every thought into captivity to Christ, as the Scriptures teach. This is particularly true of boys because of their intense sex drive. Their thoughts early on can become explicitly sexual.

Parents need to deal tenderly with teens, explaining that such thought temptations are natural. Everyone has them, but for Christians, who would be virtuous and pleasing to the Lord, they should be repented of and confessed. The human mind cannot entertain a vacuum; it must be active. Therefore, their thoughts should be directed to wholesome activities and eventually the goal of having a lifetime mate and a home of their own. The ideal would be for them to memorize Scripture so they can review their verses as they drift off to sleep rather than entertain sexually provocative fantasies. My grandmother's classic statement is still true today: "An idle mind is the devil's workshop!"

TEACH THEM HOW TO SAY NO!

It is not enough just to tell young people to say no to premarital sex; we must show them how. And we must show them while they are still young.

You should not make them wait until they get into a difficult situation to figure out what to do, but help them anticipate how to avoid such situations, which means they must follow the rules you lay down. That greatly reduces the number of sexually tempting situations they will face. Then urge them to say no emphatically. That means they say no with their mouth and body at the same time. The girl who says no but remains in a close embrace is sending the signal that she really does not mean it.

Young people need to think of dating as a time for fun, not just with one person, but several. They should not be allowed to date without specific plans on where they are going and what they are going to do. Even couples who think they are in love do not have to be alone to have fun on a date. Sure, intimacy is exciting, but it leads to the desire for more intimacy. Research has shown that even with couples who do not intend to go all the way, they will be sexually involved after spending three hundred hours alone with each other.[1]

SURROUND THEM WITH PRAYER

Most of us prayed that God would give us children in the first place. Then we dedicated them to Him soon after they were born, much as Hannah dedicated Samuel to God in the Old Testament. Now we need to surround them in prayer, asking that God will give them wisdom to hear and heed our parental advice to keep themselves pure and unspotted from the world.

At twenty years of age, after two years in the Air Force, I was more rebellious toward God than at any other time in my life. My mother's prayers kept me from going to the wrong college and instead directed me to a Christian university where I met Miss Right for my life. Together we have shared almost a lifetime of love and companionship for which we are both eternally grateful. I know you want no less for your children. Remember the words of Scripture: "The prayer of a righteous man [or woman] is powerful and effective" (James 5:16, NIV). Somehow I think God pays special attention to the prayers of parents for their children.

Taken from *Raising Sexually Pure Kids* by Tim and Beverly LaHaye. ©1998 by Tim and Beverly LaHaye. Used by permission of Multnomah Publishers, Inc. Available at your local Christian bookstore.

Raising virtuous children isn't just going to happen. You can't simply pray that they will turn out right. Prayer is just the thing you start and finish with. In the middle, you've got a lot of work to do. In many circles, it's called proactive parenting—initiating the good things with your children instead of only responding to the bad things. If you're a passive parent, you'll reap a harvest with your children you may not be too proud of. There are so many things that need to be done to encourage your children to remain virtuous that I strongly encourage you to read Tim and Beverly LaHaye's book Raising Sexually Pure Kids. *It has some very practical advice you can apply to your family.*

EVALUATION QUESTIONS

1. Take some time and evaluate where you are in experiencing this breakthrough. Where would you rate yourself on the following scale?

1	5	10
Not even close to experiencing this breakthrough.	I've begun the journey, but I've got a ways to go.	I've experienced a breakthrough, and I'm living the abundant life.

2. What would you consider to be the biggest hindrance to your experiencing this breakthrough right now?

3. What one action should you take to experience this breakthrough right now? I challenge you to do it.

1. George B. Eager, *Love, Dating, and Sex: What Teens Want to Know* (Valdosta, Ga.: Mailbox Club Books, 1989), 127.

"Children are like clocks; they must be allowed to run."
JAMES C. DOBSON

"Our tendency is to grab and hold our children and not allow them to make mistakes. Then, when they do fail, we jump forward to bail them out and prevent them from learning valuable lessons."
JAMES C. DOBSON

"When you have saved a boy from the possibility of making any mistake, you have also prevented him from developing initiative."
JOHN ERSKINE (1509–1591)

"Becoming a father is easy enough, but being one can be rough."
WILHELM BUSCH (1832–1908)

"Fathering is a marathon, not a sprint."
PAUL L. LEWIS

"One of the best legacies a father can leave his children is to love their mother."
C. NEIL STRAIT

"You don't need to be right all the time. Your child wants a man for a father, not a formula. He wants real parents, real people, capable of making mistakes without moping about it."
C. D. WILLIAMS

Fathers, Help Your Kids Stand Tall

STEVE FARRAR

I recently asked a college student on summer break the following question: "What's the biggest surprise that you've found in college?" It was an open-ended question, so I wasn't sure what to expect. Know what he said? "None of the guys in the dorms like their parents! None of them have a relationship with their parents. And it's everywhere!" What a tragedy! But, fathers, there is hope. If you have young children, you can change things right now. And if your children are grown, it's still not too late to begin applying these principles today.

When you look at your kids, what do you see? Do you see them as they are now, or as what they will become? I think a lot of guys look at their four-year-olds and just see four-year-olds. And we need to value them and appreciate them as four-year-olds. But on the other hand, we also need to clearly see that these four-year-olds won't always be four. In ten years they'll be fourteen, chompin' at the bit to get their driver's licenses in a couple of years.

They will also be under tremendous peer pressure, making some of the most critical choices of their entire lives. One decision they will make every day is whether to be a leader or a follower.

I'm convinced that we need to "Gutenberg" our kids. Just as Johannes Gutenberg took a wine press and a coin punch and turned them into a printing press, so we dads need to take our kids and shape their character so that we turn them into *moral* and *spiritual leaders.* I'm talking about turning your kids into men and women of character who can make the kind of tough choices that few leaders in our contemporary world seem able to make.

The time to begin doing that is now.

Something happens when a kid hits adolescence. When kids are small, they tend to think their dad hung the moon. When kids hit adolescence, sometimes they begin to think their dad should *go to* the moon. To take it a step further, when a boy or girl hits adolescence, one of two things is going to happen. An adolescent will either go to his peers and critique his parents, or go to his parents and critique his peers. Obviously, we want our kids to come to us.

To put it another way, a child is going to be either a leader or a follower. Teenagers are deciding this every day of their lives. There is pressure to do drugs, have sex, and do whatever it is that everyone else is doing. So how do we combat that? By turning our kids into leaders. And we get after it right away.

LEADERSHIP: WHAT IS IT?

What is leadership? A friend of mine wrote his doctoral dissertation on leadership and found 165 published definitions.

Some of those definitions are pretty complex and dazzling. Dr. Howard Hendricks, distinguished professor at Dallas Theological Seminary, has come up with the best definition of a leader I've ever heard. According to Dr. Hendricks, "A leader is someone who leads." Don't let the simplicity of that definition fool you. It is pregnant with meaning.

Recently a man handed me his business card. It listed his position as chief executive officer and president. I later found out this man is a poor excuse for a leader. Yet his card was impressive. This man has positional leadership, but an illustrious business card or title doesn't make someone a leader.

It's also important to distinguish between leading and "managing." Managing is usually tied in with some type of organizational structure. The true leader may have no organizational structure at all. He simply leads.

In 1947, Dr. Chandrasekhar, a professor at the University of Chicago, was scheduled to teach a class in advanced astrophysics. The professor was living in Wisconsin; his plan was to commute to Chicago twice a week, even though the class was held during the winter quarter, and he would encounter the very worst weather the Midwest could throw at him.

The professor had second thoughts about teaching the class when he heard that only two students had signed up for his course. He thought of the distance, the time away from his family, and the snow and ice. But then he thought of the two students and decided to follow through on his commitment. He had obviously hoped for more than two students, yet perhaps those two would be worth the time investment.

Ten years later, Dr. Chandrasekhar was very pleased to hear that those two young men were progressing quite nicely. Chen Ning Yang and Tsung-Dao Lee were both awarded the Nobel Prize in physics in 1957. In 1983, Dr. Chandrasekhar was awarded the same honor. You might say the class was worth the effort. The professor, who demonstrated his leadership in being willing to teach just two young, motivated students, obviously passed along some values and character as well as a syllabus.

Gentlemen, your kids are your students. You're teaching a class on leadership every day. And whether you realize it or not, they are watching your example like hawks. You may have only one or two students, but a man with vision knows that the opportunity to shape the lives of his children with godly character is simply too good to pass up.

I've been thinking about this process of turning kids into leaders for quite some time. I have also been *working* on it. I have some good friends who are in the same process. From time to time we will compare notes for the simple reason that none of us really have our act together. So we check in with one another as much as possible and talk shop about raising our kids to be leaders.

I have come up with seven principles that can help your kids stand tall in a culture that's trying to drag them down into the muck.

1. Be a leader yourself.

Dave Johnson is a friend of mine. For years, Dave rode a Harley, but now he rides in a patrol car. Dave is a police officer in San Jose who wrote a fascinating book about his experiences as a street cop. Dave has plenty of stories that are hilarious, but here's one that could make you weep:

> Frank and I had just finished a call and climbed into our police cars. As I started my car, I heard the police radio call out Frank's unit number. The dispatcher reported a young boy missing from his residence.

Two years old, wearing tennis shoes, coveralls, and a light blue T-shirt. The mother had fallen asleep and discovered the boy missing when she awoke fifteen minutes later.

Frank acknowledged the call and began driving to the address. I told the dispatcher I would also respond to help in the search. I was driving directly behind Frank's car. Our sergeant, Dennis Busch, heard the call, too, and radioed back that he would also respond.

Suddenly the dispatcher alerted us: "The lost boy has been located—in the next-door neighbor's swimming pool."

Adrenaline shot through my veins as I reached for the control switch to activate my red lights. I saw Frank's lights jump on at the same time. We both accelerated. I began praying that the people who found the boy knew CPR and were attempting to revive him.

As Frank and I rounded the corner near the address, we saw several men in front of a house. Dennis was just getting out of his car and talking with them. I suddenly saw him bolt toward a gate at the side of the house. As Frank and I got closer, one of the men pointed: "The boy's in the pool in that backyard." I could hardly believe what I'd heard.

Frank and I both ran through a narrow side yard. As we rounded the corner of the house we could see Dennis pulling the boy's limp body out of the pool. He laid the boy on the cold cement at the pool's edge and began administering CPR, and Frank knelt down to help.

With Frank and Dennis hovering over the motionless body, I was left with nothing to do except watch—which is hard for most police officers to do in a life-and-death situation. I searched the boy's face, looking for any sign of life that might flicker there. *If only I could do something...*

My eyes fell to the coveralls that hung wet on his little body. I thought how much they looked like the ones my girls wore when they were that age. I saw the small tennis shoes on his limp feet and noticed that one was untied. I wondered if he would ever have someone tie his shoes again.

I desperately tried to choke back the lump tightening in my throat. I turned, walked a few steps, and took out my handkerchief to wipe my eyes. As I put it back in my pocket, I saw four men standing and watching Dennis and Frank work. I recognized them as part of the group out front when we arrived.

I felt anger welling up inside me. "Who found the boy in the pool?" I asked.

They only hung their heads and stared at the ground.

Just then the fire department arrived. Soon an oxygen mask was secured around the small face that hadn't changed expression. The firefighters took over; Dennis was still kneeling, softly stroking the boy's small, closed hand and staring into his lifeless face...

I looked up again at the four men still standing in their group. Suddenly they all turned and walked out of the yard, none of them saying a word.[1]

I don't know anything else about those four men. I don't know where they worked; I don't know if they were married; and I don't know if they were Democrats or Republicans. But there's something I do know. None of those four men was a leader. Every one was a follower.

Allow me to surmise something else about these four men. If any of them had children, my guess is that you would find them doing the same things that their fathers were doing.

Standing around.

Generally speaking, men who are followers produce children who are followers. And followers are very good at just standing around in a crisis. That little two-year-old boy lost his life because four men were followers. It's my conviction that children all over America are dying emotionally, spiritually, and morally because the men in their lives are just standing around. Passivity is death!

What should you do? Sit down and write out a plan. Set some goals for your family. Take a successful dad out for breakfast and tap into his methods. Get with a small group of guys and encourage and sharpen each other. Attend a men's leadership conference. But whatever you do, don't stand around!

I don't remember who said it, but he was right on target: "There is as much risk in doing nothing as in doing something." And doing nothing with kids in regard to leadership is simply asking for tragedy in the teenage years.

So what's it going to be, Dad? Are you standing tall or just standing around?

2. *Be a spiritual submarine under the surface of your children's lives.*

Tom Clancy knows submarines. That's why he writes the following with such certainty:

> *Submarine.* The very word implies stealth and deadliness.... Since its creation in the United States some forty years ago, the nuclear attack submarine (SSN)

has become the most feared weapon in the oceans of the world.... Here is a creature that, like Ridley Scott's *Alien,* appears when it wishes, destroys what it wishes, and disappears immediately to strike again when *it* wishes.[2]

May I submit to you, gentlemen, that God has called you to be an SSN for your children. When it comes to spiritual battle, you should understand that you have been given awesomely powerful weapons.

In my estimation, Ephesians 6 is telling us that godly men who are leading their families have the potential to be nothing less than the stealth warships of spiritual warfare:

Put on the full armor of God, that you may be able to stand firm against the schemes of the devil. For our struggle is not against flesh and blood, but against... the spiritual forces of wickedness in the heavenly places. Therefore, take up the full armor of God, that you may be able to resist in the evil day, and having done everything, to stand firm. (Ephesians 6:11–13)

A man who has put on the full armor of God is a force to be reckoned with. The prayers of a man who has put on the full armor of God are lethal. Effective. Protective. God responds to the prayers of such a man who is alert to pray with perseverance for his children.

We understand, gentlemen, that we cannot be with our children twenty-four hours a day. We cannot be with them every time they encounter peer pressure. But that does not mean you are without influence. We are in spiritual warfare. A man in the full armor of God is no less a force than a SSN.

Through your prayers you have the ability to affect situations where you are not physically present. You may be undetected, but that does not mean that you are ineffective.

3. Expect your children to be leaders.

"I don't know what to do," a man said to his therapist. "My wife thinks she's a piano."

"Well then, bring her in for an appointment."

"Are you crazy?" exclaimed the husband. "Do you have any idea what it costs to move a piano?"

The moral of the story? If you *think* your kids are leaders and expect them to be leaders, then your kids will begin to see themselves as leaders.

If you expect your kids to go along with the crowd, then they most likely will. Do you expect them to fight their way upstream when everyone else is floating with the downstream current? Then they probably will. Expect your children to be leaders. If it's important to you, it will be important to them.

4. Encourage your children to be leaders.

All leaders get discouraged. That's why they need *encouragement,* which is a great word. It means "to put courage in." That's the job of a dad. It's tough being a teenager who goes against conventional wisdom; sometimes kids can become weary in well doing. That's especially when you must put courage in.

Two psychiatrists were at a convention. "What was your most difficult case?" one asked the other.

"Once I had a patient who lived in a pure fantasy world. He believed that a wildly rich uncle in South America was going to leave him a fortune. All day long he sat around and waited for a make-believe letter to arrive from a fictitious attorney."

"What was the result?"

"It was an eight-year struggle, but I finally cured him. And then that stupid letter arrived…"

The last thing we want to do is to discourage our children in any way. We don't want to discourage their dreams, their hopes, their aspirations, or their moral courage. We want to help them become optimistic about what God has in store for them to be and to do.

Thomas Fuller once said that a young trooper should have an old horse. Guess what, my friends—you are the horses. And your name isn't Trigger, Champion, or Silver. Your name had better be Encouragement.

5. *Remind your children that they are leaders.*

"Dad," a polar bear cub asked his father, "am I 100 percent polar bear?"

"Of course you are," answered the father bear. "My parents are 100 percent polar bear, which makes me 100 percent polar bear. Your mother's parents are 100 percent polar bear, so she's 100 percent polar bear. Yep, that makes you 100 percent polar bear. Why do you ask?"

"I'm *freezing* out here, Dad."

Kids need to be frequently reminded who they are. When I drop my kids off at school, I often say to them as they get out of the car, "Be a leader today." Why do I do that? Because they need to be reminded.

Young polar bears may need to be reminded who they are when they feel the cold. Our kids need to be reminded when they start following the crowd that leaders don't do that. They are *leaders,* not followers. It's your job to remind them when they begin to doubt. Leo Tolstoy once commented, "We lost, because we told ourselves we lost." Remind your kids that they are leaders. Frequently.

6. Support them in their leadership.

Professional golfers play every tournament round with a caddie. The caddie is more than an extra shoulder to hoist a bag of clubs. A caddie is there for support. A good caddie can be a tremendous support in the heat of the competition.

Tommy Bolt was one of the greatest golfers of all time. But he had a legendary temper, too. Tommy was playing in a tournament in Southern California one year, and he was still ticked off about his score from the day before. He told his caddie not to say a word to him.

Tommy hit his first tee shot, and it came to rest behind a tree. He asked his caddie what he thought about a five iron. The caddie didn't reply. Tommy hit a five iron and made an unbelievable shot that landed on the green.

Tommy turned to his caddie and said proudly, "Well, what do you think about that?"

"It wasn't your ball, Tommy," said the caddie as he picked up the bag and headed toward the green.

One of the greatest ways you can support your kids is to listen to them. When there's something eating 'em up, you find out what's going on inside their hearts. It will not be easy for your kids to be leaders when most of their friends are moral followers. And there will be times when they just need to talk. So be there, with very large ears and a very large heart. If you do that, they will know that they are supported. Because you cared enough to listen.

7. Reward them for demonstrating leadership.

When a child leads, he should be rewarded. When your child eats lunch at school with a kid whom the other kids make fun of, he should be rewarded. When your teenager stands tall in the howling winds of peer pressure and does what is right, he should be rewarded. But how?

When I say reward, I don't mean money or a gift. There is certainly a time and place for that. But there are other ways of giving a child a reward.

One of the better ways to reward your sons and daughters is with your words. Acknowledge their achievement or accomplishment verbally. There is a reason why I think this is important. Criticism always follows leaders. Men and women and boys and girls who stand tall always make the easiest targets.

A young boy had practiced for years to become a great pianist. Finally the night of his debut arrived. The auditorium was jammed. The boy played his heart out for the audience. Yet when the newspapers came out, the critics ripped apart his performance. A wise old musician put his arm around the boy and said, "Remember, young man, there is no city in the world where they have erected a statue to a critic."

Your child will have plenty of critics. Just make sure that you are not one of them.

Taken from *Standing Tall* by Steve Farrar. © 1994, 2001 by Steve Farrar. Used by permission of Multnomah Publishers, Inc. Available at your local bookstore.

At a recent men's conference, I asked how many guys there hated their fathers. The average age of the conference attendees was thirty-five, and the overwhelming majority of these men stood to their feet! The problem with fathers not relating to their children is huge. It's everywhere I look these days. Fathers in all parts of the country have failed their children. And there's only one way to fix this problem. Repentance—by the fathers! Do you realize that if you don't go back and get reconciliation from your children when you wrong them, you will do more to drive them away from the Lord than anything else in the world? That's right! Fathers have a tremendous impact on how their children respond to the Lord. If your children are leaning away from God right now, you fathers need to experience this breakthrough right away. Your children can't afford for you not to.

EVALUATION QUESTIONS

1. Take some time and evaluate where you are in experiencing this breakthrough. Where would you rate yourself on the following scale?

1	5	10
Not even close to experiencing this breakthrough.	I've begun the journey, but I've got a ways to go.	I've experienced a breakthrough, and I'm living the abundant life.

2. What would you consider to be the biggest hindrance to your experiencing this breakthrough right now?

3. What one action should you take to experience this breakthrough right now? I challenge you to do it.

1. David R. Johnson, *The Light behind the Star* (Sisters, Ore.: Questar Publishers, 1989), 93–6.

2. Tom Clancy, *Submarine: A Guided Tour Inside a Nuclear Warship* (New York: Berkley Books, 1993), xix.

"It's possible that we—in pursuit of the disciplined life — focus our eyes on larger-than-life goals. We take on three jobs at church. We memorize not only verses, but chapters. We sell the TV or get up at 4:00 every morning for devotions.... But it may be that we've overlooked more immediate and obvious things. We've passed over things like a clean room, or being on time, or curbing our tongue."

JONI EARECKSON TADA

"Let us not fool ourselves—without Christianity,
without Christian education,
without the principles of Christ inculcated into young life,
we are simply rearing pagans."

PETER MARSHALL (1902–1949)

"The parent must convince himself that discipline
is not something he does to the child;
it is something he does for the child."

JAMES C. DOBSON

"The best way for a child to learn to fear God is
to know a real Christian.
The best way for a child to learn to pray is
to live with a father and mother who know a life of friendship
with God and who truly pray."

JOHANN HEINRICH PESTALOZZI (1746–1827)

Instill the Discipline of Good Manners

ELISABETH ELLIOT

Very few parents these days realize that teaching their children manners actually has something to do with their walk with the Lord. Basically, manners are a way to extend courtesy to those around us. They say: You are so important that I wouldn't think of doing anything rude in your presence. Manners are not a trivial matter. And having rules for your children to follow is not being legalistic. As Elisabeth Elliott so eloquently explains, rules handled properly encourage relationships because they force children to put other people first, which is a characteristic of a First Chair Christian.

In many of England's tiny back gardens one sees espaliers—trees or shrubs which have been trained to grow flat against a wall, giving a two-dimensional effect. While this is drastically contrary to the direction they would have grown if left to themselves, they take up little space and produce beautiful flowers or fruit.

As the gardener who espaliers the tree cooperates with God, so parents cooperate with Him in training children in the way they should go, not in the way they would naturally go. Jesus used the metaphor of the vine to teach about our union with Him, a union meant to result in our bearing fruit that will glorify God.

"My Father is the gardener. He cuts off every branch in me that bears no fruit, while every branch that does bear fruit he prunes so that it will be even more fruitful" (John 15:1–2, NIV).

It is difficult to resist the pressures of our "have it your way" society, and even earnest Christian parents sometimes feel uncertain about the wisdom of drawing up so much as the briefest list of rules. Won't it make children rebel? Isn't it legalistic? What if we can't enforce them?

In our fear that we squeeze children into our own mold, we are in danger of allowing the world to squeeze us into its mold—something Paul sternly warned the Roman Christians to watch out for. God bestows on parents a very great trust. They are in charge of the "vineyard" that is the family. We may look upon rules laid down for children as the stakes and ties that keep the vine from rank growth and enable it to produce the best fruit, while the pruning might represent the parents' chastening. Jesus says, "If a man remains in me and I in him, he will bear much fruit; apart from me you can do nothing" (John 15:5, NIV). This "remaining" is not a vague feeling of religiosity. Jesus makes it clear that it means obedience. Union with Him is impossible without harmony with His will. "Why do you call me Lord," Jesus asked, "and do not the things that I say?"

The gardener loves his garden, knows each flower and shrub and tree, understands its special qualities and needs, and gives it tender care. Parents are given the delicate task of training an imperfect and highly impressionable child who is not their property but is entrusted to them for a time, that they may curb the natural tendencies that are useless or destructive and guide him or her instead to God.

God in His mercy told His people what to do and what not to do. My parents made rules for us, stakes and ties to help us live a peaceful and fruitful life. The keeping of these rules was our early training in that renunciation and death to self that will never be easy for any of us so long as we live in this mortal body, yet that very renunciation is the route to freedom and fulfillment. The obedient child is the happiest child.

Rules and the consequences of infringing them instilled in us a healthy fear, not only of our parents, but of authority in general. My friend Essie and I, on our way to school, once trespassed on the property of a Catholic school. I have never forgotten how I shook with fear when a nun scolded us. I think it was the first time anyone other than my parents corrected me. I never set foot on that territory again.

Although the Bible has much to say about the fear of the Lord, Christian teaching on it is rare today. Objections are raised as soon as it is mentioned. Isn't fear a base motive? Why should we fear Him who loves us as He does? If He is our Shepherd, Savior, and Friend, how can we be afraid of Him? "He is not a tame lion," C. S. Lewis says. When Moses had given the Ten Commandments there were thunder and lightning and the sound of a trumpet, and the mountain was filled with smoke. The people of Israel trembled with fear, stood at a distance, and begged Moses to do the talking rather than let God speak to them, lest they die. Note the language of Moses' reply.

"*Do not be afraid.* God has come to test you, so that *the fear of God will be with you* to keep you from sinning" (Exodus 20:20, NIV, emphasis mine). Do not be afraid—so that *the fear of God will be with you!* The words seem oddly contradictory, but I think there are two kinds of fear here: fear of physical harm, which Moses assures them is not called for, and the fear without which they would certainly come to spiritual disaster. A child's fear of physical punishment leads him to obedience, but so does his natural desire to please the people he loves. It is the beginning of respect. Until we love perfectly, which will not happen on this fallen planet, we must fear. Until perfect love casts it out, fear is a salutary thing. Fear saves us.

The fear of the Lord, according to Proverbs, is "to hate evil." It is the "fruit of humility," the "first step to wisdom," the "fountain of life." It "brings length of days" and makes him "a refuge for his children" (Proverbs 8:13; 22:4; 9:10; 14:27; 10:27; 14:26, REB).

The New Testament teaches the necessity of this fear if we want to live a holy life. "We must all have our lives laid open before the tribunal of Christ, where each must receive what is due to him for his conduct in the body, good or bad. With this fear of the Lord before our eyes we address our appeal to men and women. To God our lives lie open" (2 Corinthians 5:10–11, REB).

"If you say 'Father' to him who judges every one impartially on the basis of what they have done, you must live in awe of him during your time on earth" (1 Peter 1:17, REB).

"Let us serve God with thankfulness in the ways which please him, but always with reverence and holy fear. For it is perfectly true that our God is a burning fire" (Hebrews 12:28–29, Phillips).

Ancient writers saw the fear of the Lord as conducive to inner health; it is a lamp in a dark place, it illuminates and teaches, consumes malice, burns wrong thoughts.

George Macdonald wrote, "The fear of God will cause a

man to flee, not from Him, but from himself; not from Him but to Him, the Father of himself, in terror lest he should do Him wrong or his neighbor wrong" (*Unspoken Sermons,* 30).

I saw a film showing how a mother polar bear trained her cubs. They came stumbling out of their cave in the ice, all three of them a bit bleary from the long hibernation, the cubs dazzled by the sunshine, drunk with the freedom of the wide world spread out before them. The mother had serious business to attend to: to teach her children how to survive in a frozen world. There was no time for nonsense. She nudged them into line, showing them where to go, rolling down a snowbank (they followed fearlessly), avoiding the cracks in the ice (they jumped over them), taking them to where she could teach them to find food. Example was everything—or I should say almost everything. Verbal precepts were not needed, but a few swift cuffs to their little furry behinds certainly helped. So our loving Shepherd leads us in paths of righteousness, using His rod from time to time for correction and His staff for protection, both of which the psalmist found comforting.

In all the daily routines at home we were taught this is what we do, this is how we do it, this is where things go. Most of these were routines and habits established simply by the way in which our parents had ordered their own lives. We learned by watching. But what if our parents had not been there? What if we had seen more of some other caregiver than we saw of Daddy and Mother? The power of influence would have been diluted. "Quality time" can never substitute for ordinary days spent doing ordinary things together.

As for what we were to do, morning routines were firmly fixed on weekdays:

Get up.
Dress.
Eat breakfast.
Join family prayers.
Brush teeth.
Make bed.
Get ready for school.

How we did these things called for many more reminders and repeated precepts, for example:

Get up promptly when called.

Dress quickly (no meditation exercises in the middle of the floor), *properly* (we had clothes for school, play, and church, and very few for each, so we had to wear the right ones).

Come to breakfast punctually (at 7:10, not 7:11).

Come cheerfully. If anyone in our house appeared wearing a scowl, he might be asked to go back upstairs and "find a cheerful face." What a death to self that demanded! What a renunciation of one's nasty feelings! I remember it well. It was not a capricious requirement. The book of Proverbs supports it: "A happy heart makes the face cheerful," "A cheerful look brings joy to the heart" (15:13, 30, NIV), and this is more for the sake of others than for one's own.

Eat politely. Table manners cannot be skipped over, for if there's one area where the spiritual and emotional climate of a home is revealed, it's at the table. To my parents, politeness meant, among other things:

If you can't say something nice about the food don't say anything.

Napkin in lap, everybody.

Sonny, elbows off the table.

Sit up straight, Bets. You're slouching. That's better!

Eat what is put before you.

Pass the milk to somebody else before helping yourself.

Don't reach, Davy. Ask. Good boy.

Don't interrupt.

Ginny, hold your spoon properly—like this, not like that.

Don't make a gangplank with your knife, Tommy.

Jim, we don't eat with our knives. You have a fork—let's see if you can hold it properly. Good for you!

Don't chew with your mouth open.

Don't talk with your mouth full!

The endless repetition of these reminders can wear out the hardiest fathers and mothers and make them wonder whether it really matters how we go about ingesting our necessary daily sustenance. There was conversation at our meals. It wasn't all rules and corrections, not by a long shot. But conversation is made more pleasant when people are behaving themselves in a civilized fashion.

Being told what to do and how to do it is not all children need. They need help in the performance. God does not leave us to ourselves. Having told us what to do and how, He helps His children in all kinds of ways. Moses named his son Eliezer, which means "my God is my helper." God is a very present help in trouble. "The Lord is with me; I will not be afraid. What can man do to me? The Lord is with me; he is my helper," wrote the psalmist (Psalm 118:6–7, NIV), and in the prophetic writings Christ Himself speaks, "The Lord God will help me, therefore shall I not be confounded" (Isaiah 50:7, KJV).

"The Spirit helps us in our weakness. We do not know what we ought to pray for, but the Spirit himself intercedes for us with groans that words cannot express" (Romans 8:26, NIV). "We may receive mercy and find grace to help us in our time of need" (Hebrews 4:16, NIV). In his letter to the Ephesians the apostle Paul describes our helplessness when we were following "the spirit who is now at work in those who are disobedient…gratifying the cravings of our sinful nature and following its desires and thoughts.… But because of his great love for us, God, who is rich in mercy, made us alive with Christ even when we were dead in transgressions—it is by grace you have been saved" (Ephesians 2:2–5, NIV).

Grace did for us what we could not do for ourselves. And so parents, says my sister-in-law Lovelace Howard, do for their children what they cannot do by themselves in order that they may learn to do what they must do by themselves.

We learned the how of toothbrushing by our parents doing it for us when teeth first came in and by their helping us learn to do for ourselves. *Thoroughly* was the word. Daily, faithfully. And how about bedmaking? Smoothly.

I have already described how carefully we were trained in where things go: A place for everything, everything in its place. There was security in this routine and consistency. Life is simplified when you know what, how, where. A hook for the car keys and the car keys always on the hook eliminates frantic scrambles all over the house with everybody shouting at everybody else about who had them last.

The ordering of a peaceful home is not possible without the application of eternal principles. It is, after all, mostly little, common things that make up our lives. This is the raw material for the spiritual life. If we despise small things, regard normal household duties as burdens, routines as boring, rules too confining, we will never learn, nor can we teach our children, to live a life of holy harmony. This takes faithfulness in the troublesome details first of all, learning to do them well that we may make of them an offering to the Lord, for it is His work, after all, given to us. It is our daily bread for which we should learn to be thankful. Such faithfulness is the groundwork for all God may ever ask us to do.

Self-preoccupation, self-broodings, self-interest, self-love—these are the reasons we jar each other. Turn your eyes off yourself; look up and out! There are your brothers and sisters; they have needs that you can aid in. Listen for their confidences; keep your heart wide open to their calls and your hands alert for their service. Learn to give and not to take, to drown your own hungry wants in the happiness of lending yourself to fulfill the interests of those nearest and dearest. Look up and out from this narrow, cabined self of yours. You will find to your own glad surprise the secret of the meekness and gentleness of Jesus, and the fruits of the Spirit will all bud and blossom from out of your life.

Taken from *The Shaping of a Christian Family* by Elisabeth Elliot Gren. ©1992 by Elisabeth Elliot Gren. Published by Thomas Nelson Publishers. Used by permission. Available at your local Christian bookstore.

Encouraging your children to live their lives in the First Chair can be a tiresome job at times. Especially when you consider all the little details that go into it. While all families will have somewhat different family routines, it's important to remember that the rules we enforce in our families are not only for our own benefit or even for the benefit of our children. While there are advantages for our family in following certain rules, the foremost benefactor is God. All our actions are to glorify God, and those that put Him first and other people second glorify Him to the fullest. Let us all purpose to glorify God in all our actions, even the details. To learn more about shaping your family into a God-centered family, read Elisabeth Elliot's book The Shaping of a Christian Family.

EVALUATION QUESTIONS

1. Take some time and evaluate where you are in experiencing this breakthrough. Where would you rate yourself on the following scale?

1	5	10
Not even close to experiencing this breakthrough.	I've begun the journey, but I've got a ways to go.	I've experienced a breakthrough, and I'm living the abundant life.

2. What would you consider to be the biggest hindrance to your experiencing this breakthrough right now?

3. What one action should you take to experience this breakthrough right now? I challenge you to do it.

*"Discipline and love are not antithetical;
one is a function of the other."*
JAMES C. DOBSON

*"Ideal parenting is modeled after the relationship
between God and man."*
JAMES C. DOBSON

*"Love your children with all your hearts,
love them enough to discipline them before it is too late....
Praise them for important things,
even if you have to stretch them a bit.
Praise them a lot.
They live on it like bread and butter, and
they need it more than bread and butter."*
LAVINA CHRISTENSEN FUGAL

*"If you accept the authority of Jesus in your life, then you accept
the authority of his words."*
COLIN URQUHART

Train Your Children to Respect Authority

Ted Tripp

God's desire for your marriage is that you produce godly offspring. First, He wants you to be godly. Then He wants you to pass on your faith to your children. Unfortunately, many parents don't want the responsibility of passing on their faith. Many just hope their kids will take on their faith. A major breakthrough for Christian parents is to take responsibility for raising godly children. We, as the parents of our children, are responsible for being their authority. We are responsible for telling them about the things of God. We are responsible for showing them how to apply the things of the Lord. We are responsible. Are you ready to take charge?

The boys were out in the shed working on the go-cart. Our daughter went out to call them for dinner. "You both are to go inside, wash up, and get ready for dinner. Right now!" she announced authoritatively.

"Are the boys coming in?" my wife inquired, when our daughter had returned to the house alone.

"I called them," she said with a look that betrayed her.

Why hadn't the boys come in? Because it was their sister who had called them, and they were not about to obey her on her authority.

She returned to the shed with the same message and added two powerful words, "Mother said..."

Our daughter did not have the authority to order the boys into the house. The second time she called the boys, she called them as the agent of their mother. They knew it was time to come.

CONFUSION ABOUT AUTHORITY

Our culture does not like authority. It is not just that we don't like to be under authority, we don't like being authorities. One of the places where this is most clearly seen is in our discomfort with authority in the home.

We need a biblical understanding of authority. Questions abound. What is the nature of the parents' authority over a child? Is it absolute or relative? Is the authority vested in the parents because of the relative size difference between parents and young children? Are we in charge because we are smarter and more experienced? Are we called to rule because we are not sinners and they are? Do we have the right to tell our kids to do anything we want them to do?

If you don't answer questions such as these, you will be tentative and insecure in discharging your duty to God and to your children. If you are unsure about the nature and extent of your authority, your children will suffer greatly. They will never know what to expect from you because the ground rules will be constantly changing. They will never learn the absolutes and principles of God's Word that alone teach wisdom.

Parents in our culture often improvise because they do not understand the biblical mandate to shepherd children. Parenting goals are often no more noble than immediate comfort and convenience. When parents require obedience because they feel under pressure, obedience of children is reduced to parental convenience. Christian parents must have a clear understanding of godly parenting and children must be trained to know that God calls them to obey always.

CALLED TO BE IN CHARGE

As a parent you have authority because God calls you to be an authority in your child's life. You have the authority to act on behalf of God. As a father or mother, you do not exercise rule over your own jurisdiction but over God's. You act at His command. You discharge a duty that He has given. You may not try to shape the lives of your children as pleases you but as pleases Him.

All you do in your task as parent must be done from this point of view. You must undertake all your instruction, your care and nurture, your correction and discipline because God has called you to. You act with the conviction that He has charged you to act on His behalf. In Genesis 18:19, Jehovah says, "I have chosen him [Abraham], so that he will direct his children and his household after him to keep the way of the Lord by doing what is right and just" (NIV). Abraham is on God's errand. He is performing a task on God's agenda. God has called him to these things. He is not freelancing. Abraham does not write his own job description. God defines the task. Abraham acts on God's behalf.

Deuteronomy 6 underscores this view of parental responsibility. In verse 2, God says His goal is for Israel and their children and grandchildren to fear the Lord by keeping His decrees. The person by whom God's decrees are passed on is the parent whom God calls to train his children when they sit at home, when they walk by the road, when they lie down, and when they rise up. God has an objective. He wants one generation to follow another in His ways. God accomplishes this objective through the agency of parental instruction.

Ephesians 6:4 commands you to bring your children up in the training and instruction of the Lord. This is not simply a command to train and instruct. It is a command to provide the training and instruction of the Lord, to function on God's behalf.

Understanding this simple principle enables you to think clearly about your task. If you are God's agent in this task of providing essential training and instruction in the Lord, then you too are a person under authority. Your child and you are in the same boat. You are both under God's authority. You have differing roles but the same Master.

If you allow unholy anger to muddy the correction process, you are wrong. You need to ask for forgiveness. Your right to discipline your children is tied to what God has called you to, not to your own agenda.

YOU ALSO ARE CALLED TO OBEDIENCE

You do not come to your child demanding, for your own purposes, that he knuckle under to you and obey. No! You come with the corrections of discipline that are the way to life (Proverbs 6:23). You engage your son on behalf of God because God has first engaged you.

I recall many conversations that went like this:

"You didn't obey Daddy, did you?"

"No."

"Do you remember what God says Daddy must do if you disobey?"

"Spank me?"

"That's right. I must spank you. If I don't, then I would be disobeying God. You and I would both be wrong. That would not be good for you or for me, would it?"

"No," (a reluctant reply).

What is this dialogue communicating to the child? You are not spanking him because you are mean. You are not trying to force him to submission to you only because you hate insolence. You are not mad at him. You, like he, are under God's rule and authority. God has called you to a task you cannot shirk. You are acting under God's rule. You are requiring obedience because God says you must.

Confidence to Act

There is tremendous freedom here for a parent. When you direct, correct, or discipline, you are not acting out of your own will; you are acting on behalf of God. You don't have to wonder if it is OK for you to be in charge. You certainly do not need your child's permission. God has given you a duty to perform; therefore the endorsement of your child is not necessary.

Mandate to Act

Understanding that you are God's agent as a parent deals not only with the right to direct. It also provides the mandate to act. You have no choice. You must engage your children. You are acting in obedience to God. It is your duty.

To illustrate, the state of Pennsylvania, where I live, requires schools to report any case of suspected child abuse. This law does not simply provide the right to report abuse. It requires that abuse be reported. The school official has no discretionary right to decide whether to report child abuse. The law requires it. In the same way, the fact that you are called by God to be an authority in the training of your children not only gives you the right but also the responsibility to train.

As a school administrator, I observe that most parents do not understand the appropriateness and necessity of being in charge in their child's life. Rather, parents take the role of advisor. Few are willing to say, for instance, "I have prepared oatmeal for your breakfast. It is a good, nutritious food, and I want you to eat it. Maybe other mornings we will have something you like better." Many are saying, "What do you want for breakfast? You don't want the oatmeal I have prepared. Would you like something else?" This sounds very nice and enlightened, but what is really happening? The child is learning that he is the valid decision maker. The parent only suggests the options.

This scenario is repeated in the experience of young children in clothing choices, schedule choices, social choices, free-time choices, and so forth. By the time children are six or eight or ten, they are their own boss. By age thirteen the child is out of control. Parents can cajole, plead, urge (in frustration and anger), scream, and threaten, but the child is the boss. The parent has long since given up the decision-making prerogative in the child's life. How did it happen? It crept in at a very early age as the parent made every decision a smorgasbord of choices for the child to decide.

Some may argue, "Children only learn to be decision makers as parents allow them to make decisions. We want children to learn to make sound decisions." This misses the most important issue. Children will be good decision makers as they observe faithful parents modeling and instructing wise direction and decision making in their behalf.

Preliminary even to decision making is the importance for children to be under authority. Teach your children that God loves them so much that he gave them parents to be kind authorities to teach and lead them. Children learn to be wise decision makers by learning from you.

Parents must be willing to be in charge. You should do this with a benevolent and gracious manner, but you must be an authority for you children.

PARENTING DEFINED

Recognizing that God has called you to function as His agent defines your task as a parent. Our culture has reduced parenting to providing care. Parents often see the task in these narrow terms. The child must have food, clothes, a bed, and some quality time. In sharp contrast to such a weak view, God has called you to a more profound task than being a care provider. You shepherd your child on God's behalf. The task God has given you is not one that can be conveniently scheduled. It is a pervasive task. Training and shepherding is going on whenever you are with your children. Whether waking, walking, talking, or resting, you must be involved in helping your child to understand life, himself, and his needs from a biblical perspective (Deuteronomy 6:6–7).

If you are going to shepherd your children, you must have intimacy of relationship. You must understand what makes your children tick. If you are going to direct them in the ways of the Lord as Genesis 18:19 calls you to, you must know them and their inclinations. This task requires more than simply providing adequate food, clothing, and shelter.

CLEAR OBJECTIVES

It is instructive to ask parents what concrete training objectives they have for their children. Most parents cannot quickly generate a list of the strengths and weaknesses of their children. Nor can they articulate what they are doing to strengthen their child's weak areas or to encourage his strengths. Many moms and dads have not sat down and discussed their short-term and long-term goals for their children. They have not developed strategies for parenting. They do not know what God says about children and His requirements for them. Little thought has been given to methods and approaches that would focus correction upon attitudes of heart rather than merely on behavior. Sadly, most correction occurs as a by-product of children being an embarrassment or an irritation.

Why is this? Our idea of parenting does not include shepherding. Our culture sees a parent as an adult care provider. Quality time is considered having fun together. Fun together is not a bad idea, but it is light-years away from directing your child in the ways of God.

In contrast to this, Genesis 18 calls fathers to direct their children to keep the way of the Lord by doing what is right and just. Being a parent means working on God's behalf to provide direction for your children. Directors are in charge. Directing involves knowing and helping your children to understand God's standard for children's behavior. It means teaching them they are sinners by nature. It includes pointing them to the mercy and grace of God shown in Christ's life and death for sinners.

HUMILITY IN YOUR TASK

Understanding that you function as God's agents can keep you sharply focused and humble as parents. It is sobering to realize that you correct your child by God's command. You stand before him as God's agent to show him his sin. Just as an ambassador is conscious of functioning on behalf of the country that has sent him, so you as the parent must be aware of the fact you are God's representative to the child. I know of no realization that will sober and humble the parent like this one.

On many occasions I have had to seek the forgiveness of my children for my anger or sinful response. I have had to say. "Son, I sinned against you. I spoke in unholy anger. I said things I should not have said. I was wrong. God has given me a sacred task, and I have brought my unholy anger into this sacred mission. Please forgive me."

Your focus can be sharpened by the realization that discipline is not your working on your agenda, venting your wrath toward your children; it is your coming as God's representative, bringing the reproofs of life to your son or daughter. You only muddy the waters when the bottom line in discipline is your displeasure over their behavior rather than God's displeasure with rebellion against His ordained authority.

NO PLACE FOR ANGER

I have spoken to countless parents who genuinely thought their anger had a legitimate place in correction and discipline. They reasoned that they could only bring their children to a sober fear of disobeying if they showed anger. So discipline became the time when Mom or Dad manipulated their children through raw displays of anger. What the child learns in this is the fear of man, not the fear of God.

James 1 demonstrates the falsehood of the idea that parents should underscore correction with personal rage. "My dear brothers, take note of this: Everyone should be quick to listen, slow to speak and slow to become angry, for man's anger does not bring about the righteous life that God desires." (James 1:19–20)

The apostle James could not be more clear. The righteous life that God desires is never the product of uncontrolled anger. Human anger may teach your children to fear you. They may even behave better, but it will not bring about biblical righteousness.

Any change in behavior that is produced by such anger is not going to move your children toward God. It moves them away from God. It moves them in the direction of the idolatry of fearing man. No wonder James makes emphasis by saying, "Dear brothers, take note of this."

If you correct and discipline your children because God mandates it, then you need not clutter up the task with your anger. Correction is not your showing anger for their offenses; it is rather your reminding them that their sinful behavior offends God. It is bringing His censure of sin to these subjects of His realm. He is the King. They must obey.

BENEFITS TO THE CHILD

The parent comes to the child in God's name and on God's behalf. As parents you can teach your child to receive correction from you because it is the means God has appointed. The child learns to receive correction, not because parents are always right, but because God says the rod of correction imparts wisdom, and whoever heeds correction shows prudence (Proverbs 15:5, 29:15).

The child who accepts these truths will learn to accept correction. I have been humbled and amazed to see my children, in their late teens and early twenties, accept correction, not because I brought it to them in the best possible manner, but because they were persuaded that "he who ignores discipline despises himself, but whoever heeds correction gains understanding" (Proverbs 15:32, NIV). They understand that their dad is God's agent, used by God in the role of authority to direct in God's ways. Therefore, even though I am not a flawless instrument of God's work, they know that receiving correction will bring them understanding.

DISCIPLINE: AN EXPRESSION OF LOVE

Making small talk during a coffee break at a pastor's conference, I overheard some fathers talking about their children, and I couldn't resist listening in.

"I'm too hard on them," commented Dad #1. "I discipline them all the time. I really have to; my wife loves them too much to discipline them."

"I guess you and your wife need to strike some sort of a balance," Dad #2 observed.

"Yes," continued Dad #1 reflectively, "we need some balance between discipline and love."

I almost choked on my donut! Balance discipline and love? I thought of Proverbs 3:12: "The Lord disciplines those he loves, as a father the son he delights in" (NIV). Proverbs 13:24 rushed to mind: "He who spares the rod hates his son, but he who loves him is careful to discipline him," and Revelation 3:19, "Those whom I love, I rebuke and discipline" (NIV). How can you balance discipline and love?

The conversation that I overheard represents a view that is not uncommon. Many parents lack a biblical view of discipline. They tend to think of discipline as revenge—getting even with their children for what they did. Hebrews 12 makes it clear that discipline is not punitive, but corrective. Hebrews 12:5–6 calls discipline "a word of encouragement" that addresses sons. It says discipline is a sign of God's identification with us as our

Father. God disciplines us for our good that we might share in His holiness. It says that while discipline is not pleasant, but painful, it yields a harvest of righteousness and peace. Rather than being something to balance with love, it is the deepest expression of love.

God provides the understanding of what discipline is. Its function is not primarily punitive. It is corrective. The primary thrust of discipline is not to take revenge, but to correct. The discipline of a child is a parent refusing to be a willing party to his child's death (Proverbs 19:18).

What makes this idea so hard to get hold of? It is difficult because of what we discussed above. We don't see ourselves as God's agents. We, therefore, correct our children when they irritate us. When their behavior doesn't irritate us, we don't correct them. Thus, our correction is not us rescuing our children from the path of danger; it is rather just an airing of our frustration. It is us saying to them, "I am fed up with you. You are making me mad. I am going to hit you, or yell at you, or make you sit on a chair in isolation from the family until you figure out what you did wrong."

What I have just described is not discipline. It is punishment. It is ungodly child abuse. Rather than yielding a harvest of righteousness and peace, this sort of treatment leaves children sullen and angry. Is it any wonder that children resist the will of someone who moves against them because they have been an irritation?

Discipline as positive instruction rather than negative punishment does not rule out consequences or outcomes to behavior. Consequences and outcomes of behavior are certainly part of the process God uses to chasten His people.

While it is true that disciplined children are a joy to their parents (Proverbs 23:15–16, 24), as God's agents, you cannot discipline for mere matters of self-interest or personal convenience. Your correction must be tied to the principles and absolutes of the Word of God. The issues of discipline are issues of character development and honoring God. God's nonnegotiable standards should be the fuel of correction and discipline.

Your objective in discipline is to move toward your children, not against them. You move toward them with the reproofs and entreaties of life. Discipline has a corrective objective. It is therapeutic, not penal. It is designed to produce growth, not pain.

Taken from *Shepherding Your Child's Heart* by Tedd Tripp. ©1998 by Tedd Tripp. Used by permission of Shepherd Books. Available at your local Christian bookstore.

Raising children to live in the First Chair takes time, patience, wisdom, and a whole lot of prayer. But it also takes action. This action isn't to come because you're better, smarter, or bigger than your children. No, the responsibility to influence your children's lives for the Lord is given to you by God. When you had children you assumed this responsibility. It was given to you by God. What have you done with that responsibility? Are you taking it and helping your offspring grow in the nurture and admonition of the Lord? If not, you're not being a good shepherd. You see, your children are as helpless as little lambs, which are completely dependent on the shepherd for their survival. The other sheep can't protect them, but the shepherd can. The world wants to destroy your child with false ideas, and only you, the child's earthly shepherd, can defend your child. It is absolutely crucial that you experience this breakthrough and begin taking responsibility. And if you need more direction on being a shepherd to your child, read Ted Tripp's book Shepherding Your Child's Heart. *It will change the way you think about parenting.*

EVALUATION QUESTIONS

1. Take some time and evaluate where you are in experiencing this breakthrough. Where would you rate yourself on the following scale?

1	5	10
Not even close to experiencing this breakthrough.	I've begun the journey, but I've got a ways to go.	I've experienced a breakthrough, and I'm living the abundant life.

2. What would you consider to be the biggest hindrance to your experiencing this breakthrough right now?

3. What one action should you take to experience this breakthrough right now? I challenge you to do it.

Mothers, Fear Not!

JEAN FLEMING

This chapter was written for mothers, but fathers would do themselves a great favor to read it. Fear is a universal feeling. Some "macho" men might not want to admit it, but we've all experienced fear at some point in our lives. But God is very clear in His Word that we should not fear anyone or anything except Him. In fact, He even promises to take care of us and bless us if we are obedient to Him. Some of you may not be reaching that First Chair in your parenting because fear is keeping you from it. After reading the following words of wisdom from Jean Fleming, I'm sure you'll be most encouraged in how you raise your children. In fact, I pray it will help you experience an incredible breakthrough in your parenting.

- Does the state of the world ever make you wish you could gather your family together and run to the hills?
- Does rearing godly children in this society seem an impossible challenge?

• Do you see negative things in your children's lives that scare you to death?

As a young woman in the '60s, I heard Christian women discussing whether they would bring children into such a vile and uncertain world. Khrushchev had hammered his shoe on the table at a United Nations meeting and said that the USSR would bury the U.S. We have seen tremendous upheaval since then. Circumstances change. Today our "atheistic enemy" is now one of the most fertile mission fields in the world, more responsive to the gospel than our own country.

I suppose every generation has reasons to fear bringing up children. This world is a hostile environment, no doubt about it. But I wonder if we, like those women in the '60s, don't often worry needlessly over things that will never become reality.

A few years ago I met a mother with her infant, her first-born, in her arms, who said, "I love being a mother, but I'm so afraid of her teenage years." Perhaps our fears about the teenage years precipitate some of the problems. Undoubtedly, when we fear what may happen in the future, we rob today of strength and joy.

Fear often originates and multiplies in our minds, in our imaginations. I've known this fear; perhaps you have too. Of course, we're not the first to worry over threats that never materialize. In the Old Testament a king receives word that his enemies have formed an alliance. The news intimidates, and "the hearts of Ahaz and his people were shaken, as the trees of the forest are shaken by the wind." Quaking, trembling, quivering fear. Panic spreads and nothing had happened. God sends word to Ahaz, "Be careful, keep calm and don't be afraid. Do not lose heart because of [them]" (Isaiah 7:2,4, NIV).

After God acknowledges the threat to King Ahaz, "the Sovereign LORD says: 'It will not take place, it will not happen'" (v. 7). Then, God warns him: "If you do not *stand* firm in your faith, you will not *stand* at all" (v. 9, emphasis added).

In Hebrew whenever God repeats the same word in a sentence, it is a signal to take careful note. He is making the strongest kind of statement, issuing the most forceful kind of warning.

What are the evidences that we are standing firm in our faith? We are to be careful, keep calm, not be afraid, and not lose heart. We must focus our eyes on God, not on the armies amassing on our borders, not on the coming teenage years.

FEAR NOT, FEAR GOD

God never tells us to be afraid. He tells us to hate evil, flee evil, and to be alert and wise about evil, but not to fear evil. God does not tell us to fear the times. In fact, He commands us not to be alarmed (Matthew 24:6). God sometimes stirs fear in our enemies to accomplish His purposes, but He does not give the spirit of fear to His people (2 Timothy 1:7).

Throughout Scripture God both chides and comforts His people with the phrases "Fear not" or "Do not be afraid." From the first "Fear not" recorded in the Bible in Genesis to the last in Revelation, God unites those words to some statement about Himself. In Genesis He tells Abram, "Do not be afraid, Abram. I am your shield, your very great reward" (Genesis 15:1, NIV). In the last book of the Bible God speaks to the apostle John, "Do not be afraid. I am the First and the Last. I am the Living One; I was dead, and behold I am alive for ever and ever! And I hold the keys of death and Hades" (Revelation 1:17–18, NIV). When God says, "Do not be afraid,"

He means to lift our eyes off the circumstance and focus our gaze on Him.

"Fear not" were the very words the angel spoke to Mary, our Lord's mother (Luke 1:30, KJV), and He has been speaking those same words to mothers ever since. He knows our tendency to succumb to fear and the debilitating results on us and our children. He does not say that dangers don't exist. They do. Sometimes our worst fears do come upon us. Even then, it is Who God is, what God says, and that God is with us that really matter.

We are, unfortunately, given to fearing the wrong things and the wrong people. God tells us to fear Him. This phrase is frequently repeated in the Bible. Fearing God means we are to take God seriously, to regard Him as holy, to worship, trust, and obey Him.

I used to cling to Psalm 34:7 in my times of terror: "The angel of the LORD encamps around those who fear him, and he delivers them." But the promise for deliverance is not for those who are afraid, but for those who fear the Lord.

WHAT DOES THIS MEAN FOR US AS MOTHERS?

Fear Does More Harm Than Good

Recognize that your fears do your family more harm than good. Fears make us controlling. Fears make us tense. Fears show us, at that moment, not to be people of faith. Fears show us, at that moment, not to be people of hope. And unfortunately, fears often show us, at that moment, not to be people of love. Just as love casts out fear (1 John 4:18), it seems fear casts out love. Parents often drive their children from them and from faith by their fears.

Our fears may press us either to frenzied decision or paralyzed indecision, to rash and regrettable words or petrified silence, to unwarranted suspicions or unwise denial. For certain, our fears do our families more harm than good.

God Is in Control

Acknowledge that God has chosen you and your family to live exactly where you are at exactly this time in history. If we charted history on a graph to determine the best time to rear children, we would be hard pressed to find a good time. After Adam and Eve sinned, it was all downhill. In fact, if we were drawing our graph, I believe we would have a hard time deciding whether times were good times or bad times. Would we want to rear children during the golden age of the Old Testament when David was king?

Adultery, rape, and murder were part of the royal family's story. Would the years when Jesus walked this earth be a good time? No other period was graced with the physical presence of God come in flesh, but hundreds of babies were slaughtered in Bethlehem within two years of His birth (Matthew 2:13–18). The land where Jesus was born was under enemy occupation; the religious establishment was cold and corrupt; and God had been silent for roughly four hundred years prior to His coming. Was the first century of Christianity a good time or a bad time? The church was afire. The good news was spreading, but believers were being torn apart by lions.

Are we in a good time or a bad time? Obviously we see many grievous things in our culture. But perhaps more mothers gather to pray for their children and their schools today than any other time in history. Around the United States, high school students meet at the flagpole before class to pray. Whenever God moves His people to gather together to pray, He hears and does something extraordinary.

But suppose this really is one of worst times. God assures us that He has chosen us to live at this specific time of history for a purpose: "From one man he made every nation of men, that they should inhabit the whole earth; and he determined the times set for them and the exact places where they should live. God did this so that men would seek him and perhaps reach out for him and find him, though he is not far from each one of us" (Acts 17:26–27, NIV).

The parable of the weeds provides us with a helpful picture of life on earth (Matthew 13:24–30, 36–43). The servants of the landowner are distressed because an enemy has sown weeds among the good seed. The landowner tells his servants to wait until harvest to separate the two crops. For us as well, the bad and the good must grow up together.

God Calls Us to Faith, Hope, and Love

"Now faith is being sure of what we hope for and certain of what we do not see" (Hebrews 11:1, NIV). Faith and hope are intertwined. Both are tied to believing that what God says is true. Both have to do with unseen realities. Faith says, "I believe what God says about the invisible." Hope says, "I believe what God says about the future."

In heaven we will have no need for faith or hope; all will be visible, tangible reality. But love has a place for eternity. Perhaps this is why it is said, "And now these three remain: faith, hope and love. But the greatest of these is love" (1 Corinthians 13:13, NIV).

As mothers, we exercise our faith when we look beyond what is visible. Although Saint Augustine (354–430) had a believing, praying mother, he was involved in immoral living and dabbled in strange philosophies and sects. Augustine was thirty before he became a follower of Christ. William Wilberforce (1759–1833) grew up in a home where Christ was honored, but was absorbed in tile sporting and social life. Wilberforce came to true faith through a tutor at Queens College where the two of them read aloud to each other literary classics and the Bible and discussed what they read. After his conversion to Christ, Wilberforce was discipled by John Newton, the converted former slave ship captain who wrote the great hymn "Amazing Grace." Newton encouraged Wilberforce to memorize Scripture, do Bible study, and be Christ's man in the British Parliament where Wilberforce spent most of his public life passing legislation against slavery.

My point? Just because your children are not where you would like to see them at this point in time does not mean all hope is lost. Keep praying and trusting God to work. Pray specifically for the people that God might bring into their lives to influence them. We have all heard dramatic stories of conversion where God touched people who did not have the privilege of learning of Christ in their homes. Our hearts beat faster as we hear their stories. We exalt in the fact that God can reach down and redeem in amazing ways. But often when it comes to our own children, we need the challenge to faith: if God can create something from nothing as He did in creation, and if He can make something good from something bad, certainly He can yet touch your child as He touched Augustine and Wilberforce.

Encourage Others

God wants us to encourage each other to faith.

"Is there any particular need I should address?" I asked the woman who had arranged for me to speak to the women at her church. "Goodness! They're scaring each other to death," she said. "They're convinced it's impossible to raise good kids today."

It dishonors God when we feed one another's fears instead of encouraging each other to trust God and to take heart. God calls us to stir each other to faith and good works especially in these difficult times (Hebrews 10:24–25).

Fear may be one of the Enemy's most powerful strategies. Fear has a way of taking over, of causing us to doubt God, of pushing aside good judgment, of grabbing us by the throat and bullying us into a corner. Neither Jesus nor Paul sidestepped the reality of evil. They painted evil in dark terms, but they never suggested that the state of the world should paralyze believers with fear, nor that we should feed one another's fears. If we fear evil instead of fearing God, evil has power over us.

God has given many promises that He is stronger than evil and that He will be with us and help us. Satan is part of God's creation, inferior to God in every way and in every degree, limited by God in scope and power. The apostle John reminds us: "You, dear children, are from God and have overcome them, because the one who is in you is greater than the one who is in the world" (1 John 4:4).

It dishonors God when we talk as if the end were still up for grabs, as if we weren't sure who would win the battle between good and evil. The end is written: Jesus is victor.

God is honored when those who fear God, not evil, talk with each other. "Then those who feared the LORD talked with each other, and the LORD listened and heard. A scroll of remembrance was written in his presence concerning those who feared the LORD and honored his name" (Malachi 3:16, NIV). I see the Lord looking down on a scene that delights Him. Those who take Him seriously are talking with each other about His faithfulness, His promises, His tender mercies and loving kindness. They may be enjoying tea together or suffering in a dreary dungeon; they may be mothers rejoicing over the robust spiritual health of their children or looking to God in faith for wayward children. The situation is immaterial. The spirit and content of the meeting is everything: God is taken seriously.

The scene is so pleasing to God that He calls in heavenly scribes to record the conversation, to capture permanently this high point in the history of humanity. For after all, in God's eyes aren't the high points of history those times when His people count on His character and His Word?

God Calls Us to Live with the Tensions of Faith

To live by faith is to live with tensions, with blurred lines, and with an uncomfortable lack of definition because God wants us to look to Him for wisdom, strength, and direction as we parent our children and live our lives.

Although God gives some precise negative commands—do not lie, do not commit adultery—the body of His communication to us is presented in round, general terms. For example, God tells us to love Him with all our heart, mind, and strength; to honor our parents; to love others as ourselves. The latter injunctions are clear, but the way of applying them is not specified. The application of "do not lie" is plain, but the application of "love others as yourself" is not. Loving others might be applied by taking a needy family a casserole, not speaking while someone else is talking, rescuing a drowning child, or a million other possibilities. When we mother by faith, trusting God and seeking to implement what He asks of us, the outworking will, and should, vary from family to family, from situation to situation.

God will lead you into individualized applications tailor-made for your family. For example, should you give your child a public school, Christian school, or home school education? God bids each family to pray and seek His counsel. No one answer is right for everyone. God may in fact lead a family to use many different schooling options. The schooling issue illustrates a multitude of other areas where we may learn from God and exercise faith as we make decisions in our families.

There is no one answer as to how we handle television, music, computer, or dating. Each family must come to its conclusions before God in faith.

As we endeavor to follow God, fear often intrudes to test our faith. Fears come in many forms. We worry that God might not lead us or that we might not be able to distinguish His promptings. We worry about outside forces: the media, popular culture, and peer pressure.

Of course, peer pressure can cause problems. Unfortunately, when the phrase peer pressure is mentioned, mothers usually think solely of the destructive squeeze our children feel to conform. But mothers succumb, too. Sometimes the peer pressure of other Christian mothers wrongly dictates our actions and defines our anxieties. Instead of looking to the Lord for direction, we look around us for cues and approval.

The result is often a rigid picture of what a life following Jesus should look like. We fix upon a single picture: how kids should dress or wear their hair; whether the godly should choose Christian school, public school, or home school for their children. We must neither yield to peer pressure ourselves, nor judge parents who seek to follow the Lord but decide directions different from ours.

We need each other; we are a body. We need to challenge and encourage one another, to learn from one another. The danger comes when one specific application is held up as the only right course of action.

The Struggle to Live Relevantly in This World

If God allowed us to retreat from this world, huddled together in delightful commune with others of like mind, we would be released from some of the stresses that accompany the life of those who take His call seriously. But God calls His people to make Him known. This requires involvement in this world and brings with it complexities and tensions. The difficulty comes in trying to balance the desire to protect our children and the realization that if they can't relate to people, there is little hope of reaching them for Christ. The questions are obvious and difficult. For example, should I allow my children to watch television? If so, what programs? How will I counter the negative impact? What real food for the mind and soul will I feed them?

Once into these complex issues, I must realize that my conclusions before God may be different from those of other parents who are also seeking God's direction. God has peculiar plans for each family, each child. It only follows that we won't all look the same.

Don't run to the hills to escape the evil of this world. Raising godly children right where you are is possible. Ask God to work in your children's lives. Take heart. Be calm. Be careful. Don't be afraid. Trust God.

From *A Mother's Heart* by Jean Fleming. ©1996 by Jean Fleming. Used by permission of NavPress. Available at your local Christian bookstore.

Trusting God—it's not always easy, especially when it comes to our children. Sometimes we want to hold on so tight, thinking that perhaps we can save them from the pain of this ugly, sinful world. What we usually find is that the tighter we hold on, the more the world gets its hands around our children. Perhaps you've found this to be true in your own life. Or worse, you've grown so fearful of the world that you've decided not to bring any children into the world because "they wouldn't stand a chance." Well, as Jean Fleming has just explained, God likes those odds. In fact, it's when we don't stand a chance that God's power is most evident. All He wants us to do is trust Him. Won't you do that right now? If you will, you'll experience a breakthrough in your parenting that truly demonstrates the power of God. And mothers, if you would like to read more of Jean Fleming's wisdom, I strongly encourage you to read her book, A Mother's Heart. *You will be blessed!*

EVALUATION QUESTIONS

1. Take some time and evaluate where you are in experiencing this breakthrough. Where would you rate yourself on the following scale?

1	5	10
Not even close to experiencing this breakthrough.	I've begun the journey, but I've got a ways to go.	I've experienced a breakthrough, and I'm living the abundant life.

2. What would you consider to be the biggest hindrance to your experiencing this breakthrough right now?

3. What one action should you take to experience this breakthrough right now?

Experiencing Spiritual Breakthroughs in Your Walk with God

*"A man who has faith must be prepared
not only to be a martyr, but to be a fool."*
G. K. CHESTERTON (1874–1936)

"A perfect faith would lift us absolutely above fear."
GEORGE MACDONALD (1824–1905)

*"Don't be afraid to take a big step.
You can't cross a chasm in two small jumps."*
DAVID LLOYD GEORGE (1863–1945)

"Faith can put a candle in the darkest night."
MARGARET SANGSTER (1838–1912)

*"Faith is…doing the right thing regardless of the consequences,
knowing God will turn the ultimate effect to good."*
PAMELA REEVE

Live Life
beyond the Limits

FRANKLIN GRAHAM

It doesn't matter whether you're in the Second Chair or the Third Chair, the truth is, you're not living the life of abundance. When the children of Israel refused to enter the Promised Land the first time they approached the Jordan River, what was their fundamental sin? They refused to believe that God would do what He said He would do. They didn't trust God. However, everything they had experienced since their departure from Egypt told them that God was completely trustworthy. God was asking them to do something that seemed impossible. And by human standards, it was. For some people, moving to the First Chair may seem like a similar impossibility. But, as Franklin Graham explains, God asks us to have faith that He can do the impossible in our lives.

Mary Damron frequently entertains herself and others by singing primitive mountain music. On our trip to Bosnia, she taught all of us, including Ricky Skaggs, a song she particularly likes. When I think of Mary, I find myself humming the tune, sometimes even singing each verse. But without the twang that mountain singers have perfected, it doesn't sound quite the same. The song tells about how life sometimes takes us up on the mountain, but it can also take us down into the dark valleys. It reminds us that the God on the mountain is also the God in the valley. He's the God of the good and the bad times, and the God of the day is still God in the night.

There's a lot of truth in this song. Many of us are mountaintop Christians. We think we'll stay in sync with God as long as He keeps us on the highest plateau. But when we get used to the good times, we forget all about God. We don't have time for Him anymore.

Yet all of us inevitably come tumbling off that mountaintop and land in the depths—the valleys of illness, depression, financial insecurity, family feuds, temptation, and sin. We've all been in them. Those are the moments when we are tempted to question God's love and provision.

And yet, if we truly want to live a life beyond the limits, we need something that will keep us in step with Him, whether we're on top of a high mountain or walking in the shadows of the valley of death. That something is faith.

One of my favorite passages of Scripture has always been Hebrews 11. It begins by defining faith: "Now faith is the substance of things hoped for, the evidence of things not seen. For by it the elders obtained a good testimony" (vv. 1–2, NKJV).

You see, that's what I want in life: a good testimony. I want to hear my heavenly Father say, "Well done, thou good and faithful servant."

The book of Hebrews tells us how we can build an iron-clad testimony:

By faith Abel offered to God a more excellent sacrifice than Cain, through which he obtained witness that he was righteous, God testifying of his gifts; and through it he being dead still speaks. (11:4, NKJV)

Imagine that: Being dead, Abel still speaks. How many people wear themselves out trying to achieve some sort of earthly immortality? People try to amass great wealth, achieve unparalleled fame, or set world records just so that there will be some evidence that they existed. Politicians want to leave their mark on history. Only a few do, like George Washington, Abraham Lincoln, and Ronald Reagan. Most fade into obscurity, and their speeches and legislation are forgotten.

I understand their drive and their search for significance, but they are depositing their efforts in the wrong bank. Putting all your money and effort into an earthly inheritance is like investing in horses and buggies—the future will leave you behind. Our future—the one that counts—is in heaven. It is called life everlasting: "The earth will grow old like a garment, and those who dwell in it will die in like manner; but My salvation will be forever, and My righteousness will not be abolished" (Isaiah 51:6, NKJV). And in eternity, faith is the only currency that counts.

Hebrews 11:6 goes on to say, "Without faith it is impossible to please Him, for he who comes to God must believe that He is, and that He is a rewarder of those who diligently seek Him" (NKJV). You can be the most religious person in your town and go to church every time the door is open. But if you don't have faith, you're just playacting the Christian life.

The problem in many of our churches today is that we have lost our faith.

But you see, Hebrews 11 tells us that it was faith that kept

Noah in sync with God. When the skies were still clear, Noah got on board, didn't he?

It was faith that moved Abraham to go to a foreign country and later offer up his only son, Isaac. By putting Isaac on the altar, Abraham knew he was putting everything on the line—how could God's promise come true if Abraham sacrificed his only true heir? But Abraham's faith moved him to be obedient—he stayed in sync with God's will and purpose.

Faith leads to action.

How can we have the kind of faith that is never shaken, questioned, or doubted?

ZERO-HOUR FAITH

Over the years, I have been privileged to meet people of tremendous faith. Some of the great missionaries I have known have lived extraordinary lives of faith. My grandfather Dr. L. Nelson Bell left Virginia's Shenandoah Valley right after World War I to go to China, where he spent the next twenty-five years serving the Chinese people in Christ's name.

In the mideighties, I had a chance to go to China with my mother and father. Today in that country, there are literally tens of thousands of Christians who can trace their faith back to my grandfather's ministry as a medical missionary. When he died after many years of service to our Lord, he didn't leave his family a great wealth of earthly possessions, but what a remarkable testimony and example he left behind for his children and grandchildren.

A good friend of mine, Dr. Bob Foster, is also a man of faith. Though a Canadian citizen, Bob grew up in Africa. As a young man, Bob believed God called him to become a medical missionary. Being from a missionary family presented a major hurdle, though. He had no money.

Even so, convinced that God was calling him, Bob persevered and applied the principles of faith he had seen his parents put into practice. At seventeen, Bob completed his application to medical school. He asked the Lord to supply the fee. He waited and waited and waited some more, but not one dollar came.

As the second hand ticked closer to the deadline hour, Bob decided to submit his application minus the fee.

Standing in line at the university, he shoved his hands down into his empty pockets and wondered where he would get his fee. He knew God had called him to be a missionary doctor. Even though two fingers had been crushed while working at a shipyard that summer trying to earn enough money for his registration and tuition fees, God had allowed his fingers to be partially saved. To him, that was proof God wanted him to continue pursuing his dream to become a doctor. As the line moved slowly forward, Bob grew anxious. If he only had $450.

"What's your name?" The registrar interrupted his thoughts as he stepped up to the desk.

"Robert Livingstone Foster," he replied nervously.

He watched as she ran her finger down a list of names, then stopped and looked up at him.

"Your bill has been paid. You won a scholarship from your high school exams, and the money has already been credited to your account. All your fees have been taken care of for the year."

Stunned, Bob walked away with an overwhelming sense of gratitude. There was no doubt in his mind that God had prepared him for medical school and that He was going to pay the bills as well. In fact, in the years ahead, Bob saw such provision over and over again. Several years, he received scholarships for scholastic achievement. Three years after the accident at the shipyard, workmen's compensation called, telling him that they had made an award to him for permanent disability. The amount covered a full year of medical school.

This was a pattern that seemed to follow Bob throughout his medical training. He found himself having to wait until zero hour, when God would miraculously provide desperately needed funds in order to continue. Through the grace and provision of his heavenly Father, Bob finished medical school and set his sights on the mission field. God was developing his character and faith for the adventures he would come to experience in another part of the world.

Like his parents, Bob has served God in some of the most difficult places throughout Africa. He raised seven children on the mission field, and many of them today are serving the Lord in foreign countries. In his retirement he stays busier than ever, raising money for mission projects, traveling to Africa to relieve missionary doctors so that they can have time off, and preaching Christ at every opportunity. Without faith exercised and proven, Bob would never have accomplished on earth what God intended. He experienced firsthand what the book of James tells us: "The testing of your faith develops perseverance. Perseverance must finish its work so that you may be mature and complete, not lacking anything" (1:3–4, NIV).

To have faith like Bob Foster, we're going to have to confront the enemies of faith.

THE ENEMIES OF FAITH

One enemy of faith is our possessions. Abraham was willing to put everything on the line because "he waited for the city which has foundations, whose builder and maker is God"

(Hebrews 11:10, NKJV). We're not willing to wait. We want everything, and we want it now. Many times God provides on the last day or at the last hour, sometimes at the very last minute.

Think of the blessing Bob would have missed had he refused to deliver his application because he didn't have the money needed! What Bob did not know as he stood in line was that God had already provided days before.

I understand the lure of possessions and enticing desires. We all feel their tug. And if we're not careful, they can pull us down. I remember when Jane Austin and I were first married and we could load everything we owned in her little Ford Maverick. I recall the freedom of being packed and on the road in ten minutes. It was great! Nothing to hold us back.

Though most of us do not live as nomads, we still need to ask, Is my faith being buried by my possessions? Is my faith shattered most when my financial situation looks the bleakest? Do I define my security by what I have stored in the bank? By themselves, possessions aren't sinful, but our faith is buried when we begin to worship things. "Take heed and beware of covetousness, for one's life does not consist in the abundance of the things he possesses" (Luke 12:15, NKJV).

Another enemy of faith is experience. We limit ourselves by what we think is humanly possible. Hebrews 11:11 tells us, "By faith Sarah herself also received strength to conceive seed, and she bore a child when she was past the age, because she judged Him faithful who had promised" (NKJV). How could a woman past the age of childbearing conceive and give birth to a son? That's humanly impossible, but faith points to a God for whom nothing is too hard.

When Bob Pierce started Samaritan's Purse, people thought his vision of immediate response to the world's most urgent needs was brilliant but practically impossible. Bureaucracy would get in the way. Business meetings would block the flow of critically needed funds. Red tape would strangle his good intentions. People didn't believe in Bob's vision because they had never seen it done—a relief organization that could move quickly, immediately, and commit to providing aid virtually on the spot. People scoffed.

But Bob's vision has grown many times over in the years since. God has created a way for relief to begin flowing when and where it's needed—not just months after a lengthy approval process. Bob blew the limits that kept many others back.

One of the devil's favorite excuses is, "But that's never been done. Why try?" The faithful Christian's answer is, "If God's really calling us to do this, He'll provide a way to get it done."

Possibly the greatest lesson I learned from Bob Pierce was something he called *God room*. This was a phrase he coined that simply means recognizing a need bigger than what human limitations can meet. Yet you press on to meet the need that you believe God has placed on your heart. Trust Him to close the gap, and watch a miracle unfold by God's own provision. Before you know it, the need is met through ways that seem completely impossible.

Bob always told me, "Faith isn't required as long as you set your goal only as high as the most intelligent, most informed, and expert human efforts can reach. You don't exercise faith until you have committed more than it's possible to give." Bob Foster's story illustrates this principle so well.

I like how Charles Wesley defined faith:

> *Faith, mighty faith, the promise sees,*
> *And looks to God alone;*
> *Laughs at impossibilities,*
> *And cries, "It shall be done."*

Faith is the power that God gives us to break out of our human limitations and become the people He created us to be. Use this power to slay the enemies of faith and experience the joy of living in sync with Him.

Taken from *Living beyond the Limits* by Franklin Graham. ©1998 by Franklin Graham. Used by permission of Thomas Nelson Publishers. Available at your local Christian bookstore.

When Joshua took the Israelites into the Promised Land, he was moving them from the Second Chair to the First. The victories they experienced while conquering the land of Canaan were concrete examples of what God will accomplish in our lives when we have faith in Him. God told the Israelites to enter the land and take possession of it. The task looked impossible, but God told them to do it. Has God ever told you to do something that seemed impossible? Perhaps you have your own Jericho that needs to be conquered. I can assure you that God will never tell you to do something that cannot be done—with faith. When God tells you to do something, He also promises to enable you to accomplish it. What is it in your life that God is telling you to do? If you're reading His Word, I'm sure He's telling you something. Won't you do as it says and sit in the First Chair today? Living in the First Chair requires us to live beyond the limits that humans are normally bound by. In his book, Living Beyond the Limits, *Franklin Graham makes it very clear that you can live an exciting life that is limited only by God—not man.*

EVALUATION QUESTIONS

1. Take some time and evaluate where you are in experiencing this victory. Where would you rate yourself on the following scale?

1	5	10
Not even close to experiencing this breakthrough.	I've begun the journey, but I've got a ways to go.	I've experienced a breakthrough, and I'm living the abundant life.

2. What would you consider to be the biggest hindrance to your experiencing this breakthrough right now?

3. What one action should you take to experience this breakthrough right now? I challenge you to do it.

*"I find doing the will of God
leaves me no time for disputing about his plans."*
GEORGE MACDONALD (1824–1905)

"I want what God wants, that's why I am so merry."
SAINT FRANCIS OF ASSISI (C. 1181–1226)

"The center of God's will is our only safety."
BETSIE TEN BOOM (1885–1944)

"To walk out of his will is to walk into nowhere."
C. S. LEWIS (1898–1963)

*"There are no disappointments to those whose wills
are buried in the will of God."*
FREDERICK WILLIAM FABER (1814–1863)

Obey the Will of God

WARREN WIERSBE

For many Second Chair believers, the will of God seems to be an elusive thing. They seem to be waiting for God to come down from the heavens and speak to them face-to-face. Few people have actually had that happen—and you can read about these folks in the Bible. For the rest of us, God has chosen to speak to us through His Word and by the counsel of the Holy Spirit. Many Christians seem to think that the Bible is not completely sufficient for giving them direction. But it is! The Word of God, in the form of the Scriptures and with the help of the Holy Spirit's illumination, has every answer to every question. The answer may be located in a specific command or principles of biblical wisdom applied to the issue at hand in direct answer to the prayer of wisdom in James 1. But, as Warren Wiersbe explains, it's not as easy as simply opening the Bible and pointing to a verse.

*O*nly he who believes is obedient; only he who is obedient believes." That was written by the German pastor and martyr Dietrich Bonhoeffer, and it's a statement that shows insight into the relationship between personal faith in Christ and obedience to the will of God. We've just thought about what it means to live by faith; now let's consider what it means to obey by faith and do the will of God.

Four principles should govern our attitude toward the will of God: (1) The will of God is planned from the heart of God; (2) the will of God is for the glory of God; (3) the will of God is revealed through the Word of God; and (4) we appreciate the will of God more as we trust Him and obey what He tells us to do.

FROM THE HEART OF GOD

The first principle is that the will of God comes from the heart of God. "The counsel of the Lord stands forever, the plans of His heart to all generations" (Psalm 33:11, NKJV).

Note that phrase "the plans of His heart." It takes care of any nightmares you may have about merciless masters, heartless robots, and faceless machines. If the will of God comes from the heart of God, then His will is the expression of His love. Rebellious nations see God's will as chains to be broken, and they shout in unison, "Let us break Their bonds in pieces and cast away Their cords from us" (Psalm 2:3, NKJV). But God doesn't shackle His children with chains; He draws us "with gentle cords, with bands of love" (Hosea 11:4, NKJV). God wants to guide us like children, with His counsel and His eye, not like animals with a bit and a bridle (Psalm 32:8–9).

The will of God isn't a faceless machine that comes to a sudden halt if I disobey the Lord. The will of God is a living relationship between me and the Lord. What He has willed proves His love for me; my obedience to that will proves my love for Him, "and His commandments are not burdensome" (1 John 5:3, NKJV).

God's will is more like a warm human body than like a piece of cold machinery. If one part of my body rebels, the rest of my body compensates for it until the doctor and I can get the malfunctioning part fixed. When my gallbladder declared war on me a few years ago, I became a very sick man, but my heart kept beating and my breathing didn't stop. Within a week, my rebel gallbladder had been taken out, and I was on the mend.

FOR THE GLORY OF GOD

The second principle is that the will of God is for the glory of God.

Most of us are prone to think of God's will only as His plan for getting something done. That's why we pray, "Your will be done on earth as it is in heaven" (Matthew 6:10, NKJV). Getting things done may be the immediate purpose of His will, but the ultimate purpose is His glory, and the glory of God is the highest purpose that can occupy the human heart and life.

God's immediate purpose in opening the Red Sea was to rescue Israel from the pursuing Egyptian army, but His ultimate aim was to reveal His glory to a pagan nation whose ruler had flippantly asked, "Who is the Lord, that I should obey His voice to let Israel go?" (Exodus 5:2, NKJV). As they watched the Egyptian army drown, no wonder Israel sang,

> I will sing to the Lord,
> For He has triumphed gloriously!…
> He is my God, and I will praise Him.
> (Exodus 15:1–2, NKJV)

What I want to emphasize here is that we dare not separate the will of God from the glory of God. Jesus put them together in the Lord's Prayer: "Hallowed be Your name. Your kingdom come. Your will be done" (Matthew 6:9–10, NKJV).

Maturing believers aren't content merely to know what God wants them to do; they also want to know how to do it so that God will be glorified. David's desire to bring the ark to Jerusalem was a noble venture, but his first attempt failed because he didn't glorify God (2 Samuel 6). Paul's prayer to be delivered of his thorn in the flesh wasn't answered because having the thorn and depending on God's grace brought more glory to God (2 Corinthians 12:7–10). When Mary and Martha sent word to Jesus that Lazarus was sick, He didn't immediately come to their aid. By waiting until Lazarus died, Jesus was able to bring more glory to God (John 11:4, 40).

When the Assyrian army surrounded Jerusalem and threatened to capture it, King Hezekiah prayed to God for help, and when you read his prayer (Isaiah 37:14–20), you see that his great burden was the glory of God as opposed to the vanity of the Assyrian idols. He prayed, "You are God, You alone, of all the kingdoms of the earth" (v. 16, NKJV). Sennacherib sent his army "to reproach the living God" (v. 17, NKJV). And what a grand climax to his prayer: "Now therefore, O Lord our God, save us from his hand, that all the kingdoms of the earth may know that You are the Lord, You alone" (v. 20, NKJV). God answered the prayer, delivered His people, and glorified His name.

When our prayers focus on the glory of God, we're in league with all creation, for "the heavens declare the glory of God" (Psalm 19:1, NKJV). We're also cooperating with God in the great goal of salvation, "to the praise of the glory of His grace" (Ephesians 1–6:, NKJV), and we're keeping in step with the Holy Spirit who was given that Jesus might be glorified (John 16:14).

THROUGH THE WORD OF GOD

The third principle is that the will of God is revealed through the Word of God. "Your word is a lamp to my feet and a light to my path" (Psalm 119:105, NKJV).

Perhaps the psalmist had the nation of Israel in mind when he wrote that statement, for God guided His people by means of a glorious cloud by day and by night (Exodus 13:21; 40:34–38; Nehemiah 9:12). In times of perplexity, I've wished I had such visible and obvious means of guidance. But then I have had to remind myself that God's children can't mature unless we walk by faith and not by sight.

However, we must not think that the Bible is some kind of magical book that reveals the future, like a deck of tarot cards or a cup of tea leaves. Opening the Bible at random and pointing to a verse is gambling, not seeking God's will; and the consequences could be disastrous. It's not random use of the Bible that gives us guidance but reading the Word daily, systematically, and obediently. "Let the word of Christ dwell in you richly in all wisdom" is God's commandment (Colossians 3:16, NKJV).

Through its admonitions, promises, warnings, and examples, the Bible makes very clear what pleases God and what displeases Him. In fact, some verses state, "This is the will of God." "For this is the will of God, your sanctification: that you should abstain from sexual immorality" (1 Thessalonians 4:3, NKJV). Nobody has to pray about committing fornication or adultery because God says these acts are sins and must be avoided. "In everything give thanks; for this is the will of God in Christ Jesus for you" (1 Thessalonians 5:18, NKJV). That takes care of our complaining! "For this is the will of God, that by doing good you may put to silence the ignorance of foolish men" (1 Peter 2:15, NKJV). The best way to handle criticism and slander is to do good works and let God do the rest.

I can't prove it statistically, but I'm sure that 90 percent of the decisions I make daily are covered in the Scriptures—I don't have to ask God what to do. I've read my Bible enough to know that it's wrong to steal, to lie, to hate, to avenge myself, to gossip, to lose my temper, to harbor resentment, and to be unkind to people. But what about the other 10 percent? Although it gave me plenty of counsel concerning marriage and the Christian home, my Bible didn't tell me exactly the girl I should marry. It didn't name the school I should go to, the city I should live in, or the local church my family and I should attend. How do we handle these everyday practical decisions?

It's here that we trust God for the sanctified common sense that comes from the renewing of the mind (Romans 12:2). Believers who spend time daily in the Word and in prayer gradually develop a spiritual radar, a practical wisdom[1] from the Holy Spirit that gives us direction when we need it. Sometimes that direction comes from a promise or warning in Scripture, sometimes from God's providential working in circumstances, and sometimes from the Spirit's witness in our hearts. Even a chance remark by a friend can be used of God to guide us if our minds and hearts are prepared and we're willing to obey God's leading.

Determining God's will also depends on knowing God's character, and His character is revealed in His Word. It doesn't take long for a child to learn what Mother and Father are really like, and the child's behavior is based on that knowledge. Students study their instructors as much as they study their books, and they try to do the kind of work that will please their teachers the most. That's the way to get a better grade.

It isn't enough to read the Bible and discover what God did; we also need to learn why God did it. God "made known His ways to Moses, His acts to the children of Israel" (Psalm 103:7, NKJV). The Israelites knew what God did because they saw it happen, but Moses knew why God did it. That's because Moses prayed, "If I have found grace in Your sight, show me now Your way, that I may know You and that I may find grace in Your sight" (Exodus 33:13, NKJV).

When the Lord revealed Himself to Moses on the mount, He answered Moses' prayer by reciting His glorious attributes: "The Lord, the Lord God, merciful and gracious, longsuffering, and abounding in goodness and truth" (Exodus 34:6, NKJV). And when Moses interceded for the disobedient nation at Kadesh-Barnea, he reminded God of His holy character and obtained pardon for them (Numbers 14:11–25). When you know the character of God, you find it easier to pray in the will of God.

When circumstances or people want to direct us, we must trust the Spirit of God within us to bear witness and give us guidance from the Word. We must always test circumstances by the Word of God; otherwise, we'll find ourselves going on detours. On two occasions, David had opportunity to kill King Saul, and some of his men encouraged him to do it. But David refused because he knew it was wrong to avenge himself by laying hands on God's anointed leader, even though that leader was rejected by God. (see 1 Samuel 24; 26). When the south wind blows softly (Acts 27:13), we need great discernment, and that discernment can come only through the Spirit of God using the Word of God.

AS WE TRUST AND OBEY

Our fourth principle is that we appreciate the will of God more as we trust Him and obey what He tells us to do. "Do not be conformed to this world, but be transformed by the renewing of your mind, that you may prove what is that good and acceptable and perfect will of God" (Romans 12:2, NKJV).

The word translated "prove" means "to prove by experience." It describes the testing of metal in the furnace and suggests to us that discerning the will of God is something we learn by practical experience in the furnace of life. Sometimes children don't believe their parents' warnings or instructions and have to learn the hard way that fire burns, knives cut, too much candy can make you sick, and electricity is dangerous to play with. But Paul isn't advising us to learn the hard way; rather, he is telling us how to learn to discern God's will in the daily experience of life and avoid the problems.

Words like "be transformed" and "renewing" describe an ongoing process rather than something completed. God doesn't hand us the latest road atlas, complete with maps, photographs, and directions. Rather, He gives us a compass and a goal, and we learn the rest along the way.

God's "good and acceptable and perfect will" is one will and not three. The will of God isn't like a mail-order catalog that offers the customer "good-better-best," the only difference being the price and the quality of the merchandise. A young man said to me, "I think I'll settle for God's good will because I don't want to make the sacrifices necessary for His perfect will." But a holy and loving God could never will for His beloved children anything other than what is perfect. If we settle for second best, it isn't God's second best because He wills only what is the very best for us. "The renewal of the mind," writes Leon Morris, "enables the believer to discern what is good, what is pleasing to God, and what is perfect."[2]

If you keep in mind that discerning the will of God means developing a personal relationship with the Lord, not receiving a series of memos from heaven, then you will better understand how this demanding but delightful process works. The better we get to know the Lord, the better we understand His ways and His character, and therefore, the better we know how to please Him. However, at the same time we get to know ourselves better and we discover the things that need special attention. It's similar to the kind of personal growth that spouses experience during their first year or two of marriage.

When I was in pastoral ministry, during premarital counseling sessions I would give the man and the woman each a piece of paper and say, "Would you please write down the three things that you enjoy the most and then the three things you think your prospective mate enjoys the most." The results were sometimes devastating!

"If you two don't know how to please each other now," I'd say, "what will happen after you're married?" Sometimes this led to another counseling session, which I hope led to a happier marriage.

This adventure of getting to know God and ourselves better makes doing the will of God exciting, far more exciting than sinning. When we sin, we become blind to ourselves and to God, and there is no growth in character. Like the Prodigal Son, we find ourselves lonely and perishing while there is plenty back at the Father's house. What Dr. Theodore Epp called "adventuring by faith" is the most exciting kind of life anybody could ever experience.

QUESTIONS ABOUT GOD'S WILL

We've examined the four principles relating to the will of God. What remains now is to deal with some practical questions that often arise when you discuss this topic.

What if I've prayed, read the Word, and waited on God, but no answer has come? What do I do next?

You keep waiting. If there is no answer, you assume God wants you to stay where you are. Remember that God is more concerned about building the worker than getting the work done. If He wants to grow a mushroom, He can do it overnight, but it takes a few years to build an oak. In our waiting, God works in our lives to prepare us for what He is preparing for us.

What about "putting out a fleece?"

What Gideon did was a sign not of faith but of unbelief (Judges 6:36–40), and I don't recommend that you follow his example. God had already made it clear to Gideon that He would use him to deliver Israel from the Midianites, and there was no need for Gideon to test God's will further. Who are we to tell God how He should communicate with us? How do I know that the test I'm proposing is a valid one? I've heard people say, "Well, if I get a phone call by such and such a time, I'll know this is God's will." So we allow the phone company to determine God's will for us! Better to depend on the Word and wait on the Lord. Gideon didn't have a complete Bible as we do, so perhaps we can excuse him. But beware! Use a fleece and the devil may pull the wool over your eyes!

I have a friend who determines God's will by taking a card out of her promise box. Is this dependable?

No. I call that religious roulette. The purpose of a promise box is to give us a promise a day that we can carry with us, memorize, and learn to appreciate. But pulling out a card to determine God's will is like opening your Bible at random and pointing to a verse. If you were planning a trip, would you open the road atlas just anywhere and point to a highway? A promise can encourage us after we've made a decision, but pulling out a card is a dangerous way to make that decision.

Does God want to guide us in little things or only in big things?

He wants to guide us in everything, but He also expects us to use our common sense. I had a friend who became unbalanced emotionally because he wanted God to tell him what breakfast cereal to eat, what color tie to wear, and what side of the street to walk on. There are no trivial things in the Christian life, but some things are more important than others. God can use a casual word or a new acquaintance to help us determine His will. If we yield ourselves to God each day and ask Him to guide us, we'll have the direction we need when we need it. If we don't, then we wait. God leads in little things and big things because He is making all things work together for good.

Taken from *Being a Child of God*, ©1996 by Warren W. Wiersbe. Published by Thomas Nelson Publishers. Used by permission. Available at your local Christian bookstore.

How many times have you heard that Christianity is not a religion, it's a relationship? The statement is very true. But many times we try to circumvent the relationship and do things the easy way. This is the case with finding the will of God. It's so much easier to find a verse that justifies what we want to do, or say that we heard a voice telling us to do something, than it is to actually have a relationship with the Lord, know His Word and His character, and act accordingly. If you want to experience a breakthrough in knowing the will of God, then take the time to build that relationship—it's the only way to go! So if you're struggling to find the will of God, take the time to read His Word, pray, think, and wait on Him. I also recommend that you read Warren Wiersbe's book Being a Child of God. *It has some timeless principles about knowing and loving God as one of His children.*

EVALUATION QUESTIONS

1. Take some time and evaluate where you are in experiencing this spiritual breakthrough over pride. Where would you rate yourself on the following scale?

1	5	10
Not even close to experiencing this breakthrough.	I've begun the journey, but I've got a ways to go.	I've experienced a breakthrough, and I'm living the abundant life.

2. What would you consider to be the biggest hindrance to your experiencing this breakthrough right now?

3. What one action should you take to experience this breakthrough right now? I challenge you to do it.

1. The wisdom discussed so fully in the book of Proverbs is the kind of spiritual radar that I'm referring to. Spiritual wisdom is the practical skill we learn from God for guiding our lives so that we avoid the pitfalls of sin and make the most of the many opportunities God gives us along the way. That's why I called my exposition of the book of Proverbs *Be Skillful* (Victor Books, 1995). When we yield ourselves to God, meditate on His Word, and obey what we read, He renews our minds so that we start to think His thoughts and gradually incorporate His ways. This gives the Holy Spirit something to use in our hearts and minds when we turn to God for guidance.

2. Leon Morris, *The Epistle to the Romans* (Grand Rapids, Mich.: Eerdmans, 1988), 436.

"We shall be made truly wise if we be made content; content not only with what we can understand, but content with what we do not understand—the habit of mind which theologians call, and rightly, faith in God."

CHARLES KINGSLEY (1819–1875)

"True contentment is a real, even an active, virtue— not only affirmative but creative. It is the power of getting out of any situation all there is in it."

G. K. CHESTERTON (1874–1936)

"To have what we want is riches; but to be able to do without is power."

GEORGE MACDONALD (1824–1905)

"The contented man is never poor, the discontented never rich."

GEORGE ELIOT (1819–1880)

"The children of Israel did not find in the manna all the sweetness and strength they might have found in it; not because the manna did not contain them, but because they longed for other meat."

JOHN OF THE CROSS (1542–1591)

Experiencing Spiritual Breakthroughs in Your Walk with God

Gaining Contentment

JONI EARECKSON TADA AND STEVEN ESTES

There is one attribute that characterizes 100 percent of the people sitting in the Second Chair, and it keeps them from serving the Lord with their whole heart. It's a heart of covetousness. Scripture tells us that covetousness is simply idolatry, desiring anything above God and His will. Whether it be for physical possessions, physical attributes, or anything else, the person in the Second Chair puts gaining these things in front of living a godly life and raising a godly family. And the breakthrough that must occur is that the love of other people's things or attributes must be broken at God's feet, or you will never experience victory in your walk with God, because God hates idolatry.

contented man is the one who enjoys the scenery along the detours."[1]
A quote like this deserves a story....
Your heart is racing as you sketch out plans for a move. A move to Rome, Italy. You study the language,

food, and art, and buy history books of the Basilica and Sistine chapel. You flip through home buyers' guides and picture breakfast on a balcony overlooking a sunny bay. Your hopes are soaring. It'll be the adventure of a lifetime.

Winging your way to Rome, the plans change. Your 747 lands in Holland. You stumble out of the Amsterdam airport bewildered, clasping Italian brochures and asking, "Where am I? What's going on?" The landscape is flat; the weather cold and damp. You gag on Dutch brussels sprouts and learn how to say *tot ziens* rather than *arrivederci*. Even though disappointment stings, you may as well get used to wearing wooden shoes. Holland is now your home. Shelve your shattered hopes and get on with living. Once in a while you miss Italy, but you learn to survive in Holland. It's not unbearable, just different.[2]

That's life. You're flying along at a good clip, then plans change. A heart attack sidelines your brother or AIDS infects your son. God may part the heavens with a miracle, but more than likely, you will have to accept the obvious. You will bear the pain and hang on. You will spend weekends helping your brother's family. You will push aside prejudice and change the sheets on your son's bed. Or you will change the diapers of your twelve-year-old who is mentally handicapped. You will hold on to marriage vows despite a cold shoulder and an empty bed. Stick to a budget and forgo vacation. Clamp the lid on raging hormones and make a date with the TV and dinner for one.

You resign yourself to the way things are.

Once in a while you wonder what it would be like—or was like—to live without the dull ache of constant pain. But most of the time, you block it out. You cope with a new language, different ways of doing things—not the ways you prefer—and you learn to survive in a world you'd never choose.

I can't live—really *live*—that way. I don't believe you can either. Maybe pets who are trained for the leash can and horses who are schooled for the bit, but not humans. Animals submit. Horses yield to the heavy harness and resign themselves to the plow. But we are not animals. God weeps when He sees us put the blinders on, like horses with spirits broken. He weeps because He never intended us to live lives of solemn resignation. For one reason, stoics unwittingly place themselves at the center of everything. For another, our souls are too significant. Even in the desperation of silence, inside the shell of a hardened heart, passion pulsates like a dying ember. A warm breeze revives a distant memory. A song stirs a faraway hope. A hand on the shoulder awakens desire. We long to be fully human. We ache. We taste bitterness and gall. We taste tears. Animals don't cry, or if they do, they don't wonder, "Is there more to life than survival?"

Maybe we can survive, but it can't stop there.

"Will I ever be happy—really happy—again?"

Yes and no. You can be "sorrowful, yet always rejoicing; poor, yet making many rich; having nothing, and yet possessing everything" (2 Corinthians 6:10, NIV). In other words, you may end up enjoying Holland. Perhaps more than Italy.

WHEN YOU CAN'T ESCAPE

Will I ever be happy in this place? It's all I could think of after I got out of the hospital and wheeled through the front door of my home. Doorways were too narrow. Sinks were too high. Three little steps were a roadblock preventing access to the living room. I sat at the dining-room table, my knees hitting the edge. A plate of food was placed in front of me, but lily hands remained limp in my lap. Someone else—at least for the first few months—fed me. I felt confined and trapped. Our cozy home had become an adverse and foreign environment.

My confinement forced me to look at another captive.

The apostle Paul had seen the inside of more than one small room from which there was no escape. For over two years, Paul had been shifted from pillar to post as one Roman leader after another disclaimed any responsibility for him. Nobody—neither Felix nor Festus—wanted to touch him with a ten-foot pole. So he was shipped to Rome.

Once there, Paul, shadowed by a guard, continued to be under house arrest. He thanked the believers in Philippi for their concern and reassured them with his words in the fourth chapter of his epistle: "I have learned to be content whatever the circumstances. I know what it is to be in need, and I know what it is to have plenty" (Philippians 4:11–12, NIV).

Paul was talking about an internal quietness of heart, supernaturally given, that gladly submits to God in all circumstances. When I say "quietness of heart," I'm not ruling out the physical stuff like prison bars, wheelchairs, unjust treatment, and disease. What I am ruling out is the internal stuff: thinking peevish thoughts, plotting ways of escape, and vexing and fretting that only lead to a flurry of frantic activity. Contentment is a sedate spirit that is able to keep quiet as it bears up under suffering. Paul understood how to live this way.

He learned it. It meant acquiring skills. Understanding something and then practicing it. What did he understand? "I have learned the secret of being content in any and every situation, whether well fed or hungry, whether living in plenty or in want" (Philippians 4:12, NIV).

What was the secret Paul learned? In his seventeenth-century classic *The Rare Jewel of Christian Contentment,*

Jeremiah Burroughs notes that the New Testament word tendered as "contentment" in our English Bibles carries the idea of sufficiency. Paul uses the same Greek root in 2 Corinthians 12:9: "My grace is sufficient for you, for my power is made perfect in weakness" (NIV). Paul's secret was simply learning to lean on the Lord of grace for help. "Let us then approach the throne of grace with confidence, so that we may receive mercy and find grace to help us in our time of need" (Hebrews 4:16, NIV).

Paul had to master this. It meant making tough choices—deciding this, not that; going in this direction, not that one. Why does the secret involve such hard work? Because "approaching the throne of grace with confidence" is not our natural bent. Finding grace to help in time of need doesn't come automatically. Just take a look at a few of Paul's well-chosen words in Philippians: "I *press on*...I strive...I stand firm."

In a small way, I understand making choices like these. I got tired of being fed at our dinner table. But when I tried to feed myself with paralyzed arms, I wanted to give up. A bent spoon was inserted into a pocket on my leather arm splint. With weak shoulder muscles, I had to scoop food on the spoon, then balance and lift it to my mouth. It was humiliating to wear a bib, smear applesauce all over my clothes, and have it land more times on my lap than in my mouth.

I could have surrendered, it would have been easy—and many wouldn't have blamed me for quitting. But I had to make a choice. A series of choices. Was I going to let embarrassment over my food-smeared face dissuade me? Was I going to let disappointing failures overwhelm me? I decided the awkwardness of feeding myself outweighed the fleeting satisfaction of self-pity. It pushed me to pray, *Oh, God, help me with this spoon!* My secret was learning to lean on the Lord for help. Today, I manage a spoon with my arm splint quite well.

I didn't get back use of my arms or hands.

But I did learn to be content.

Christ is not a magic wand that can be waved over our heartaches and headaches to make them disappear. "In [Him] are hidden all the treasures of wisdom and knowledge" (Colossians 2:3, NIV). Wisdom and knowledge, including knowing how to be content, are hidden in him, like a treasure that needs to be searched for. To search for something concealed requires hard work: "You will seek me and find me when you seek me with all your heart" (Jeremiah 29:13, NIV).

God doesn't leave us on our own. "I have learned the secret of being content.... I can do everything through Him who gives me strength" (Philippians 4:12–13, NIV). As we wrap our hands around a task and, in faith, begin to exert force, eureka! Divine energy surges through us. God's strength works in us at the moment we exercise faith for the task. "I have strength for all things in Christ, Who empowers me—I am ready for anything and equal to anything through Him Who infuses inner strength into me [that is, I am self-sufficient in Christ's sufficiency]" (Philippians 4:13, Amplified).

You make the choices and God gives you the strength. He gives you the strength to hold your tongue when you feel you have cause for complaining even when your husband hasn't attended his fair share of PTA meetings. He imparts the strength to look out for another's interests before your own—even when it's the coworker in your office who uses you as a stepladder to the top. He infuses the strength to choose a bright attitude when you wake up in the morning, even though it's another day of the same old routine as you care for your disabled child.

You still have an irresponsible husband, a greedy coworker, and a handicapped kid, but you have quietness of heart.

GAINING THROUGH LOSING

Suffering is having what you don't want and wanting what you don't have. Subtract your wants and you'll have contentment. It's a way of equalizing your desires and circumstances.

The apostle Paul was an expert at this arithmetic. For example, he was glad his Philippian friends were sending him gifts. "I rejoice greatly" he says, but quickly adds, "I am not saying this because I am in need" (Philippians 4:10–11, NIV).

Not in need? In a jail? "I am amply supplied," he assures his friends (Philippians 4:18, NIV). Good grief, Paul, why then are you rejoicing greatly? "I am not looking for a gift," he explains, "but I am looking for what may be credited to your account" (v. 17, NIV). Paul subtracted his desires and, in so doing, increased his joy over supplying the needs of others.

Paul wasn't living in denial in that dank dungeon; he simply adjusted his longings in light of Christ's sufficiency. Christ was more than enough whether Paul was "well fed or hungry, whether living in plenty or in want" (Philippians 4:12, NIV).

The world is clueless to this sort of math. The world will try to improve its circumstances to match its desires— increase its health, money, beauty, and power. It's wiser to subdue your heart to match your circumstances. Christians may not be able to rule their life situations, but they can rule their hearts: "The brother in humble circumstances ought to take pride in his high position. But the one who is rich should take pride in his low position, because he will pass away like a wild flower," says James 1:9–10 (NIV). Burroughs wrote, "Here lies the bottom and root of all contentment: When there is an evenness and proportion between our hearts and our circumstances."[3]

Cecile Van Antwerp has lived in a wheelchair many more years than I, plus she resides in a nursing home. When I went to visit her, I was struck by the small size of her living alcove—just enough room for a bed and a chest of drawers in the corner by a window. Yet with photos, a flower arrangement, a colorful afghan, and a plaque on the wall above her headboard, she has made it her home. She has scaled down her heart's desires and fashioned a small, cozy nest out of a tight, cramped space. She's content.

How do we become skilled in such arithmetic? How do we get this kind of "subtraction"? By feeding the mind and heart on those things that bring contentment rather than arouse desire. I'm not talking about rule keeping. Rules only lead to the arousal of cravings. (You can't help but dabble in desire as soon as you see, Don't Touch This and Don't Do That.) I am talking about common sense.

Or call it behavior modification. Don't want to get hurt? Then stay away from things that cause hurt. You'll never catch me lingering in the lingerie department where they display tall, elegant mannequins wearing beautiful silk negligees. I don't care if it's a Styrofoam model. It's standing up and I'm not. And it's gracefully wearing things that hang like a sack on me! Being paralyzed, it's not practical to wear lacy garter belts or brocade bedroom slippers. Gazing at these gorgeous garments makes me think restlessly, *Boy, I'd love to wear that!* And so I only remain on third-floor lingerie long enough to purchase a few necessities, and then I'm out of there.

It's the same with sixties psychedelic music. Those weird, crazy sounds were background music to my suicidal despair when I would wrench my head back and forth on my pillow, hoping to break my neck at a higher level. Now I turn the dial whenever I hear screeching guitars or a hard, angry beat. I cannot listen. I'm not living in denial or refusing to face up to reality. I merely have a healthy respect for the powerful effect of music. I am as paralyzed now as I was then, and I'm asking for trouble if I expose my mind to music that conjures dark thoughts.

Food is another thing. Because I can't exercise like most people, I have to watch my calories more closely. In the evening when I leave the office, I occasionally catch the enticing aroma of charbroiled steak wafting from the Wood Ranch Barbecue Pit across the freeway. It's murder. I'm a pushover for their fried Maui onion rings. I avoid that restaurant when I'm starving, just as I bypass the French pastry aisle at the supermarket.

Gaining contentment does not mean losing sorrow or saying good-bye to discomfort. Contentment means sacrificing itchy cravings to gain a settled soul. You give up one thing for another. It's hard. Hard, but sweet. You are "sorrowful, yet always rejoicing." You "have nothing, yet possess everything." First Timothy 6:6 says, "Godliness with contentment is great gain" (NIV) and the gain always comes through loss.

No wonder contentment requires enormous strength!

CONSIDER HIM

If you only try to stave off discontentment, you will fail miserably. Unless you add the massive promise of superior happiness in God, you can subtract all the desires you please, and you'll still be restless.

When it comes to contentment, God must be our aim. Whether it's wayward thoughts, bad-mouthing our circumstances, or comparing ourselves with others whose lot in life is easier, the battle involves more than eschewing evil; it involves pursuing God. Hebrews 11:24–25 says,

> It was by faith that Moses...chose to share ill-treatment with God's people instead of enjoying the fleeting pleasures of sin. He thought that it was better to suffer for the promised Christ than to own all the treasures of Egypt, for he was looking forward to the great reward that God would give him. (TLB)

I am still learning this. What my body can't have, my mind will shift into overdrive to deliver. But fantasies only frustrate. I must fight to stay satisfied with God, and so I glut myself on the promises of Christ. Dr. John Piper has written superbly on this subject in *The Pleasures of God*:

> We must swallow up the little flicker of [earthly] pleasure in the conflagration of holy satisfaction. When we make a covenant with our eyes, as Job did, our aim is not merely to avoid something erotic, but to gain something excellent.... We do not yield to the offer of sandwich meat when we can smell the steak sizzling on the grill.[4]

In the quest for contentment, we should not give up so easily and get detoured by earthly pleasures when there is the promise of maximum, full-forced joy in the Lord. After all, "in thy presence is fullness of joy; at thy right hand there are pleasures for evermore" (Psalm 16:11, KJV). Contentment has the upper hand in your heart when you are satiated in Christ. When, with Paul, you see him as sufficient. As enough. "Whom have I in heaven but you? And having you, I desire nothing else on earth" (Psalm 73:25, REB).

It is what Jesus means when he says, "I am the bread of life. He who comes to me will never go hungry" (John 6:35, NIV).

Contentment is being full.

Never wanting more.

We need not ever be hungry for "man does not live on bread alone but on every word that comes from the mouth of the Lord" (Deuteronomy 8:3, NIV). The role of the Word of God is to feed faith's appetite for Christ.

SUBTRACT ONE MORE THING

The Lord once preached a superb sermon on the promises of superior happiness in God. He whets our appetite for God as He lists through his beatitudes in Matthew 5:3–12.

When I was a kid, the Beatitudes baffled me. I wanted to get excited about God and be blessed and happy as much as anyone, but Jesus seemed to make it a minus rather than a plus. He employed more of the same gaining-through-losing arithmetic.

If I wanted the Kingdom, I'd have to know persecution. Subtraction.

If I longed to be comforted, I'd have to mourn. More subtraction.

Inherit the earth? Be meek. Subtract again.

The beatitude especially linked to contentment is verse 3, "Blessed are the poor in spirit, for theirs is the kingdom of heaven" (NIV).

Do you want to know contentment pure and deep? Become poor in spirit like this: "Search me, O God, and know my heart; test me and know my anxious thoughts. See if there is any offensive way in me, and lead me in the way everlasting" (Psalm 139:23–24, NIV). See yourself as spiritually impoverished and you'll find satisfaction in God.

"Godly sorrow brings repentance that leads to salvation and leaves no regret" (2 Corinthians 7:10, NIV). Why no regrets? The one who recognizes his low estate before a good God has low expectations, much like the Prodigal Son, who said to his father, "I am no longer worthy to be called your son; make me like one of your hired men" (Luke 15:19, NIV). I would say it this way, "I would rather be in this chair knowing Him, than on my feet without Him." No regrets. Even the apostle Paul, the most contented yet most maligned Christian who ever lived, saw himself as the least of the apostles, the least of all saints, and the chief of sinners.

When you realize you are among the least, the littlest, the last, and the lost, God becomes everything. To be caught up in His superior happiness is to see His love infused in and entertained around everything. Absolutely everything.

Satisfaction in life arises from knowing you are where you belong. Discontented people strive to be somewhere else or someone else. Contentment comes from many great and small acceptances in life. "Every day we experience something of the death of Jesus, so that we may also show the power of the life of Jesus in these bodies of ours" (2 Corinthians 4:10, Phillips).

When life isn't the way you like it, like it the way it is...one day at a time with Christ. And you will be blessed.

Taken from *When God Weeps*, ©1997 by Joni Eareckson Tada and Steven Estes. Used by permission of Zondervan Publishing House. Available at your local Christian bookstore.

I love how Joni describes suffering. She says, "Suffering is having what you don't want and wanting what you don't have. Subtract your wants and you'll have contentment." Do you realize what a breakthrough she wants you to experience? It's what the Scriptures have been wanting you to do since the day you were born: put off your own desires and take on the desires of the Lord. That is true contentment. And when our wants take over, we move instantly into the Second Chair. When we put our own desires above those of our Lord's, we are filled with covetousness. Ultimately, that means we are worshiping ourselves and desiring what we have to offer ourselves more than we desire what God has to offer us. When you put it in that light, it seems pretty foolish, doesn't it? True contentment is found only in the Lord. Won't you break through your heart of covetousness today. And if you are still suffering, read Joni Eareckson Tada and Steven Estes' book When God Weeps. *It will help you find the comfort and contentment that only God can give.*

EVALUATION QUESTIONS

1. Take some time and evaluate where you are in experiencing this breakthrough. Where would you rate yourself on the following scale?

1	5	10
Not even close to experiencing this breakthrough.	I've begun the journey, but I've got a ways to go.	I've experienced a breakthrough, and I'm living the abundant life.

2. What would you consider to be the biggest hindrance to your experiencing this breakthrough right now?

3. What one action should you take to experience this breakthrough right now? I challenge you to do it.

1. George Herbert, as quoted in Edythe Draper, *Draper's Book of Quotations for the Christian World* (Wheaton, Ill.: Tyndale House, 1992), 101.

2. The idea for this story came from Carol Turkington in the *Washington State School for the Deaf Newsletter*.

3. Jeremiah Burroughs, *The Rare Jewel of Christian Contentment* (Carlisle, Penn.: The Banner of Truth Trust, 1992), 46.

4. Dr. John Piper, *The Pleasures of God* (Portland, Ore.: Multnomah Press, 1991).

"Idolatry is not only the adoration of images...but also trust in one's own righteousness, works and merits, and putting confidence in riches and power."
MARTIN LUTHER (1483–1546)

"Idolatry: trusting people, possessions or positions to do for me what only God can do."
BILL GOTHARD

"Whenever we take what God has done and put it in the place of himself, we become idolators."
OSWALD CHAMBERS (1874–1917)

"O senseless man who cannot make a worm, and yet makes gods by dozens."
MICHEL EYQUEM DE MONTAIGNE (1533–1592)

Day 26

Experiencing Spiritual Breakthroughs in Your Walk with God

Keep Yourself from Idols

JOHN WESLEY

"Little children, keep yourselves from idols."

1 JOHN 5:21

We discovered yesterday that idolatry is what keeps many carnal Christians from moving into the First Chair. We see this truth embodied so clearly in the book of Exodus, when the Israelites worship the golden calf. But how pervasive is idolatry in your life? The following chapter by John Wesley may help you answer that question. But I have to warn you, this could be a very difficult chapter for you to read. In fact, if you're not serious about moving into the First Chair, this chapter could very well make you angry because of how deeply it cuts. So before you read on, take a moment and ask the Lord to prepare you to hear what He would have you to hear. Then, after you've done this, read John Wesley's words with a view to his heart. I think you'll see that his words are coming from a heart full of God.

A n ancient historian relates that when the Apostle John was so enfeebled by age as not to be able to preach, he was frequently brought into the congregation in his chair, and would just utter, "Beloved children, love one another." He could not have given more important advice. And equally important is this which lies before us; equally necessary for every part of the Church of Christ: "Beloved children, keep yourselves from idols."

Indeed there is a close connection between them: One cannot subsist without the other. As there is no firm foundation for the love of our brethren except the love of God, so there is no possibility of loving God except we keep ourselves from idols. But what are the idols of which the Apostle speaks? This is the first thing to be considered. We may then, in the second place, inquire, "How shall we keep ourselves from them?"

GIVE ME THY HEART

We are first to consider, "What are the idols of which the Apostle speaks?" I do not conceive him to mean, at least not principally, the idols that were worshiped by the heathens. They to whom he was writing, whether they had been Jews or heathens, were not in much danger from these. There is no probability that the Jews now converted had ever been guilty of worshiping them: As deeply given to this gross idolatry as the Israelites had been for many ages, they were hardly ever entangled therein after their return from the Babylonian captivity. From that period the whole body of Jews had shown a constant, deep abhorrence of it: And the heathens, after they had once turned to the living God, held their former idols in the utmost detestation. They abhorred to touch the unclean thing; yea, they chose to lay down their lives rather than turn to the worship of those gods whom they now knew to be devils.

Neither can we reasonably suppose that he speaks of those idols that are now worshiped in the Church of Rome; whether angels, or the souls of departed saints, or images of gold, silver, wood or stone. None of these idols were known in the Christian Church till some centuries after the time of the apostles. Once, indeed, St. John himself "fell down to worship before the face of an angel" that spake unto him; probably mistaking him, from his glorious appearance, for the Great Angel of the Covenant; but the strong reproof of the angel, which immediately followed, secured the Christians from imitating that bad example: "'See thou do it not.' As glorious as I appear, I am not thy Master. 'I am thy fellowservant, and of thy brethren the Prophets: Worship God'" (Revelation 22:9).

Setting then pagan and Roman idols aside, what are those of which we are here warned by the Apostle? The preceding words show us the meaning of these. "This is the true God," the end of all the souls he has made, the center of all created spirits; "and eternal life," the only foundation of present as well as eternal happiness. To him, therefore, alone, our heart is due. And he cannot, he will not, quit his claim, or consent to its being given to any other. He is continually saying to every child of man, "My son, give me thy heart!" And to give our heart to any other is plain idolatry. Accordingly, whatever takes our heart from him, or shares it with him, is an idol; or, in other words, whatever we seek happiness in independent of God.

Take an instance that occurs almost every day: A person who has been long involved in the world, surrounded and fatigued with abundance of business, having at length acquired an easy fortune, disengages himself from all business, and retires into the country, to be happy. Happy in what? Why, in taking his ease. For he intends now,

To sleep, and pass away,
In gentle inactivity the day!

Happy in eating and drinking whatever his heart desires: perhaps more elegant fare than that of the old Roman, who feasted his imagination before the treat was served up; who, before he left the town, consoled himself with the thought of "fat bacon and cabbage too!"

Happy, in altering, enlarging, rebuilding, or at least decorating, the old mansionhouse he has purchased; and likewise in improving everything about it: the stables, outhouses, grounds. But, meantime, where does God come in? Nowhere at all. He did not think about him. He no more thought of the King of heaven, than of the King of France. God is not in his plan. The knowledge and love of God are entirely out of the question. Therefore, this whole scheme of happiness in retirement is idolatry, from beginning to end.

THE DESIRES OF THE FLESH

If we descend to particulars, the first species of this idolatry is what St. John terms the desire of the flesh. We are apt to take this in too narrow a meaning, as if it related to one of the senses only. Not so: this expression equally refers to all the outward senses. It means the seeking happiness in the gratification of any or all of the external senses; although more particularly of the three lower senses, tasting, smelling, and feeling. It means the seeking happiness herein, if not in a gross, indelicate manner, by open intemperance, by gluttony or drunkenness, or shameless debauchery; yet, in a regular kind of epicurism; in a genteel sensuality; in such an elegant course of self-indulgence as does not disorder either the head or the stomach; as does not at all impair our health, or blemish our reputation.

But we must not imagine this species of idolatry is confined to the rich and great. In this also, "the toe of the peasant" (as our poet speaks) "treads upon the heel of the courtier." Thousands in low as well as in high life sacrifice to this idol; seeking their happiness (though in a more humble manner) in gratifying their outward senses. It is true, their meat, their drink, and the objects that gratify their other senses, are of a coarser kind. But still they make up all the happiness they either have or seek, and usurp the hearts which are due to God.

THE DESIRES OF THE EYE

The second species of idolatry mentioned by the Apostle is the desire of the eye. That is, the seeking happiness in gratifying the imagination (chiefly by means of the eyes), that internal sense, which is as natural to men as either sight or hearing. This is gratified by such objects as are either grand or beautiful or uncommon. But as to grand objects, it seems they do not please any longer than they are new. Were we to survey the Pyramids of Egypt daily for a year, what pleasure would they then give?

Beautiful objects are the next general source of the pleasures of the imagination: The works of nature in particular.

Others are pleased with adding art to nature; as in gardens, with their various ornaments: Others with mere works of art; as buildings, and representations of nature, whether in statues or paintings. Many likewise find pleasure in beautiful apparel, or furniture of various kinds. But novelty must be added to beauty, as well as grandeur, or it soon palls upon the sense.

Must we not refer to the head of novelty, chiefly, the pleasure found in most diversions and amusements; which were we to repeat them daily but a few months would be utterly flat and insipid? To the same head we may refer the pleasure that is taken in collecting curiosities; whether they are natural or artificial, whether old or new. This sweetens the labor of the virtuoso, and makes all his labor light.

But it is not chiefly to novelty that we are to impute the pleasure we receive from music. Certainly this has an intrinsic beauty, as well as frequently an intrinsic grandeur. This is a beauty and grandeur of a peculiar kind, not easy to be expressed; nearly related to the sublime and the beautiful in poetry, which give an exquisite pleasure. And yet it may be allowed, that novelty heightens the pleasure which arises from any of these sources.

From the study of languages, from criticism, and from history, we receive a pleasure of a mixed nature. In all these, there is always something new; frequently something beautiful or sublime. And history not only gratifies the imagination in all these respects, but likewise pleases us by touching our passions; our love, desire, joy, pity. The last of these gives us a strong pleasure, though strangely mixed with a kind of pain.

The love of novelty is immeasurably gratified by experimental philosophy; and, indeed, by every branch of natural philosophy; which opens an immense field for still new discoveries. But is there not likewise a pleasure therein, as well as in mathematical and metaphysical studies, which does not result from the imagination, but from the exercise of the understanding? unless we will say, that the newness of the discoveries which we make by mathematical or metaphysical researches is one reason at least, if not the chief, of the pleasure we receive therefrom.

I dwell the longer on these things, because so very few see

them in the true point of view. The generality of men, and more particularly men of sense and learning, are so far from suspecting that there is, or can be, the least harm in them, that they seriously believe it is matter of great praise to give ourselves wholly to them. Who of them, for instance, would not admire and commend the indefatigable industry of that great philosopher who says, "I have been now eight-and-thirty years at my parish of Upminster; and I have made it clear, that there are no less than three-and-fifty species of butterflies therein: But if God should spare my life a few years longer, I do not doubt but I should demonstrate, there are five-and-fifty!" I allow that most of these studies have their use, and that it is possible to use without abusing them. But if we seek our happiness in any of these things, then it commences an idol. And the enjoyment of it, however it may be admired and applauded by the world, is condemned by God as neither better nor worse than damnable idolatry.

THE PRIDE OF LIFE

The third kind of love of the world the Apostle speaks of is "the pride of life." It is usually supposed to mean the pomp and splendor of those that are in high life. But has it not a more extensive sense? Does it not rather mean the seeking happiness in the praise of men, which, above all things engenders pride? When this is pursued in a more pompous way by kings or illustrious men, we call it "thirst for glory;" when it is sought in a lower way by ordinary men, it is styled "taking care of our reputation." In plain terms it is seeking the honor that cometh of men, instead of that which cometh of God only.

But what creates a difficulty here is this: We are required not only to "give no offence to anyone," and to "provide things honest in the sight of all men," but to "please all men for their good to edification." But how difficult is it to do this, with a single eye to God! We ought to do all that in us lies to prevent "the good that is in us from being evil spoken of." Yea, we ought to value a clear reputation, if it be given us, only less than a good conscience. But yet if we seek our happiness therein, we are liable to perish in our idolatry.

WHAT ABOUT MONEY?

To which of the preceding heads is the love of money to be referred? Perhaps sometimes to one, and sometimes to another; as it is a means of procuring gratifications, either for "the desire of the flesh," for "the desire of the eyes," or for "the pride of life." In any of these cases money is only pursued in order to a further end. But it is sometimes pursued for its own sake without any farther view. One who is properly a miser loves and seeks money for its own sake. He looks no further, but places his happiness in the acquiring or the possessing of it. And this is a species of idolatry distinct from all the preceding; and indeed, the lowest, basest idolatry of which the human soul is capable. To seek happiness either in gratifying this or any other of the desires above mentioned is effectually to renounce the true God, and to set up an idol in his place. In a word, so many objects as there are in the world, wherein men seek happiness instead of seeking it in God, so many idols they set up in their hearts, so many species of idolatry they practice.

CAN OTHER PEOPLE BE IDOLS?

I would take notice of only one more, which, though it in some measure falls in with several of the preceding, yet, in many respects, is distinct from them all; I mean the idolizing a human creature. Undoubtedly it is the will of God that we should all love one another. It is his will that we should love our relations and our Christian brethren with a peculiar love; and those in particular whom he has made particularly profitable to our souls. These we are commanded to "love fervently;" yet still "with a pure heart." But is not this "impossible with man?" to retain the strength and tenderness of affection, and yet, without any stain to the soul, with unspotted purity? I do not mean only unspotted by lust. I know this is possible. I know a person may have an unutterable affection for another without any desire of this kind. But is it without idolatry? Is it not loving the creature more than the Creator? Is it not putting a man or woman in the place of God—giving them your heart? Let this be carefully considered, even by those whom God has joined together; by husbands and wives, parents and children. It cannot be denied that these ought to love one another tenderly: they are commanded so to do. But they are neither commanded nor permitted to love one another idolatrously. Yet how common is this! How frequently is a husband, a wife, a child, put in the place of God. How many that are accounted good Christians fix their affections on each other so as to leave no place for God! They seek their happiness in the creature, not in the Creator. One may truly say to the other, "I view thee, lord and end of my desires."

That is, "I desire nothing more but thee! Thou art the thing that I long for! All my desire is unto thee, and unto the remembrance of thy name." Now, if this is not flat idolatry, I cannot tell what is.

HOW WE KEEP OURSELVES FROM IDOLS

1. Be deeply convinced that none of them bring happiness.
No thing, no person under the sun, no, nor the amassment

of all together, can give any solid, satisfactory happiness to any child of man. The world itself, the giddy, thoughtless world, acknowledge this unawares, while they allow, nay, vehemently maintain, "No man upon earth is contented."

And if no man upon earth is contented, it is certain no man is happy. For whatever station we are in, discontent is incompatible with happiness.

Indeed not only the giddy, but the thinking part of the world allow that no man is contented; the melancholy proofs of which we see on every side, in high and low, rich and poor. And, generally, the more understanding they have, the more discontented they are. For,

> They know with more distinction to complain,
> And have superior sense in feeling pain.

It is true, everyone has (to use the cant term of the day, and an excellent one it is) his hobbyhorse; something that pleases the great boy for a few hours or days, and wherein he hopes to be happy! But though

> Hope blooms eternal in the human breast;
> Man never is, but always to be, blest.

Still he is walking in a vain shadow that will soon vanish away! So that universal experience, both our own and that of all our friends and acquaintance, clearly proves that as God made our hearts for himself, so they cannot rest till they rest in him; that till we acquaint ourselves with him we cannot be at peace. As "a scorner" of the wisdom of God "seeketh wisdom, and findeth it not;" so a scorner of happiness in God seeketh happiness but findeth none.

2. Stand and consider what you are about. Will you be a fool and a madman all your days? Is it not high time to come to your senses! At length awake out of sleep and shake yourself from the dust! Break loose from this miserable idolatry and "choose the better part!" Steadily resolve to seek happiness where it may be found; where it cannot be sought in vain. Resolve to seek it in the true God, the fountain of all blessedness; and cut off all delay! Straightway put in execution what you have resolved! Seeing "all things are ready," "acquaint thyself now with him, and be at peace."

But do not either resolve or attempt to execute your resolution trusting in your own strength. If you do you will be utterly foiled. You are not able to contend with the evil world, much less with your own evil heart; and least of all with the powers of darkness. Cry, therefore, to the Strong for strength. Under a deep sense of your own weakness and helplessness trust thou in the Lord Jehovah, in whom is everlasting strength. I advise you to cry to him for repentance in particular; not only for a full consciousness of your own impotence, but for a piercing sense of the exceeding guilt, baseness, and madness of the idolatry that has long swallowed you up. Cry for a thorough knowledge of yourself; of all your sinfulness and guiltiness. Pray that you may be fully discovered to yourself; that you may know yourself as also you are known. When once you are possessed of this genuine conviction all your idols will lose their charms. And you will wonder how you could so long lean upon those broken reeds, which had so often sunk under you.

What should you ask for next?

"Jesus, now I have lost my all,
Let me upon thy bosom fall!
Now let me see thee in thy vesture dipped in blood!

Now stand in all thy wounds confest,
And wrap me in thy crimson vest!

Hast thou not said, 'If thou canst believe, thou shalt see the glory of God?' Lord, I would believe! Help thou mine unbelief. And help me now! Help me now to enter into the rest that remaineth for the people of God; for those who give thee their heart, their whole heart; who receive thee as their God and their All. O thou that art fairer than the children of men, full of grace are thy lips! Speak that I may see thee! And as the shadows flee before the sun, so let all my idols vanish at thy presence!"

From the moment that you begin to experience this, fight the good fight of faith; take the kingdom of heaven by violence! Take it as it were by storm! Deny yourself every pleasure that you are not divinely conscious brings you nearer to God. Take up your cross daily: Regard no pain, if it lies in your way to him. If you are called thereto, scruple not to pluck out the right eye, and to cast it from you. Nothing is impossible to him that believeth: You can do all things through Christ that strengtheneth you. Do valiantly; and stand fast in the liberty wherewith Christ hath made you free. Yea, go on in his name, and in the power of his might, till you "know all that love of God that passeth knowledge:" And then you have only to wait till he shall call you into his everlasting kingdom!

Taken from John Wesley's sermon "Spiritual Idolatry." Published in *Great Sermons*, Vol. 1 (Barbour & Co.).

Now do you understand why I gave you warning at the outset? These are some tough words. But they are words that cannot be ignored. In fact, they demand to be heeded. It has been said that John Wesley has done more to advance the kingdom of God than any person in the last 1,000 years. If his life exhibited the depth of commitment his words convey (which it did), then this statement becomes very believable. You see, John Wesley chose whom he would serve, and it wasn't anyone or anything. He chose to serve God wholeheartedly. Now that you've read these challenging words, won't you ask God to search your heart and show you anything that you have given your heart to other than God himself? Once you've seen what God has shown you, repent of it and turn your heart back to God. This is not an easy breakthrough to experience, but the rewards will be truly heavenly.

EVALUATION QUESTIONS

1. Take some time and evaluate where you are in experiencing this breakthrough. Where would you rate yourself on the following scale?

1_____5_____10

Not even close to experiencing this breakthrough.	I've begun the journey, but I've got a ways to go.	I've experienced a breakthrough, and I'm living the abundant life.

2. What would you consider to be the biggest hindrance to your experiencing this breakthrough right now?

3. What one action should you take to experience this breakthrough right now?

*"If thou intend not nor seek nothing else but the pleasing of God
and the profit of thy neighbor thou shalt have inward liberty."*
THOMAS À KEMPIS (C. 1380–1471)

"Measure your growth in grace by your sensitiveness to sin."
OSWALD CHAMBERS (1874–1917)

*"Growth is demanding and may seem dangerous,
for there is loss as well as gain in growth."*
MAY SARTON

"The stronger and deeper the roots, the less visible they are."
CHARLES R. SWINDOLL

"The mature believer is a searching believer."
JOHN POWELL

*"There are no shortcuts to spiritual maturity.
It takes time to be holy."*
ERWIN W. LUTZER

"Spiritual maturity: the quiet confidence that God is in control."
CHARLES R. SWINDOLL

Enlarge Your
Longing for God

JERRY BRIDGES

I seek you with all my heart;
do not let me stray from your commands.
PSALM 119:10, NIV

Devotion to God is something that only Christians can possess. However, the believer who sits in the Second Chair has only a cursory devotion to God that prevents him from fully appreciating the God of the universe. The First Chair Christian, on the other hand, has a deeper devotion to God that enables him to not only appreciate the God of the universe but also to put into full effect the grace of God. However, that's not where the differences end. While the First Chair Christian already has a deeper devotion to God than the person in the Second Chair, he desires to have an even deeper devotion than he already does, whereas the person stuck in the Second Chair may not even give a second glance to his devotion. So this chapter is both a challenge and an encouragement. It is a challenge to the Second Chair person to experience a breakthrough in his devotion to God, and it is an encouragement to the First

Chair Christian that he can, in fact, have an even deeper devotion than he already has.

cripture defines unbelievers as totally godless. Paul tells the Romans that they have no fear of God, are hostile to Him, are unwilling to submit to His law, and are unable to please Him. This is just as true of the morally upright unbeliever as it is of the most corrupt profligate. The former worships a god of his own mind, not the God of the Bible. When confronted with the claims of the sovereign God of the universe, he often reacts with greater hostility than an unbeliever living in open sin.

At the time of our salvation, God through His Holy Spirit deals with this godless spirit within us. He gives us a new heart and moves us to obey Him, He gives us a singleness of heart and inspires us to fear Him, and He pours out His love into our hearts so that we begin to comprehend His love for us. All of this is bound up in the blessings of the new birth, so we may safely say that all Christians possess, at least in embryonic form, a basic devotion to God. It is impossible to be a Christian and not have it. The work of the Holy Spirit at regeneration assures this. God has given us everything we need for life and godliness.

But though all of us as Christians possess a basic God centeredness as an integral part of our spiritual lives, we must grow in this devotion to God. We are to train ourselves to be godly; we are to make every effort to add godliness to our faith. To grow in godliness is to grow both in our devotion to God and in our likeness to His character.

We can illustrate devotion to God by an equilateral triangle whose three points represent the fear of God, the love of God, and the desire for God. To grow in our devotion to God is to grow in each of these three areas. And as the triangle is equal on all three sides, so we should seek to grow equally in all of these areas; otherwise our devotion becomes unbalanced.

To seek to grow in the fear of God, for example, without also growing in our comprehension of His love can cause us to begin to view God as far-off and austere. Or to seek to grow in our awareness of the love of God without also growing in our reverence and awe of Him can cause us to view God as a permissive and indulgent heavenly Father who does not deal with our sin. This latter unbalanced view is prevalent in our society today. That is why many Christians are calling for a renewed emphasis on the biblical teaching of the fear of God.

A crucial characteristic of our growth in godly devotion, then, must be a balanced approach to all three of the essential elements of devotion: fear, love, and desire. Another crucial characteristic must be a total dependence upon the Holy Spirit to bring about this growth. The principle of Christian ministry that Paul states in 1 Corinthians 3:7, "neither he who plants nor he who waters is anything, but only God, who makes things grow" (NIV), is just as true as a principle of growth in godliness. We must plant and water through whatever means of grace God has given us, but only God can make godly devotion increase within our hearts.

PRAYING FOR GROWTH

We express this vital dependence on God by praying that He will cause us to grow in our devotion to Him. David prayed, "Give me an undivided heart, that I may fear your name" (Psalm 86:11, NIV). Paul prayed that the Ephesian Christians might be able to grasp how wide and long and high and deep is the love of Christ (Ephesians 3:17–18). And David prayed that he might dwell in the house of the Lord, to behold His beauty and to seek Him in His temple (Psalm 27:4). Each of these prayers is a recognition that growth in devotion to God is of Him.

If we are committed to the practice of godliness, our prayer life will reflect it. We will be regularly asking God to increase our fear of Him, to deepen our understanding of His love for us, and to heighten our desire for His fellowship. We would do well, for example, to put the three verses mentioned above, or similar passages, on our list of prayer requests and pray over them regularly.

Meditating on God

Although all of the Bible should instruct us in the fear of God, I have found there are certain passages that are especially helpful to me in drawing my attention to the majesty and holiness of God, the attributes particularly suited to stimulate our hearts in the fear of God. Here are some passages I refer to frequently:

Isaiah 6; Revelation 4—God's holiness
Isaiah 40—God's greatness
Psalm 139—God's omniscience and omnipresence
Revelation 1:12–17; 5—The majesty of Christ

These Scripture selections are intended only as suggestions. You may find others that are more meaningful to you. Use them. The important point is that God uses His word to create in our hearts the sense of reverence and awe of Him that causes us to fear Him. It is vain to pray for an increase of the fear of God in our hearts without meditating on passages of Scripture that are particularly suited to stimulate that fear.

There are also specific passages that will help us grow in our awareness of Gods love. I find these especially helpful: Psalm 103, Isaiah 53, Romans 5:6–11, 2 Corinthians 5:14–21, Ephesians 2:1–10, 1 Timothy 1:15–16, and 1 John 4:9–11.

In commending certain passages of Scripture to you, I cannot emphasize too strongly, however, that it is not just the bare reading, or even memorizing, of these passages that accomplishes the desired result of growth in godliness. We must meditate on them, but even that is not sufficient. The Holy Spirit must make His Word come alive to our hearts to produce the growth, so we must meditate in prayerful dependence upon Him to do His work. Neither meditation nor prayer by themselves are sufficient for growth in devotion: We must practice both.

WORSHIPING GOD

Still another essential part of our practice of devotion to God is worship. By worship I mean the specific act of ascribing to God the glory, majesty, honor, and worthiness that are His. Revelation 4:8–11 and 5:9–14 give us clear illustrations of the worship that goes on in heaven and which should be emulated by us here on earth. I almost always begin my daily quiet time with a period of worship. Before beginning my Bible reading for the day, I take a few minutes to reflect upon one of the attributes of God or to meditate upon one of the passages about Him mentioned above, and then ascribe to Him the glory and honor due to Him because of that particular attribute.

I find it helpful to assume a kneeling position for this time of worship as a physical acknowledgment of my reverence, awe, and adoration of God. Worship is a matter of the heart, not of one's physical position; nevertheless, the Scriptures do frequently portray bowing the knee as a sign of homage and adoration. David said, "In reverence will I bow down toward your holy temple" (Psalm 5:7, NIV). The writer of Psalm 95 says, "Come, let us bow down in worship, let us kneel before the Lord our Maker" (v. 6, NIV). And we know that one day every knee shall bow before Jesus as a sign of homage to His lordship (Philippians 2:10).

Obviously, it is not always possible to bow before God in our times of worship. God understands this and surely allows for it. But when we can do so, I strongly recommend bowing before God not only as a sign of reverence to Him but also for what it does in helping us prepare our minds to worship God in a manner acceptable to Him.

In emphasizing the value of worship, I have dealt solely with the practice of private worship, that which we should do in our personal quiet time. I do not mean to ignore public, corporate worship; I simply do not feel qualified to speak on that subject. I would plead with ministers of congregations to give us more instruction in the nature and practice of corporate worship. I sense that many Christians go through the motions of a worship service without actually worshiping God.

FELLOWSHIP WITH GOD

All that has been said thus far about the importance of prayer, of meditating on the Word of God, and of having a specific time of worship, implies the value of a quiet time. The expression *quiet time* is used to describe a regular period each day set aside to meet with God through His Word and through prayer. One of the great privileges of a believer is to have fellowship with almighty God. We do this by listening to Him speak to us from His Word and by speaking to Him through prayer.

There are various spiritual exercises we may want to use during our quiet time, such as reading through the Bible in a year and praying over certain requests. But the primary objective of our quiet time should be fellowship with God: developing a personal relationship with Him and growing in our devotion to Him.

After I have begun my quiet time with a period of worship, I next turn to the Bible. As I read a passage of Scripture (usually one or more chapters), I talk to God about what I am reading as I go along. I like to think of the quiet time as a conversation: God speaking to me through the Bible and my responding to what He says. This approach helps to make the quiet time what it is intended to be: a time of fellowship with God.

Having worshiped God and fellowshipped with Him, I then take time to go over various prayer requests I want to bring before Him that day. Following this order prepares me to pray more effectively. I have thought about who God is; therefore, I do not rush into His presence casually and demandingly. At the same time I am reminded of His power and love, and my faith regarding His ability and delight to answer my requests is strengthened. In this way, even my time of asking actually becomes a time of fellowship with Him.

In suggesting certain Scriptures for meditation, or certain modes of worship, or a particular practice for a quiet time, I do not want to give the impression that growing in devotion to God is merely following a suggested routine. Neither do I want to suggest that what is helpful to me ought to be followed by others or will even be helpful to others. All I want to do is demonstrate that growth in devotion to God, although a result of His ministry in us, comes as a result of very concrete practice on our part. We are to train ourselves to be godly, and training involves practice: the day-after-day exercise that enables us to become proficient.

THE ULTIMATE TEST

Thus far we have looked at specific activities that help us grow in our devotion to God: prayer, meditation on the Scriptures, worship, and the quiet time. There is still another area that is not an activity but an attitude of life: obedience to the will of God. This is the ultimate test of our fear of God and the only true response to His love for us. God specifically states that we fear Him by keeping all His decrees and commands (Deuteronomy 6:2), and Proverbs 8:13 tells us, "To fear the Lord is to hate evil" (NIV). I can know if I truly fear God by determining if I have a genuine hatred of evil and an earnest desire to obey His commands.

In the days of Nehemiah, the Jewish nobles and officials were disobeying God's law by exacting usury from their countrymen. When Nehemiah confronted them he said, "What you are doing is not right. Shouldn't you walk in the fear of our God to avoid the reproach of our Gentile enemies?" (Nehemiah 5:9, NIV). He could just as well have said, "Shouldn't you obey God to avoid the reproach of our enemies?" Nehemiah equated walking in the fear of God with obedience to God. If we do not fear God, we will not think it worthwhile to obey His commands, but if we truly fear Him—if we hold Him in reverence and awe—we will obey Him. The measure of our obedience is an exact measure of our reverence for Him.

Similarly, Paul affirmed that his awareness of Christ's love for him compelled him to live, not for himself, but for Him who died for us. As God begins to answer our prayer for a deeper realization of His love, one means He often uses is to enable us to see more and more of our own sinfulness. Paul was nearing the end of his life when he wrote these words: "Christ Jesus came into the world to save sinners—of whom I am the worst" (1 Timothy 1:15, NIV). We realize that our sins as Christians, though perhaps not as outwardly gross as before, are more heinous in the sight of God because they are sins against knowledge and against grace. We know better and we know His love, and yet we sin willfully. And then we go back to the cross and realize that Jesus bore even those willful sins in His body on the tree, and the realization of that infinite love compels us to deal with those very sins and to put them to death. Both the fear of God and the love of God motivate us to obedience, and that obedience proves they are authentic in our lives.

A DEEPER LONGING

As we concentrate on growing in our reverence and awe for God and in our understanding of His love for us, we will find that our desire for Him will grow. As we gaze upon His beauty, we will desire to seek Him even more. And as we become progressively more aware of His redeeming love, we will want to know Him in a progressively deeper way. But we can also pray that God will deepen our desire for Him. I recall reading Philippians 3:10 a number of years ago and realizing a little bit of the depth of Paul's desire to know Christ more intimately. As I read I prayed, "O God, I cannot identify with Paul's longing, but I would like to." Over the years God has begun to answer that prayer. By His grace I know experientially to some degree Isaiah's words, "My soul yearns for you in the night; in the morning my spirit longs for you" (Isaiah 26:9, NIV). I am grateful for what God has done, but I pray I will continue to grow in this desire for Him.

One of the wonderful things about God is that He is infinite in all of His glorious attributes, so never in our desire for Him will we exhaust the revelation of His person to us. The more we come to know Him, the more we will desire Him. And the more we desire Him, the more we will want to fellowship with Him and experience His presence. And the more we desire Him and His fellowship, the more we will desire to be like Him.

Paul's heartfelt cry in Philippians 3:10 vividly expresses this longing. He desires both to know Christ and to be like Him. He wants to experience both His fellowship—even the fellowship of suffering—as well as the transforming power of His resurrection. He wants both Christ-centeredness and Christlikeness.

This is godliness: God-centeredness, or devotion to God, and Godlikeness, or Christian character. The practice of godliness is both the practice of devotion to God and the practice of a lifestyle that is pleasing to God and that reflects His character to other people.

Taken from *The Practice of Godliness,* ©1998 by Jerry Bridges. Used by permission of NavPress. Available at your local Christian bookstore.

As I said at the beginning of this chapter, this was meant to be both a challenge and an encouragement. If you are still sitting in the Second Chair, you've been challenged. But if you're in the First Chair, I hope that you now realize that just because you're in the First Chair you don't have to stop experiencing spiritual breakthroughs. In fact, the deeper your devotion to God, the more you'll want to experience breakthroughs that encourage your relationship with the God of creation. To further encourage you (or challenge you—depending on where you're at), I suggest you read Jerry Bridges' book The Practice of Godliness *and discover additional breakthroughs you can experience.*

EVALUATION QUESTIONS

1. Take some time and evaluate where you are in experiencing this breakthrough. Where would you rate yourself on the following scale?

1	5	10
Not even close to experiencing this breakthrough.	I've begun the journey, but I've got a ways to go.	I've experienced a breakthrough, and I'm living the abundant life.

2. What would you consider to be the biggest hindrance to your experiencing this breakthrough right now?

3. What one action should you take to experience this breakthrough right now? I challenge you to do it.

*"Beware of saying, 'I haven't time to read the Bible, or to pray';
say rather, 'I haven't disciplined myself to do these things.'"*
OSWALD CHAMBERS (1874–1917)

"Rule your mind or it will rule you."
HORACE (65–8 B.C.)

*"Some people regard discipline as a chore.
For me, it is a kind of order that sets me free to fly."*
JULIE ANDREWS

*"Self-discipline never means giving up anything,
for giving up is a loss. Our Lord did not ask us to give up
the things of earth, but to exchange them for better things."*
ARCHBISHOP FULTON J. SHEEN (1895–1979)

*"I cannot be the man I should be without times of quietness.
Stillness is an essential part of growing deeper."*
CHARLES R. SWINDOLL

*"If we bring our minds back again and again to God,
we shall be gradually giving the central place to God, not only in
our inner selves, but in our practical everyday lives."*
PAUL TOURNIER (1898–1986)

Day 28
Experiencing Spiritual Breakthroughs in Your Walk with God

Practice the
Spiritual Disciplines

KENNETH BOA

Why would I put an article about the spiritual disciplines in a book about spiritual breakthroughs? The answer is actually quite easy: Pursuing the spiritual disciplines will lead you into more spiritual breakthroughs than anything else I can think of. That's right! As you'll soon see, the benefits of adding the disciplines to your life are so extraordinary that I would think it foolish not to implement as many of them as you possibly can. You'll notice that none of the disciplines are listed or explained here. That is because I could not do them justice in this small amount of space. My purpose is simply to get you excited about the disciplines and what they can do for your relationship with the heavenly Father. If I accomplish that, you will have experienced a vital spiritual breakthrough.

t is easy to slip into one of two extremes regarding the Christian life. The first extreme over-emphasizes our role and minimizes God's role. This position is characterized by the mentality of striving for and living for Jesus. It emphasizes knowledge, rules, rededication efforts, and human activities, and virtually ignores the ministry of the Holy Spirit. The second extreme overemphasizes God's role and minimizes our role. This position is characterized by a "let go and let God" form of passivity. It stresses experience, the supernatural, and the person of the Holy Spirit, and downplays the human side of the coin.

The biblical balance is that the spiritual life is both human and divine. Paul places these back to back in Philippians 2:12–13: "So then, my beloved, just as you have always obeyed, not as in my presence only, but now much more in my absence, work out your salvation with fear and trembling; for it is God who is at work in you, both to will and to work for His good pleasure" (NASB). On the human side, we are responsible to work out (not work for) our salvation, but on the divine side, God is the one who gives us the desire and empowerment to accomplish His purposes.

(Exercise: Read the following passages to see the interrelationship of the human and the divine in the working out of the Christian life: John 14:15–17; 15:4–11, 26–27; Romans 12:1–8, 17–21; 15:30–32; 1 Corinthians 15:10; 2 Corinthians 2:14; 3:16; 6:16–17:1; Galatians 2:20; Ephesians 6:10–20; Philippians 4:13; Colossians 1:9–12, 28–29; 1 Thessalonians 5:22–24; 2 Thessalonians 2:13–17; Hebrews 4:14–16; 10:19–25; James 4:7–10; 1 Peter 1:22–25; 4:11; 5:6–10; 2 Peter 1:1–11; 1 John 2:36.)

DEPENDENCE

The life of Christ can only be reproduced in us by the power of the Holy Spirit. As an inner work of God, it is not achieved by human effort, but by divine enabling. Apart from Christ and the power of His Spirit, we can accomplish nothing in the sight of God (John 15:4–5; Acts 1:8). Therefore, it is crucial that we develop a conscious sense of dependence upon the Spirit's power in all that we do (see Ephesians 1:19; 3:16; 5:18). "But I say, walk by the Spirit, and you will not carry out the desire of the flesh" (Galatians 5:16, NASB). "If we live by the Spirit, let us also walk by the Spirit" (Galatians 5:25, NASB). The word for "walk" in the first verse is general and refers to life in its totality. The word for "walk" in the second verse is specific and refers to the step-by-step process of daily life. Just as Jesus walked in total dependence upon the life of His Father (John 6:57, 14:10), so we must rest in the same source of power. We were never meant to create life but to receive and display the life of Christ.

DISCIPLINE

Dependence is critical, but there is no growth in the Christian life apart from discipline and self-control. "Discipline yourself for the purpose of godliness" (1 Timothy 4:7, NASB). Spirituality is not instantaneous or automatic; it is developed and refined. The Epistles are full of commands like believe, obey, walk, present, fight, reckon, hold fast, pursue, draw near, and love. The spiritual life is progressively cultivated in the disciplines of the faith. You and I will not wake up one morning to find ourselves suddenly spiritual. This is why Paul uses the metaphors of the athlete, soldier, and farmer to illustrate the discipline of the Christian life (see 1 Corinthians 9:24–27; Ephesians 6:10–18; 2 Timothy 2:3–6). We grow in godliness as we hear and obediently respond to the Word. Spiritual maturity is characterized by the ability to recognize and apply the principles of Scripture to daily experience (Hebrews 5:11–14). The Bible comes alive when its precepts are put into practice, but this does not happen apart from human choice. We must actively choose to have our minds and emotions guided and strengthened by the Holy Spirit.

THE BENEFITS OF THE DISCIPLINES

For many people, the word *discipline* reeks with negative connotations. We often associate it with tyranny, external restraint, legalism, and bondage. But a closer look at Scripture and the lives of the great saints in the history of the faith reveals precisely the opposite. The whole book of Proverbs, for instance, argues that far from limiting our freedom, personal disciplines actually enhance it and give us options we could never have had otherwise. Wisdom is a skill that is developed through instruction and discipline, and this skill in the art of living life with each area under the Lord's dominion frees us to become the people God intended us to be. The pursuit of wisdom, discernment, understanding, and the knowledge of God requires not only an appetite, but also a willingness to pay the necessary price (see Proverbs 2).

For years, I have desired the ability to sit before the keyboard of a piano and make it ring with glorious music. But my craving to do so has never been matched by a willingness to invest the time, energy, and discipline to make it happen. Only those who pay this price have the freedom to make the instrument sing. Thus, discipline is the pathway to freedom rather than bondage. Like the children's story about the impulsive train who wanted to break loose from the rails and go in its own direction, we may not discover the true "freedom of the rails" until we get bogged down in the earth of our own pursuits in disregard of God's design.

In the New Testament, a quick survey of the Gospels through the lens of discipline reveals that the Lord Jesus engaged in all the classic disciplines such as solitude, silence, simplicity, study, prayer, sacrificial service, and fasting. Jesus understood that these practices were not optional for those who have a passion for the Father's pleasure and honor. Our Lord did not engage in these disciplines as ends in themselves but as means to know and obey His Father. They moved Him in the direction of the foremost commandment: "You shall love the Lord your God with all your heart and with all your soul and with all your might" (Deuteronomy 6:5, NASB).

IMITATING OUR LORD

Yet somehow we have bought the illusion that we can be like Christ without imitating His spirituality. Clearly, if we wish to be like our Master, we must imitate His practice; if we believe He knew how to live, we must seek the grace to live like Him. To ask the question, What would Jesus do? without practicing the habits we already know He practiced is to attempt to run a marathon without prior training. What is evident to us on the physical plane is often obscure to us on the spiritual level. It is clearly absurd to think that we could excel at any sport such as golf or tennis without investing the needed time, training, and practice. But when it comes to living the Christian life, we somehow suppose that we are doing well if we attend church and crack open a Bible once or twice a week. If believers expended the same time and energy in cultivating their spiritual lives as they are willing to invest in becoming reasonably skillful at any sport or hobby, the world would look with wonder at the power of the body of Christ.

We desire to know Christ more deeply, but we shun the lifestyle that would make it happen. By relegating the spiritual to certain times and activities, we are ill prepared to face the temptations and challenges of daily living in a Christlike way. It is easy to deceive ourselves into thinking that without the active and painful formation of godly character, we will still have the capacity to make the right choices whenever we really need to. But if we have not been exercising and training and practicing behind the scenes, we will not have the skill (wisdom) to perform well when it counts. The disciplines off the stage prepare an actor to perform well when the curtain rises, and the hours of training off the field give an athlete the freedom to play well when the game begins. Similarly, the daily regimen of the spiritual disciplines equips us to live well during the uncertainties and vicissitudes of life. This is what Dallas Willard called the law of indirect preparedness; the disciplines in the background of our lives prepare us for the unexpected times when we will need to respond in appropriate ways. Willpower alone will not be enough, unless our wills have been trained and strengthened through ongoing practice.

There is no shortcut to spiritual formation. After the initial burst of enthusiasm, we soon discover that beginning the process is much easier than following through. As anyone who attempts to learn a new skill quickly realizes, the early learning stages can be particularly challenging, because everything seems no unnatural. Only those who are willing to persevere reach the point where they begin to get the hang of it. But in the spiritual arena, we never really arrive. Scripture encourages us to continually press on toward the goal and to reach forward to what lies ahead so that we may lay hold of that for which Christ Jesus laid hold of us (Philippians 3:12–14). This requires a lifelong commitment to the disciplines that Jesus, the apostles, and the godly followers of the Way have practiced through the centuries. None of the people whose spiritual vitality we have admired regarded these disciplines as optional, and it would be naive to suppose that we are history's first exceptions.

The disciplines of the faith are never ends in themselves but means to the end of knowing, loving, and trusting God. As we implement them in a consistent way, we cultivate holy habits. As these habits grow, they guide our behavior and character in such a way that it becomes more natural for us to live out our new identities in Christ. Our daily choices shape our habits, and our habits shape our character. Our character, in turn, guides the decisions we make in times of stress, temptation, and adversity. In this way, the godly actions of maturing believers are outward displays of increasing inner beauty.

The spiritual disciplines are the product of a synergy between divine and human initiatives, and the disciplines serve us as means of grace insofar as they bring the totality of our personalities under the lordship of Christ and the control of the Spirit. By practicing them, we place our minds, temperaments, and bodies before God and seek the grace of His transformation. In this way, we learn to appropriate the power of kingdom living. These disciplines are both active and passive, both initiatory and receptive; they connect us to the power of the indwelling Holy Spirit, who manifests the life of Christ in us and through us. Thus, we should work hard but receive everything we are and have by God's grace. It takes the touch of God on our lives for us to form habits that are alive and pleasing to God.

If we fail to see these disciplines and habits as responses to divine grace, we will slip into the trap of thinking that they have value in themselves. Those who think this way suppose that when they meditate or fast that they are spiritually superior to those who do not. Their disciplines become external, self-energized, and law driven. They are tempted to quantify spirituality by reducing it to a set of external practices rather than an internal, grace-drawn process of transformation. Instead, we must see the disciplines as external practices that reflect and reinforce internal aspirations. Spiritual growth is inside out, not outside in; our focus should be more on the process of inner transformation than on outward routines. This understanding will free us from thinking that the disciplines we practice are magical in themselves or that others should be engaging in the same activities that we practice. Spiritual disciplines are good servants but poor masters; they are useful means but inadequate ends.

What Do the Disciplines Mean for You?

To summarize, here are a few of the many benefits of practicing the spiritual disciplines:

1. They encourage the imitation of Christ and allow us to act in ways that are centered in God's will.
2. They personally connect us with an ongoing tradition of time-tested ways of incarnating the spiritual life.
3. They give us a rule of conduct that directs us in the path of growing skill in living before God.
4. They equip us with resources to fight on the battlefronts of the world, the flesh, and the demonic.
5. They confer perspective and power, and they encourage us to embrace God's purpose for our lives.
6. They bestow a controlled freedom to respond to changing circumstances in a more biblical manner; they allow our lives to be dominated more by the things above than the things below.
7. They remind us daily that the spiritual life is a balance between radical dependence and responsible

action—both grace and self-discipline are required for spiritual maturity.

8. They are vehicles for internal transformation. Given enough time, an average person who consistently practices spiritual disciplines will achieve spiritual productivity and proficiency.

9. They replace habits of sin by cultivating habits that lead to character (e.g., integrity, faithfulness, and compassion).

10. They increase our willingness to acknowledge the daily cost of discipleship and remind us that whatever comes quickly and cheaply is superficial, while the insights that we learn from pain will endure.

Taken from *That I May Know God*, ©1998 by Kenneth D. Boa. Used by permission of Multnomah Publishers, Inc. Available at your local Christian bookstore.

Deciding to begin a regular practice of some of the spiritual disciplines is a huge spiritual breakthrough that will lead to many other spiritual breakthroughs. And this list of benefits from Ken Boa's book That I May Know God *should be enough to light your fire to get started. As I said earlier, this chapter's purpose is not to explain each spiritual discipline and how to use it in your walk with God. It is to get you excited about the disciplines in general. To understand the various disciplines, which include prayer, fasting, meditation, journaling, and many others, I strongly suggest that you read one of the many books on this subject that are available at your local Christian bookstore. The two most widely read books on the disciplines are Richard Foster's book* Celebration of Discipline *and Dallas Willard's book* The Spirit of the Disciplines. *Of course, the disciplines are only one part of the spiritual life. Kenneth Boa addresses many of the other aspects of the Christian life in his book,* That I May Know God. *It would be a great addition to your library.*

EVALUATION QUESTIONS

1. Take some time and evaluate where you are in experiencing this breakthrough. Where would you rate yourself on the following scale?

1	5	10
Not even close to experiencing this breakthrough.	I've begun the journey, but I've got a ways to go.	I've experienced a breakthrough, and I'm living the abundant life.

2. What would you consider to be the biggest hindrance to your experiencing this breakthrough right now?

3. What one action should you take to experience this breakthrough right now? I challenge you to do it.

*"When I came to believe in Christ's teaching,
I ceased desiring what I had wished for before.
The direction of my life, my desire, became different.
What was good and bad had changed places."*
LEO TOLSTOY (1828–1910)

*"Today is not yesterday. We ourselves change.
How then can our works and thoughts,
if they are always to be the fittest, continue always the same?
Change, indeed, is painful, yet ever needful; and
if memory has its force and worth, so also has hope."*
THOMAS CARLYLE (1795–1881)

"People can cry much easier than they can change."
JAMES BALDWIN (1924–1987)

Translate Your Good Intentions into Life-Changing Action

HOWARD G. HENDRICKS AND WILLIAM D. HENDRICKS

If you'll remember clear back to the beginning of this book, Dr. Howard Hendricks is the man who helped me experience a spiritual breakthrough during one of the toughest times of my life. Dr. Hendricks has now laid out a plan of attack so you can experience breakthroughs on a regular basis. Breakthroughs don't come easy, and they rarely come without any forethought. That means you need to do some legwork, some sweat equity, if you will, in your walk with the Lord. In your pilgrimage to the First Chair (and to stay in the First Chair) you need to experience breakthroughs frequently. But sometimes you just get stuck. That's where a plan of attack comes in. The next time it feels like you just can't get out of the mud, get some godly counsel and draw up a game plan to get you moving.

*T*he church retreat had come to an end. Participants were packing bags into cars and saying their good-byes. What an outstanding weekend they'd had, with lots of fun and good food and a rich time of study in the book of Philippians. Pastor Jones wore a wide smile as he received words of appreciation from grateful members.

Up came Larry, one of the congregation. "Pastor," he said, "this weekend has been...well, it's really changed my life. I'll never be the same."

"I'm glad to hear that, Larry," replied the minister. "Tell me, what was the most significant thing?"

"Well, I don't know. All of it, really." He laughed. "I've realized that I just have so much to learn. When I get home I'm going to start reading my Bible more. And I'm really going to change the way I treat people. And I think I may sign up to help out in Sunday school. And I think I need to take a look at my giving. I was really touched by your message on missions."

"It sounds like you got a lot out of this retreat," Pastor Jones said enthusiastically. "I'll be praying for you." The two men shook hands and parted.

On the surface, this exchange sounds wonderful. On the basis of Pastor Jones's teaching of Philippians, Larry identified a few specific areas for spiritual growth and action. That's great. But the bright picture dims a bit when we find out that Larry has been to at least a dozen retreats like this one over the years. He has made similar remarks after each one. But has he changed? Not one whit. He gets pumped up by the enthusiasm of the moment. But when he gets back home, his good intentions evaporate, and he never gets started on a process of change.

WHERE DO I BEGIN?

The problem for Larry is one from which countless people suffer—the problem of a plan. We could state it in the form of a question: Where do I begin? That may be the most determinative question to ask about application.

You see, anybody can come up with a grandiose scheme for change. One person says he wants to reach the world for Christ. Somebody else wants to study every book in the Bible over the next five years. Somebody else plans to memorize a hundred verses. Somebody else is going to become a Christlike spouse.

Wonderful. Where are you going to begin?

Until you answer that, all you have are good intentions. Those have about as much value as a worthless check. After all, what good does it do to dream of reaching the world with the gospel it you can't share Christ with the person in the office next to you? How are you going to study the entire Bible when you don't even know what verse you're going to study tomorrow? How can you memorize a hundred verses when you've never even tried to memorize one? And rather than fantasize about a Christlike marriage, why not start with something simple, such as doing the dishes if you're a husband, or encouraging your husband if you're a wife?

Too much application stays at the level of good intentions because we talk about the end of the journey without specifying when, where, and how we're going to take the first step. As someone has well said, we don't plan to fail, we fail to plan.

So I want to give you a simple framework to use in planning your own process of life change. In doing so, I don't mean to oversimplify things. Obviously, life is complex, and many elements of growth cannot be charted easily. But I also know that many Christians stall out in their spiritual development because they don't know how to get started. They know all about the glorious promises that are supposed to be theirs someday. But the real question is, what will they do today to start heading in that direction.

So here are three steps for translating good intentions into life-changing action.

1. MAKE A DECISION TO CHANGE

In other words, make up your mind. Determine what sort of change you need to make, and then choose to pursue it. This is largely a matter of setting objectives. That is, how will you be different as a result of making this change? What will you look like at the end of the process?

Robert Mager, a specialist in learning and education, says that a well-stated objective describes what a person will be doing once he achieves the intended outcome. For example, the objective of our book, *Living by the Book,* to help you ask observational questions of the biblical text, explain what a passage means, and then describe practical ways to use what you've learned in everyday life. This statement points to specific behaviors that we could measure if we wanted to know whether we had accomplished our objectives. For instance, we could listen to you probing the text with questions. We could read an interpretation that you might write. We could look at your schedule to see whether you were taking action.

So what objectives are you prepared to set in order to accomplish change? Describe what you'll be doing when you reach that objective. Do you want to become a better parent? What does that look like? Can you state it in terms of noticeable, measurable behaviors? For instance, better parenting might involve spending more time with your kids. It might mean organizing and managing the family schedule. We can measure these behaviors, and we can use them to plan (see below).

The more clear and demonstrable your objectives are, the more likely it is that you will accomplish them. Fuzzy objectives lead to fuzzy results. If you say you are going to "evangelize more," you will have a hard time knowing when you've evangelized more. But if you say you're going to initiate conversations about Christ with your neighbors John and Mary, you'll know exactly when and whether you've accomplished the task.

Does this seem too rigid, too confining? If so, may I suggest that you might be settling for a decaffeinated form of Christianity—one that promises not to keep you awake at night. You see, God gives us His Word not to make us comfortable but to conform us to the character of Christ. And that goes way beyond pious feelings and good intentions. It penetrates to the level of our schedules and checkbooks and friendships and jobs and families. If our faith makes no practical difference there, then what difference does it make?

Clearly defined objectives help us see actions, not abstractions. Likewise, they keep our expectations on the ground, within reach. Is your aim to develop the compassion of a Mother Teresa? Wonderful. But don't make that your objective. A better place to start is with a soup kitchen in your own community. Determine some practical ways to meet the needs of those around you. That's achievable. That's something you can do right now. That's a realistic step in the right direction.

2. COME UP WITH A PLAN

This is the step where you ask how. How am I going to accomplish the task? If you've done a good job of stating your objectives, this should be fairly easy to answer. If not, you may need to go back and revise your objectives, making them clearer and more doable.

A plan is a specific course of action for how you're going to reach you objectives—and I do mean specific. Think it through in terms of all that it's going to take to do what you say you intend to do. Who are the people involved? What resources will you need? When are you going to plan it in your schedule? What's the best timing?

For example, suppose your objective is to become a better parent by spending more time with your children. How are you going to accomplish that? Maybe it means taking your son out for pizza and telling him about your own childhood. That could be an excellent plan. But what will it take to pull it off? When will you schedule it? Is your son agreeable to that? When would be the best timing? How long do you plan to take? Where will you go so that you can talk? What are you going to say?

Or suppose "better parenting" means organizing and managing the family schedule. How will you accomplish that? Maybe it means putting up a calendar in the kitchen. So when will you get a calendar? How big does it need to be? Where are you going to put it? How often are you going to update it? How will you know what to put on it?

Again, suppose you decide that you need to engage your neighbors John and Mary in conversation about Christ. You know that they have questions in that regard. How can you initiate that? One way might be to give them a copy of C. S. Lewis's *Mere Christianity* as a way of stimulating discussion. If so, when will you get a copy to give them? When will you give it to them? How do you plan to follow up? Will you have them over for dessert some evening to talk about it? If so, when? Are they agreeable to that?

Planning a course of action means coming up with specific ways to achieve an objective and then thinking through what you need to do to run the plan. It assigns names, dates, times, and places to your intentions. The more specific your plan, the more likely it is that you'll succeed in it.

3. FOLLOW THROUGH

In other words, get started. Does your plan begin with a phone call? Then pick up the phone. Does it start by having your secretary rearrange your schedule? Then ask her to rearrange it. Do you plan to evaluate your giving habits in light of your budget? Then sit down and update your budget so that you'll have the information you need.

The first step is always the hardest. But take it. Don't put it off. If you've come this far in the process, reward your efforts with solid follow-through. Pay yourself the respect of carrying out your commitments.

Three strategies can help you in this process. First, consider using a checklist, especially if your plan calls for repeated activity or a number of progressive steps. For instance, if you plan to memorize Scripture, you would be wise to list all of the verses you intend to memorize, and the dates by when you plan to memorize them. Then, as you commit the verses to memory, you can check them off the list. Over time, you'll be able to see and celebrate your progress, which will spur you on in your efforts.

A second strategy is to set up some relationships of accountability. These could be formal or informal. Informal accountability might involve telling your spouse or a close friend about what you plan to do. Then, as you work your way through the process, you can keep him or her aware of your progress, your struggles, and your victories.

However, for long-term spiritual growth, I recommend a formal accountability group. Jeanne and I have been part of such a group for years, and we wouldn't trade it for anything. A group of people committed to each other brings encouragement and wisdom to the growth process. And the dynamic of the group helps one follow through on the commitments he or she makes.

A third way of ensuring that you carry out your plans is to evaluate your progress. Keeping a journal is an ideal way to do that. As you set your objectives and accomplish them, write the process down. Record why you wanted to make changes and why you took the course of action that you did, and then review where you've been. You'll notice where you've made progress and where you still need to grow.

Another way to do this is to get away periodically for a time of personal reflection and evaluation. Take your journal, your Bible, your calendar, and any other records of what you've been up to during the past few months or so. Ask yourself questions such as, What have been the three greatest challenges to my walk with the Lord during this period? How did I respond? What victories do I have to celebrate? What failures do I need to consider? What specific answers to prayer can I recall? Have I changed for the better or for the worse? In what ways? Where have I spent my time? My money? What has happened in my relationships?

The point is, devise ways to measure your stride as you walk through life. Know yourself and how God has worked in your experience.

God Is at Work in You

The last part of Philippians 2:12 used to engender a lot of fear in me as a boy: "Work out your salvation with fear and trembling" (NIV). The planning process that I've described in this chapter is a form of "working out your salvation." You have to take responsibility for making choices and taking action in order to grow as a believer.

But never forget the other side: "For it is God who is at work in you, both to will and to work for His good pleasure" (Philippians 2:13, NASB). As you set your objectives, make plans, and carry them out, God is right there with you. That's the encouraging thing about the spiritual life—you're never alone. God provides His resources to help you in the process. He won't make decisions for you nor do what you are able to do. But He does work in ways known and unknown to help you become like Christ.

Taken from *Living by the Book*, ©1991 by Howard G. Hendricks and William D. Hendricks. Used by permission of Moody Press. Available at your local Christian bookstore.

Walking with God can be difficult at times, but it's even more difficult if you try to do it without a plan. The next time you're reading through Scripture (you are reading the Bible on a regular basis aren't you?) and you read something that convicts you of some sin in your life that is keeping you or threatening to move you out of the First Chair, apply the principles you've just read. You could almost say that this is a breakthrough in experiencing break-throughs. Dr. Howard Hendricks, with William Hendricks, has written a book titled Living by the Book *that will help you live your life according to the Word of God—and in the First Chair. Next time you're at a Christian bookstore, I suggest you pick up a copy.*

EVALUATION QUESTIONS

1. Take some time and evaluate where you are in experiencing this breakthrough. Where would you rate yourself on the following scale?

1	5	10
Not even close to experiencing this breakthrough.	I've begun the journey, but I've got a ways to go.	I've experienced a breakthrough, and I'm living the abundant life.

2. What would you consider to be the biggest hindrance to your experiencing this breakthrough right now?

3. What one action should you take to experience this breakthrough right now? I challenge you to do it.

Conclusion

Day 30
Experiencing Spiritual Breakthroughs

Live a Life of Ongoing Spiritual Breakthroughs

BRUCE H. WILKINSON

y now you've seen that the pattern of the Three Chairs affects the entire fabric of a person's life. No matter where you peel back the fabric, the differences are obvious. Whether you are a First Chair believer or a Second Chair believer, the chair in which you sit influences your entire life.

At this point, you are also acquainted with a number of the differences between the Three Chairs. But to make it easy for you to always distinguish the First Chair from the Second, I'd like to boil it all down to one simple passage of Scripture. With this Scripture, you can evaluate every action you make to see if it is the action of a First Chair believer or Second. Paul told us in 2 Corinthians 10:5 to take "every thought captive to the obedience of Christ," and this passage I'm about to give you will help you do just that.

The Scripture is nothing new to you; in fact, you probably already have it committed to memory:

"'You shall love the Lord your God with all your heart, and with all your soul, and with all your mind.' This is the great and foremost commandment. The second is like it, 'You shall love your neighbor as yourself.'" (Matthew 22:37–39, NASB)

Pretty simple, isn't it? Now let me explain why these two commands are the litmus test for everything we do.

LOVE THE LORD YOUR GOD

Remember back in the introduction I used Joshua as an example of a First Chair believer. His statement, "But as for me and my house, we will serve the Lord" is exactly what Jesus was referring to in Matthew when he told us to "love the Lord your God."

These words that Joshua spoke were not empty of intention. His words come during the closing season of his life. He had served the Lord all of his life, he was presently serving the Lord, and he knew he would continue to serve the Lord.

Now that's commitment! Whenever you look at a person who sits in the First Chair, you will always find this type of commitment. So, in your mind, embroider the word *commitment* into the well-worn fabric of this First Chair. Commitment is what loving "the Lord your God with all your heart, and with all your soul, and with all your mind" is all about.

1. The committed fully choose the Lord to be their Lord.

In the same speech where Joshua expresses his commitment to the Lord, he challenges the people to choose the Lord for themselves: "So Joshua said to the people, '...You have chosen the Lord for yourselves'" (Joshua 24:22, NKJV). You cannot be committed to something unless you make the initial decision to be committed voluntarily. You need to choose Jesus as your personal Lord. Not just God. Not just Savior. You must take it a step further and willfully pledge yourself to be under His authority and direction. No one can make you take that step except you.

Early in Joshua's leadership he faced the issue of making this choice for himself. The Lord wanted to revalidate who was ultimately in charge before the Israelites moved in to conquer the Promised Land. Up ahead of the group was the dangerous city of Jericho, with its high and formidable walls. The battle was just about to begin. But when Joshua was close to Jericho, perhaps scouting for the upcoming battle, he looked up, "and behold, a Man stood opposite him with His sword drawn in His hand. And Joshua went to Him and said to Him, 'Are You for us or for our adversaries?'" (Joshua 5:13, NKJV). Since Joshua was preparing for battle and the man had his sword drawn, that was an obvious question. But the answer he received was totally unexpected:

"No."

No? How could he not be for one or the other—especially with the drawn sword? The rest of the sentence reads, "As Commander of the army of the Lord I have now come." The next verse captures the spirit of someone who is sitting in the First Chair: "And Joshua fell on his face to the earth and worshiped, and said to him, 'What does my Lord say to His servant?'" Joshua was one of the committed.

He was willing to obey his Lord, come what may. Joshua immediately fell on his face and worshiped. He knew what to do in the presence of God. Joshua also used the words "my Lord" in response. The committed have already decided that Jesus will be their Lord. They have chosen the Lord for themselves. Joshua enlarges this concept in 22:5 when he exhorts the people to "love the Lord your God" and "hold fast to Him." This commitment isn't merely an intellectual one, nor is it simply a volitional one. It is emotional as well: "Love the Lord your God." And it's loyal: "Hold fast to Him." The commitment to follow Christ is ongoing and comes from a heart in love with the Lord. The committed see the Lord through the eyes of their love and loyalty. They see the Lord as "my Lord."

2. The committed wholeheartedly serve the Lord.

With the rest of verse 22:5, Joshua tells us what this love of the Lord naturally leads to: "serve Him with all your heart and with all your soul."

Is this beginning to sound familiar?

Joshua not only saw the Lord as his Lord, but he also saw himself as the Lord's servant. That's the other side of commitment. To sit in the First Chair, to be one of the committed, means that you are willing to obey His commands. When a person moves into the First Chair, he moves into a completely different mind-set.

Look again at Joshua's real question: "What does my Lord say to His servant?" (Joshua 5:14, NKJV). Joshua is requesting marching orders from his Commander. "What do you want me to do, Lord?"

That's how First Chair Christians live their lives, asking "What do you want me to do, Lord?" Every minute of every day is committed to doing what the Lord would have them do. They put aside their own desires and anything that demands their undivided loyalty.

A First Chair husband loves his wife because the Lord tells him to do so. And he does it even when his own desires would have him do otherwise.

Likewise, a First Chair wife serves and submits to her husband because the Lord tells her to. And she does it even when her fleshly desires would push her to do otherwise.

This is what it means to "love the Lord your God with all your heart, and with all your soul, and with all your mind." You see, the best way to identify those sitting in the First Chair is to see if they are wholeheartedly committed to the Lord. Every action is orchestrated to identify themselves with their Master. Nothing can persuade them to do otherwise.

3. The committed regularly fellowship with the Lord.

It stands to reason that if you love the Lord and wholeheartedly serve Him, you would want to fellowship with him as well. Therefore, one of the surest marks of a First Chair believer is the existence of a committed prayer life.

One's prayer life doesn't just happen at a particular time of the day, though the day will almost always begin or end with a formal prayer time. No, a committed prayer life is constant. First Chair believers are in constant communion with God throughout the day. They are always open to the nudging of the Holy Spirit, and they are regularly lifting words of admonition or supplication up to the Lord. They also see the Lord's hand working in many different ways. Whether it be in nature, in their business, or in the lives of the people around them, committed believers are always aware of the Lord's presence.

YOU SHALL LOVE YOUR NEIGHBOR

The first way to tell if you are sitting in the First Chair is to ask yourself, "Do I love the Lord with every part of my being?" But loving the Lord is not all there is to identifying a First Chair Christian. The second part of Christ's command is vital: "You shall love your neighbor as yourself."

How does this translate into evaluating whether you're sitting in First Chair or not? Simply ask yourself, "Do I love people?" Not just your friends and family. Not just the people who are lovable. But people in general.

Whenever First Chair believers are nearby, their love for people is apparent. Whether they are introverts or extroverts, quiet or expressive, humorous or sober, they are always looking for ways to care for the needs of others. They invite people into their homes, they get together with them elsewhere, and they reach out to be with people in many other ways as a main theme of their lives.

The early church understood this, so when they got together they shared everything. Christians sold their possessions to take care of one another. They gave generously to assist churches going through hard times, and they unselfishly supported Paul and other evangelists who took the gospel to an unsaved world. Rather than thinking of their own needs, they thought of others first. And their own needs were taken care of in the process.

When you commit to the Lord, you become committed to what He is committed to. That is why First Chair believers love people. But they don't just love them with emotions, they love them with their actions. First Chair people humbly serve others and they also pray for others.

A great example of this in the Bible is Stephen, who was one of the first deacons (a position of service). Stephen's ministry was a ministry of service. But it didn't end there. Acts 7:59–8:1 shows us that Stephen was definitely sitting in the First Chair:

> And they stoned Stephen as he was calling on God and saying, "Lord Jesus, receive my spirit." Then he

knelt down and cried out with a loud voice, "Lord, do not charge them with this sin." And when he had said this, he fell asleep. (NKJV)

Stephen loved people so much that he could pray for their forgiveness even as they were putting him to death. Love people and pray for them. Those are the marks of a First Chair person.

Naturally, the more you love, the more you serve the people you love. The more wholly you serve, the more you pray. The more you pray, the more impact you have in the lives of those you pray for.

THE SECOND CHAIR PERSON

As you can see, the First Chair believers are committed to their Lord—loving Him, serving Him, and praying to Him—and to other people—loving them, serving them, and praying for them—in that order. How does all of this differ from Second Chair people?

To put it plainly, Second Chair people do things just the opposite of how Christ commanded. Instead of loving God, they love themselves with all their heart, and they love their neighbor as they do their God, which is much less than they love themselves. You could almost make this into a manifesto for the Second Chair believer:

Love yourself with all your heart, with all your soul, and with all your might. And secondly, love others and the Lord if you have anything left over.

That doesn't sit very well, does it? I hope not. If you're sitting in the Second Chair, it's time to break through the shackles of sin and self. These shackles have kept you from entering the Promised Land that God has prepared for you. They have banished you to the wilderness for years and prevented you from enjoying the milk and honey of God's blessing.

Your spirit may have been set free from slavery when you were saved, but your mind and body have remained in slavery. If you've noticed a pattern in your life of putting your desires and pleasures ahead of the will of God (who desires obedience and fellowship), and ahead of the needs of others, then now is the time to get down on your knees and repent.

Repentance is the greatest breakthrough you can ever experience. Whether you're sitting in the Second Chair or the Third Chair, repentance can take you straight to the First Chair. You may not be a mature First Chair believer right away, but you'll still be sitting where you need to be. From there, make sure you're reading the Bible, going to a church that preaches the Bible, and making friends with those who do the same. Soon, Christ's commands to love God and to love others will be a natural part of who you are.

But let me warn you, living in the First Chair isn't easy. It will require commitment, submission, and a total reliance on God. But if you'll do it, if you'll allow the power of God to change your life, you'll have begun a legacy that can live on for generations!

Multnomah Publishers®

The publisher and author would love to hear your comments about this book. *Please contact us at:*
www.thebreakthroughseries.com